Governors State University
Library
Hours:
Monday thru Thursday 8:30 to 10:30
Friday and Saturday 8:30 to 5:00
Sunday 1:00 to 5:00 (Fall and Winter Trimester Only)

DEMCO

VIRTUAL DESTINATIONS AND STUDENT LEARNING IN MIDDLE SCHOOL

Virtual Destinations and Student Learning in Middle School

A Case Study of a Biology Museum Online

Mindi Donaldson

CAMBRIA PRESS

YOUNGSTOWN, NEW YORK

No part of this publication may be reproduced, stored in or introduced into a retrieval system, or transmitted, in any form, or by any means (electronic, mechanical, photocopying, recording, or otherwise), without the prior permission of the publisher. Requests for permission should be directed to permissions@cambriapress.com, or mailed to Permissions, Cambria Press, PO Box 350, Youngstown, New York 14174-0350.

Library of Congress Cataloging-in-Publication Data
Donaldson, Mindi.
    Virtual destinations and student learning in middle school : a case study of a biology museum online / Mindi Donaldson.
        p. cm.
    Includes bibliographical references and index.
    ISBN 978-1-934043-27-1 (alk. paper)
    1. Biology—Study and teaching (Middle school) 2. Biology—Computer-assisted instruction. I. Title.

QH315.D64 2006
570.285—dc22

2006039340

To the late Dr. Richard B. Forbes

TABLE OF CONTENTS

LIST OF FIGURES

LIST OF TABLES

FOREWORD

In 2001 Mindi Donaldson, a graduate student at Portland State University in the Department of Curriculum and Instruction, set up a display table at the annual Oregon Science Teachers Conference. She sought feedback and participation from science teachers in her study of a truly innovative concept—an online museum about animals and their native habitats available for students in their classrooms. Driven by her desire to put a powerful technological tool in the hands of resource-starved science teachers, she offered them an opportunity to collaborate with her on the research and share *Museum Explorer* with their students. This is a case study of two of those science classes. It is the result of her vision and perseverance in creating an online science classroom resource, and then studying its impact. The study found there was indeed a positive impact, not only on student content learning but also on student engagement with science and computer technology.

There is a growing need to evaluate the way students learn. The design of this study is a step to a more complete understanding of how students learn in complex classroom environments. Dr. Donaldson gathered data from student content knowledge tests, attitude surveys, email responses, teacher observations, and student journals. Using a funneling metaphor, she compared and contrasted the results across the data and provided a rich picture of student response and learning.

A key question for teachers is "Did students learn?" And yes, indeed, the students in this study did learn about science. However, they also seemed to learn some other important things for a generation growing up in an increasingly information-driven society. They learned to work interactively with a computer program to get some of their questions answered, about how to email a museum curator to gain further knowledge, and about going to a museum after being introduced to ideas online. They also learned about keeping a classroom journal to record their learning. The teacher was pleased with the results and the online resource that facilitated learning, *Museum Explorer*. He states:

> Yes, I'm sure *Museum Explorer* contributes to student learn-
> ing. I overheard conversations that indicated learning, and
> watching kids take the quizzes showed me that they were
> mastering some of the material at the time. Coupled with
> other learning experiences, I believe that *Museum Explorer*
> can help develop learning that is retained over time...

This study contributes to our knowledge about the use of innovative technology in real classrooms and how students respond to it. We can be thankful that graduate students are willing to persevere and ask new questions about classroom learning.

Professor Danelle Stevens
Portland State University

ACKNOWLEDGEMENTS

I am deeply indebted to my son Joel for sharing his technical skill and creative insight in the design and development of the virtual biology museum used in this case study. His unfailing patience and persistent effort as we worked together on the creation of the website was an unforgettable experience. My younger son Jonan, a teacher, also contributed support in many practical ways. When my determination to complete this book faltered, my loving and resilient husband was a constant bearer of courage and support. Finally, I thank my dear sister for believing in me.

Virtual Destinations and Student Learning in Middle School

CHAPTER ONE

INTRODUCTION

New methods of learning and instruction promise to improve the teaching of science and help define a better model. The inquiry-based learning paradigm focuses on student learning rather than on fact-based teaching. This model focuses on the student being able to question, think critically, and problem-solve as opposed to receiving passively information from lecture-based teaching.

Education historically has been thought of as a banking process using students, teachers, and books (Freire, 1972). Books are the cornerstone repositories of information, and teachers use those books to disseminate knowledge to students who bank that knowledge to become educated. This didactic style of teaching dominated the educational field for the past two centuries (Aksoy, 1998). John Dewey, the American philosopher and educator, believed that knowledge is a mode of intelligent practice or a habitual disposition of mind (1915). The child must construct, create, and actively inquire. Science has often been taught as an accumulation of ready-made material and not enough as a method of thinking or attitude of mind.

Krajcik, Soloway, Blumenfeld, Marx, and Fishman (2000) identify several age-old challenges in learning and teaching that can be addressed by combining approaches from new learning paradigms with computer applications crafted to meet the unique needs of learners. Software constructed using learner-centered design guidelines can incorporate "scaffolding" to present information in a fashion that supports deeper student understanding. Scaffolding provides temporary supporting structure that will help the students develop new understandings and abilities. As the students develop control of these, the program withdraws support and only provides further support for extended or new tasks.

In science, one innovative approach is the use of virtual biology museums in instructional settings. Virtual museums are database-driven websites where students can explore organized collections of electronic representations of artifacts while learning in an interactive manner.

A good virtual museum allows the student to search information ranging from simple questions to those of greater depth. A virtual biology museum has information on the species housed within a physical museum. The visitor is able to view images of skulls, skins, and skeletons instead of merely tables or spreadsheets as in a typical database. In addition, virtual museums can provide various means of presentations of information unavailable in a physical museum, thus enhancing educational value. Students can see pictures of habitats, videos of living animals, and hear the sounds of the animals. Distribution and density maps are available. Computer-generated rendering allows the visitor to rotate and view specimens from any angle or visually walk around a skeletal articulation of the animal.

A virtual biology museum can provide the structural framework for an active partnership between a university biology museum and middle schools. Museum educators have an unprecedented opportunity to work with teachers to realize the potential of the incorporation of virtual museums as classroom instructional resources. Also, to further their understanding of the learning potential of museums in classrooms, teachers can benefit from investing time to communicate with museum personnel.

THE EFFECT OF AN ONLINE MUSEUM

Middle school life science teachers need suitable computer technology resources to support their science instruction. A science teacher's job is to interest and instruct students in science so that the students meet state science standards. However, recent studies report that science is a subject in which teachers feel unprepared. Further, teachers feel they lack sufficient resources. Half of the grade school teachers in a nation-wide five-year study sponsored by the National Science Foundation responded that they are only somewhat qualified to teach science (Templeton, 1999). They also admit that science is the subject they feel least qualified to teach. Yet 50 % of the students surveyed in this study stated that they spend most of their time in science classes listening to a teacher lecture. Given this lack of sufficient science resources and teachers feeling unprepared to teach science, computer technology may provide a promising teaching supplement. Computer technology, in particular Internet-based science instruction, can relieve teachers in areas they feel less qualified to teach, introduce interactive multimedia that is interesting to students, and save money by building museum / school partnerships that deliver instruction over the Internet.

Only a handful of colleges with biology museums have entered into museum / school partnerships, and even fewer are using computer technology such as a virtual museum as a teaching interface and vehicle of instruction. It is important to introduce to middle school science teachers the opportunities available using technology in the classroom. A virtual biology museum that appropriately meets the needs of middle school science teachers and students, and integrates smoothly and efficiently with the curricula may help meet national and statewide goals. Partnerships between formal and informal science educational settings combined with technology as a teaching tool can further students' understanding of science and promote inquiry-based learning.

Computer technology use in middle school science classrooms warrants more investigation. Partnerships between museums and schools using virtual museums are potential solutions to address the problems of learning in science classrooms. Making primary resources available through innovations such as a virtual museum could inspire teachers and students throughout the community, and facilitate acquisition of knowledge and engagement.

Arguably, university museums can assume leadership roles through an innovative approach of a virtual biology museum linked to classrooms. True educational museums extend the reach of their collections beyond the confines of the physical walls to the community. Students and teachers experience an enriched sense of community through the collaboration.

Museum Explorer, an online virtual biology museum designed for middle school grades, was developed by the researcher. The online museum was designed to be used in conjunction with a museum / school partnership with a biology museum on an urban university campus to supplement current science middle school curricula. *Museum Explorer* provided students with a one-of-a-kind close-up view of animals of the Northwest with the varied multimedia experiences of video, sound, 3D images, lectures, and the accumulated store of facts on northwest vertebrates.

The purpose of this case study was to examine the effect of an online virtual museum in conjunction with a university biology museum on middle school students' content knowledge and learning engagement. Specific goals of the study were to: (a) identify the learning content effect on middle school students of a virtual biology museum implemented through a museum / school partnership, (b) examine the learning engagement of students using *Museum Explorer*, an online biology museum, and (c) determine what further engagement is generated by field trips to the museum and communication with an assistant curator through email correspondence. The researcher used a mixed methodology approach to gain insight on the effect of a virtual museum on student learning and engagement.

To date, little research addresses the use of a virtual biology museum in middle school classrooms implemented through a university museum / school partnership. This study provides a useful lens for science educators as they learn to integrate computer technology into the curricula. Further, it contributes practical information to teachers as they endeavor to apply methods of computer technology use in the classroom. The findings from this study may help educators better understand the effects of computer technology in classrooms linked through a partnership with a local university biology museum.

The research questions that guided this study are:

1. What is the effect of *Museum Explorer* (a virtual biology museum used in conjunction with a museum / school partnership) on middle school students' content knowledge?

2. What is the effect of *Museum Explorer* on student learning engagement?
3. What further engagement is generated by a field trip to the Portland State University biology museum and communication with an assistant curator via email?

ASSUMPTIONS, LIMITATIONS, AND BENEFITS OF THE STUDY

A major assumption of this study was that the data collected by the researcher would reflect genuinely the views of the participants as they self-reported. The small sampling size of 50 participants and limited time span of ten weeks, however, restricted the ability to generalize the findings. Further, the full effect of the intervention of *Museum Explorer* could not be compared to no intervention at all because the new experience mid-year for these students could explain some variations. The participants of this study were middle school students of Latino heritage who were learning English as a second language. A weakness of questionnaires is that data are open to misinterpretation due to cultural differences (Marshall & Rossman, 1999). This may have been a factor of increased importance in this study since all the students were of Latino origin. Further, questionnaires are limiting in that the researcher must rely totally on the honesty and accuracy of the responses. Yin (1993) suggests using multiple sources of evidence, thus establishing a clear chain of evidence to establish the linkages between the research problems through to the study's conclusion. There may have been biases, not only in the selection of the subjects to be studied, but also because the researcher had designed the online museum, thus reflecting personal preferences in the design and choice of measuring instruments and in the creation of the pre- and post-tests.

The benefits of this study were numerous. The students had an enriched learning experience using the online biology museum and enjoyed correspondence with the university assistant curator at the museum. The field trip offered a real-life experience for the students where they saw first-hand the things they had been looking at online. The questionnaires gave both teacher and students time for introspection as they answered the questions regarding their own attitudes toward computers. Metacognition is an important aspect in learning. The ability of students to reflect on their own performance and attitudes is a crucial element for developing successful learning strategies (Bransford, Brown, & Cocking, 2000). The various instruments such as the computer attitude questionnaires and the open-ended questionnaires provided this type of reflection. Finally, the experience provides insight in ways to enhance classroom science learning and teaching and may provide a useful lens for science educators as they learn to integrate computer technology into the curricula. Accessible resources for science teachers and their students can increase student engagement and positively impact student learning.

Definitions of Terms

- Computer Enjoyment: The amount of pleasure a student derives from using computers.
- Computer Importance: The perceived value or significance of knowing how to use computers.
- Computer Learning Engagement: Engaged students using computers are actively involved in their own learning. They actively participate and show increased interest as they interact with the computer software. Improved academic performance may result from increased student engagement.
- Computer Motivation / Persistence: Students display unceasing effort and perseverance as they work with the software programs. They never give up.
- Content Knowledge: For the purposes of this research project, content knowledge will be defined as knowledge acquired from the context of an interactive online medium, contact using email with biology students at a local university, and a field trip to a biology museum at an urban university.
- Museum / School Partnership: A mutually beneficial relationship between a school and a museum that has resources to use. Museums provide schools with something they do not have, primary resources and professional museum educators. The schools provide the museums with something they do not have, the students.

- Virtual Biology Museum: A virtual museum with information on the biological species housed within the physical museum. The visitor is able to view images of skulls, skins, and skeletons instead of merely tables or spreadsheets as in a typical database. Students can see pictures of habitats, videos of living animals, and hear the sounds of the animals. Distribution and density maps are available. Computer-generated rendering allows the visitor to rotate and view specimens from any angle or visually walk around a skeletal articulation of the animal.
- Virtual Museum: A database-driven website where the visitor can explore and learn in an interactive manner. The website provides an organized collection of electronic artifacts and information resources – virtually anything that can be digitized (McKenzie, 1997). A good virtual museum will allow the visitor to perform searches ranging from simple questions to those of greater depth.

CHAPTER TWO

BACKGROUND

The following background identifies the various implications of research on technology use in the science classroom and the implementation of university museum / school partnerships. Topics include: (a) historical background of museums in education, (b) seeing, understanding, and learning with museums, (c) university museum / school partnerships, (d) learning engagement, (e) computer technology in the science classroom and science inquiry, (f) predictors of computer usage by teachers in classrooms, and (g) the learning cycle curriculum model. Key issues are discussed as well as an overview of method designs employed in the research including a discussion of the study's weaknesses, strengths, and limitations.

The following section provides a brief examination of the history of natural history museums for educational purposes. The section begins with the introduction and growth of natural history museums in the U.S., an often overlooked resource for classroom science teaching.

HISTORICAL BACKGROUND OF MUSEUMS IN EDUCATION

One third of America's natural history museums are more than fifty years old, with four percent founded before 1900 (Melber & Abraham, 2002).

In the 19th century, museums were often a primary source of education for the general public. Slowly, the role of museums in education declined. Building museum collections took precedence over public education, with museum personnel looking towards the expansion of knowledge through larger collections as their primary focus (Skramstad, 1999).

In the 1920s and 1930s, John Dewey's educational philosophy brought a new spirit of innovation into the application of museums to learning. Dewey invigorated education, and this same spirit of innovation found its way into museum education. Many museums hired educators to develop interactive exhibits for their visitors (Hein, 2001). Another major innovation introduced in the 1920s and 1930s was the use of field trips as a principal educational component for classroom students. The field trip approach dominated the museum / school relationship for several decades (Frankel, 1995). Typically, students were taken on a quick tour through the museum, and the museum staff let the objects and exhibitions speak for themselves.

As early as the 1950s and 1960s, issues such as the Cold War, the Civil Rights Movement, and the lack of stable financial support resulted in the fading of museum educational programs (Yellis, 1990). However, during the late 1960s and 1970s, as educational theories such as discovery learning were expanded within museums, museums once again became part of educational programs.

Discovery learning is a cognitive instructional approach of learning developed by Jerome Bruner (Slavin, 1986). Students are encouraged to ask questions and formulate answers through activities and observations. Hands-on or discovery rooms are introduced in museums to involve students more closely in their learning. The focus is to make learning real and interesting by building a relationship between students, teachers, and the subject of inquiry (Frankel, 1995).

Slowly museums began offering tangible assistance to the educational needs of the schools. Museums made their collections accessible to students for hands-on learning. Museum staff mentors would come into the classrooms, visit with students, and then lead those students on personal tours of museum resources. Over time these uses of museums evolved into a common activity in many classrooms. Today, however, many museums and schools still have only an informal relationship without systemic support for teaching in museums.

Seeing, Understanding, and Learning with Museums

The overarching educational function of museums should be to provide supplemental educational experiences for their communities. These experiences can serve as a counterbalancing educational approach that offer a new way of seeing, understanding, and learning. The numerous children's museums and science and technology centers are examples of the successful creation of such alternative learning opportunities (Skramstad, 1999). The teachings of Piaget and Bruner have been influential in building the foundation for children's museums and discovery learning (Tomic & Kingma, 1998). Experiential and content-based problem-solving activities are combined with the real objects of art, history, and science through hands-on learning.

University-based natural history museums are unique among museums in that they are ideally suited to connect with their communities (Tirrell, 2001). Linda Cordell (2000) emphasizes that these museums should not only be involved in public education but should take a leadership role in informal teaching by offering programs for the lay public and classrooms, as well as learning workshops for teachers. University-based museums have at least one more function than for-profit museums, which is university training. This includes formal training for students inside the museum facilities. Further, they consider research intrinsic to their mission (Lourenco, 2001). University museums compete for state and national educational dollars, and there is a current trend that they are being asked to demonstrate the expertise required to develop nationally competitive programs. This level of expertise comes from an institutional commitment to strive for exceptional quality and creativity, and demonstrates that they can be effective in creating educational change. For all of the efforts made to convey factual information to children, museums must provide evidence that they help children understand more and feel more positive about learning science (Diamond, 2000).

University Museum / School Partnerships

The museum is a place where the best resources of the past are gathered, maintained, and organized (Dewey, 1915). Here the student can not only become acquainted with truths as they were in the past, but also as they relate in today's world. It was not until the 1990s that more formal educational collaborations between museums and schools began. Museums began organizing more substantial programs and invited active participation by making their collections accessible and providing first-hand experiences with real objects. Through partnerships, a web of meaning takes shape in a real-world context (Hirzy, 1996). Partnerships help create a multi-dimensional quality to learning that is similar to Dewey's school children going out to the garden to plant, grow, and harvest food. Partnerships and contact with primary resources can lead to more inquiry-based thinking and a deeper relationship within the culture of inquiry. Dewey states that children are led on to larger fields of investigation and to the intellectual discipline that is the accompaniment of such research. An online virtual biology museum used in conjunction with a museum / school partnership would utilize the various components of successful education such as collaboration, cooperation, communication, active engagement with the subject, construction, and inquiry.

The National Science Education Standards (NSES) specify that the school science program must extend beyond the walls of the school to include the resources of the community (National Research Council, 1996). The NSES emphasize that science is for all students, and learning science is an active process. Further, school science reflects the intellectual and cultural traditions that characterize the practice of contemporary science.

Meeting the challenge put forth by the NSES involves educational strategies such as partnerships between informal and formal settings. Hannon and Randolph (2001) identify six different types of partnerships between museums and schools: professional development, outreach, pilot programs, field trips, residencies, and the creation of museum schools. The type of partnership selected is determined by the purpose of the collaborators.

Numerous partnerships between for-profit museums and schools have existed through the years. These partnerships, however, are seldom sustained. Frankel (1995) has expressed the need for twelve conditions to be met for partnerships to be successful. These conditions range from understanding the schools' needs and having a shared vision to promoting dialogue and open communication. Frankel states that effective and sustained partnerships succeed because the partners have identified a problem to be solved or a need to be fulfilled and then worked to match what is happening in the classroom with museum resources.

One relevant study was a partnership with the Ann Arbor, Michigan, Hands-on Museum, community schools, and the local university (Paris, Yambor, & Packard, 1998). These researchers used a mixed methodology approach to assess the effects of a museum / school / university partnership. Their research demonstrated how community agencies could collaborate for mutual benefits. They noted that future research should assess the long-term consequences of these innovative partnerships, and that longitudinal research is needed to determine if these partnerships can maintain students' scientific knowledge and interest in their subsequent schooling. This partnership, however, like the handful of others that had come before, was considered a one-time research project not to be sustained.

While there are a number of museum / school partnerships between classrooms and museums-for-profit, few partnerships are established between a university biology museum and public school classrooms. There are fewer partnerships using computer technology as the vehicle of instruction. The first Museums and the Web Conference was held in 1997. By 2003, the Museums and the Web Conference (Museums and the Web, 2003) had more than 170 speakers from all over the world, which was considerably larger than the 1997 conference with only 50 speakers in attendance. Upon examination of the conference topics, however, partnerships with schools appear not to be one of the more popular subjects.

One of the earliest formal collaborations between museums and schools began in 1988 and ended in 1992 (David & Matthews, 1995). The Teacher Internship Program for Science (TIPS) was a four-year program where first-year teachers were paired with experienced science teachers. Teachers rotated their time teaching in the museum, working on exhibits, guiding class trips through the museum, and teaching in the school classroom. According to David and Matthews (1995), the partnership arose out of a growing need to develop recruiting strategies for science teachers.

Another good example of a technologically structured partnership in science was The Kids Network Program, started by the National

Geographic Society (NGS) in the late 1980s. This partnership between scientists from the NGS and students focused on the promotion of science and discovery in elementary classrooms. Students in the classrooms connected via the Internet with other students from different parts of the world. They compared and shared data on various subjects. Teachers were given information on student projects, and the introductory unit introduced students to scientific research methods. Students then gave the data they collected to scientists at the NGS who analyzed the data, pointed out patterns, and made graphs and charts to send back to the classrooms (Bradsher & Hagan, 1995). Such partnerships and Internet communities are valuable to teachers and students. However, the advantage of personal contact with primary resources at the other end of the technology was missing.

University-based museums today are becoming rare, with only about twelve natural history museums remaining with high profile large collections (West, 2000). Most university biology museums do not have programs for the lay public or partnerships with local K-12 classrooms. Today in America there are around 50 university-based natural history museums, but many of these museums have given up part of their collections (Cordell, 2000). The university biology museum that participated in this case study has a substantial collection and is located on the Portland State University campus in Portland, Oregon.

The specimens housed in the Portland State University biology museum serve the scientific community in several ways. They are available as instructional resources for PSU classes, as objects for faculty and graduate student research, and for examination by visiting scientists, artists, agency personnel, and school groups at all levels. Unfortunately, few teachers in Multnomah County are aware of the existence of this museum, let alone the instructional resources this collection offers.

A virtual biology museum available to Portland area classrooms can be an invaluable means of outreach. Making comprehensive information on each of the museum's specimens available to classrooms through an engaging and interactive multimedia virtual biology museum offers a unique integration of science, education, and technology. More importantly, this kind of educational innovation may directly engage the community and the university in a shared future of educating children.

Internet access to a museum increases outreach by bringing the museum to the student. Facilitated by technology, the museum / school partnership between the Portland State University biology museum and local area classrooms could generate a prolonged and vibrant relationship, making biology more interesting, fun, and accessible for students. It could bring the students' understanding to an entirely new level. Such partnerships could help create new energy and promote innovative ideas about the mission and meaning of schools and museums (McKenzie, 1997).

Melber and Cox-Peterson (2001) suggest that these museum environments provide untapped potential to engage teachers in professional enhancement that integrates professionalism, content, and pedagogy. The use of computer technology in the classroom further enhances opportunities for learning and engagement. One step to understand how to further these partnerships is to study the effect of an interactive web-based software program on student engagement and learning.

LEARNING ENGAGEMENT

Engaged students make a psychological investment in learning and are involved in their own learning (Newmann, 1992). The Apple Classrooms of Tomorrow (ACOT) longitudinal research study defines engagement to include variables for indicators such as initiative, motivation, independent experimentation, and enthusiasm or frustration (Sandholtz, Ringstaff, & Dwyer, 1994). This study looked at the engagement indicators of computer importance, computer enjoyment, motivation / persistence, and email use.

One longitudinal study (Smith, Butler-Kisber, LaRocque, Portelli, Shields, Sparkes, & Vibert, 1998) investigated secondary student engagement in learning and school life. The intent of the study was to try to see through the eyes of students and teachers and to convey their experiences. One teacher in the study indicated that student engagement means getting the students involved in learning and having them take responsibility for their learning. The teachers used terms such as "facilitator" and "guide" to describe their role with reference to student engagement in curriculum. Instead of being passive in the learning process, the students were very much involved and were actively engaged. The essence of student engagement for the teachers in this study was active learning, as well as student choice and independence.

Becker (2000a) notes that a student's attention and engagement are critical variables in determining if positive outcomes are attained. He states that students are more "on-task" and express more positive feelings when using computers, and therefore are more "engaged." Lepper (1985) examined the theoretical literature on intrinsic motivation and suggested that students are motivated to seek solutions to problems if computer activities provide intellectual challenge, stimulate curiosity, and give a sense of independent control and mastery. These factors influence the impact of learning in the classroom. Newman (1986) describes engagement in an intriguing way:

> Engagement is difficult to define operationally; but we know it when we see it, and we know when it is missing. Students are engaged when they devote substantial time and effort to a task, when they care about the quality of their work, and when they commit themselves because the work seems to have significance beyond its personal instrumental value. (p. 242)

Some studies report that students are more engaged while working with computers. The following section will discuss how computer technology usage in the classroom may effect student engagement.

COMPUTER TECHNOLOGY AND LEARNING ENGAGEMENT

According to Wasserstein (1995), engagement in learning takes place when educators equip students with the tools to become self-motivated. This self-motivation comes from a desire to understand things of interest or from the enjoyment of learning to achieve personal goals (Bowen, 2003). Computer technology is one resource that can affect the engagement of students and their achievement, but the research on how this technology affects achievement and engagement is inconsistent (Hede, 2002). Further, Hede states that this is because of the many contingent factors that have been shown to moderate multimedia effects. For example, some studies reveal that using both visual and auditory modes may cause a "split-attention" effect, and the students divide their attention across multiple inputs (Mousavi, Low, & Sweller, 1995).

Some researchers stress guiding principles to help educators know how to use multimedia (Mayer & Moreno, 1998). Bangert-Drowns and Pyke (2002) suggest that student-software interactions resemble engaged literate activity, and that when students make sense of educational software, they employ the same interpretive skills needed in paper-based tasks. These researchers developed a scale of engagement with educational software. The seven modes of engagement are disengagement, unsystematic engagement, frustrated engagement, structure-dependent engagement, self-regulated interest, critical engagement, and literate thinking. This scale will be discussed in detail in Chapter Three.

Research has shown that the success of computer technology is strongly related to the teacher's enthusiasm, initiative, and sense of improvement (Mann & Schafer, 1997). Interestingly, in Mann and Schafer's study the high school teachers were more positive than the middle school teachers about computer technology's ability to contribute to both school reform and their own work.

The Apple Classrooms of Tomorrow (ACOT) research project was initiated at five school sites in 1985. The purpose of the research was to examine the impact of interactive technologies on teaching and learning. ACOT provided students and teachers with Apple computers both at school and at home (Baker, Gearhart, & Herman, 1993). The project concluded in 1998 and was one of the longest continuing educational studies of its kind. The research demonstrated that use of computer technology in the classroom could increase significantly student learning and engagement. ACOT longitudinal research study found that increased student engagement using computer technology occurred in certain settings (Sandholtz, Ringstaff, & Dwyer, 1994). These settings are those where:

- Computer use was not a separate curricular focus.
- Teachers emphasized tool applications like desktop publishing and hypermedia authoring.
- Teachers were more willing to give responsibilities to students for determining specific learning tasks and how to accomplish them.

- Computers were used as only one set of tools for learning.
- Teachers were more willing to break down disciplinary and unity bound-aries to permit content to be investigated across those boundaries.
- Teachers provided for individualized computer experience that was responsive to individual student interest and ability.

While positive findings of the ACOT research point to new learning experiences requiring higher level reasoning and problem solving, as well as a positive effect on student attitudes, the negative findings show that computer-rich environments do not always point to increased learning (Schacter, 2001). In subjects such as vocabulary, reading comprehension, and mathematical concepts, the standardized tests show that the ACOT students performed no better than comparison groups with no access to computers.

Mark Lepper (1985) of Stanford University examined the theoretical literature on intrinsic motivation and predicted that: (a) if computer activities provide challenges, students will be motivated to seek solutions, (b) if computer activities stimulate curiosity, students will be motivated, and (c) if computer activities provide a sense of independence, students will be inspired to sustained and intense effort.

Not all computer activities, however, attract the same amount of student engagement and effort. Becker states that there is little nationally descriptive evidence about the relationship between various patterns of computer use and student motivational outcomes (Becker, 2000b). Many of the studies concerning engagement have involved self-report questionnaires from the teachers rather than the students. The true indication of the kinds of effects that computer experience may be having on students will come from further sustained research on learning environments.

In his meta-analysis, James Kulik (1994) summarized more than a decade of studies on the effects of computer use for instruction. One positive finding was that students like their classes more and develop more positive attitudes when their classes include computer-based instruction. However, computers did not have positive effects in every area in which they were studied.

At first glance, student engagement appears to be critical to motivation during the learning process. However, research findings are inconsistent.

Computers have at times been characterized as a panacea for educational ills because they provide a teacher-independent means of keeping students engaged in "something." Literature suggests, however, that various factors contribute to computer-rich learning environments to help students learn. One of these significant factors is defining what that something is that the student is engaged in while using the computer. There is an important difference between computer access in classrooms and quality learning applications. Learning applications which simply mimic books miss the learning potential computers provide for interactive learning. This study attempted to present and study the consequences of engaging students in the often missing interactive element. While the results of this study are clearly positive, more longitudinal research over time will be necessary. Further research is needed to build the required quantitative evidence to predict accurately the benefits and effects of computer use in the classroom.

Computer Technology in the Science Classroom and Scientific Inquiry

Computer technology has added a new element to the basic educational trio of teacher, student, and subject. It offers unique and dynamic opportunities for learning in the science classroom. Whereas a few decades ago computers were largely used by the research community, the students of today have almost unlimited access to information on the Internet. Seymour Papert, an internationally recognized seminal thinker on how computers can help students learn, states that students today have the opportunity to be more participatory in their learning and not merely recipients (Papert, 1993). Teachers can facilitate learning using computer technology designed to enhance the collaborative and interactive experience of the students.

Computer technology has captured the imagination and interest of educators across America. This new information system is now causing educators from all levels to rethink the very nature of learning and teaching. Papert (1993) refers to the computer as the "children's machine" because most students do not know a world without the computer. He states that while it may baffle adults, it is an integral part of the world of today's children, as opposed to yesterday's children. Today's children play, are entertained by, and learn with the computer. Integrating technology into science school communities successfully, however, means that it must match pedagogical theories as well (Lento, O'Neill, & Gomez, 1998).

Cuban (1986) discusses the history of technology use in schools. Telephones appeared in the principals' offices in the latter part of the 1920s. Classroom speaker-boxes allowed administrators to make school-wide announcements, and electronic bells kept the schoolrooms to a daily schedule. Time-saving mimeograph machines became available to teachers. In the 1950s educational television stations were licensed by the Federal Communications Commission for programs to be broadcast to schools. With the introduction of computers in the classrooms came the possibilities of enhanced teaching and learning. Cuban states that claims predicting extraordinary changes in teacher practice and student learning, mixed with promotional tactics, dominated the literature in the initial wave of enthusiasm for each new technology. Seldom, he states, did teachers initiate these innovations.

Molnar (1997) noted that in the late 1960s the National Science Foundation supported the development of regional computing networks, and by 1974 more than two million students used computers in their classes. Today's science teachers have the challenge of using these learning tools in a manner that supports current curricula and goals. The results of a 1999 national profile of teacher quality focused on teachers' pre-service and continued learning and the environments in which they work (Schacter, 1999). The study states that few teachers (20%) report feeling well prepared to integrate educational technology into classroom instruction. The National Science Education Standards (NSES) serve as a useful lens for science educators.

The NSES (National Research Council, 1996) provided four major goals for science education in K-12 classrooms: (a) students should learn to use appropriate scientific process and principles, (b) students should be able to engage intelligently in public discourse and debate about matters of scientific and technological concerns, (c) students should experience the excitement and richness of knowing about the natural world, and (d) economic productivity of students should increase through the use of the acquired skills, understanding, and knowledge.

To reach these goals, teachers must be at the center of reform in science education. The NSES describe extraordinary teachers who are not dependent on vocabulary-dense textbooks and encourage student inquiry, and therefore make science relevant to students' lives. The successful implementation of the NSES goals may improve student learning outcomes. Integrating computer technology into the curricula could speed up the process of implementing and reaching these goals.

The National Science Teachers Association (2002) takes the position that computers should have a large role in the teaching and learning of science. Their position statement asserts that computers should enhance, but not replace essential "hands-on" laboratory activities. The National Middle School Association (NMSA, 2003) suggests that learning activities be integrated and connected to life, challenge students, use a full range of communication skills and technologies, engage students in problem solving, and allow students to experience success. NMSA also recommends that teachers phase out excessive lecturing, drill and practice, rote learning, and the dominant use of worksheets and textbooks. The incorporation and utilization of computer technology in the classrooms is in tune with these recommendations. Various factors, however, influence teacher computer use in the classroom such as availability, teacher training, time, ability to select appropriate software, administrative support, and technical support. Any of these factors missing could impact computer technology use in the classroom (Iding, Crosby, & Speitel, 2002). Further, these factors directly influence the initiation and sustainability of innovative practices such as a virtual museum specifically designed for integration into the curricula.

The National Science Education Standards (NSES) state that instructional time spent on science should be comparable to the time spent on reading, writing, and mathematics (National Research Council, 1996). If this is the ideal, the increased instructional time should include innovative approaches that combine hands-on experiences, practical problem solving, and use of computer technology with sound educational objectives. Reform efforts should engage students in inquiry and collaboration around real-life problems, which would help build a richer and deeper understanding (Krajcik, Soloway, Blumenfeld, Marx, & Fishman, 2000). These can be furthered by the use of computer technology. Unlike passively learning from books, students become more active participants in the learning process. Computer technology offers an opportunity for interaction, which may lead to more inquiry-based learning.

Acquiring skills of inquiry in the field of science requires more than simply posing questions and seeking answers. The student must experience inquiry directly to gain a deep understanding of the subject (Olson & Loucks-Horsley, 2000). Teachers need to introduce students to the elements of inquiry and assist them as they reflect on characteristics of the inquiry. Computer technology could be used to improve investigations. There could be a de-emphasis on didactic instruction focusing on memorizing de-contextualized scientific facts with a new emphasis placed on inquiry-based learning that focuses on having students develop a deep understanding of the science that makes up our everyday world.

Students who have the opportunity to personally construct their own meaning, pose their own questions, and design and conduct investigations will be engaging in science inquiry. One of the main tenets of inquiry is that students take an active role in their learning (Hinrichsen & Jarrett, 1999). Inquiry is a multifaceted activity that involves the student to make observations, pose questions, examine information, plan investigations, review what is already known, gather, analyze, and interpret data, propose answers, offer explanations, and make predictions (Olson & Loucks-Horsley, 2000).

Science should be taught as a method of thinking and inquiring, and an attitude of mind (Dewey, 1915). Few educators in science education believe that science education should exclusively involve rote fact memorization (Byers & Fitzgerald, 2002). Since the days of Dewey, inquiry learning has been suggested as a solution to the problem of content knowledge alone being unable to advance the methods and habits of thinking and inquiry. Students who develop this method of thinking and attitude of mind will have had experience working directly with natural phenomena. They will have experience using their senses to observe and use instruments to extend the power of their senses.

Computer technology may help activate the student's curiosity, wonder, and the desire to search for solutions. Although research on the effect of computer technology use in the science classroom is inconsistent, many studies stress the need for computers to play a large role in the teaching and learning of science. A major component in understanding how to increase computer use in the science classroom is to study the effect of computer technology on student engagement and learning.

Predictors of Computer Usage by Teachers

Not all research findings on computer usage in middle school classrooms are consistent. There are, however, a number of commonly accepted predictors of successful computer use in the classroom (Becker, 2000b). One of the major predictors is availability and connectivity to the Internet. A recent report reveals that 99% of the public schools in America have access to the Internet, up from 35% in 1994 (National Center for Education Statistics, 2003). However, high poverty schools have fewer rooms with Internet access. Overall, the ratio of students to computers with Internet access is 5.4 to 1. Some researchers, however, state that computers and connectivity are seen by many as magical devices or silver bullets to solve problems in the classrooms (Dede, 1998). Dede suggests that computers and connectivity are a cost-effective investment only in the context of systemic reform.

Another predictor for teacher computer use in the classroom is computer expertise and comfort level. While Oregon has not established specific content standards and benchmarks in technology, the State Board of Education adopted revisions to the State's Technology Common Curriculum Goals (Oregon Department of Education, 2003). These goals included such things as the teacher's ability to demonstrate skill in using computer technology, using computer technology to enhance learning, and ability to design, prepare, and present unique works using this technology to communicate information.

Oregon's goals are in alignment with the National Educational Technology Standards for Teachers (NETS, 2003). Oregon's educational technology plan (Wade, 1999) states that all teachers should be prepared to meet the following standards: (a) teachers demonstrate a sound understanding of technology operations and concepts, (b) teachers plan and design effective learning environments and experiences supported by computer technology, (c) teachers implement curriculum plans that include methods and strategies for applying computer technology to maximize student learning, (d) teachers apply computer technology to facilitate a variety of effective assessment and evaluation strategies, (e) teachers use computer technology to enhance their productivity and professional practice, and (f) teachers understand the social, ethical, legal, and human issues surrounding the use of technology in middle schools and apply that understanding in practice.

While these standards are important for teachers to set as goals, teachers are often not effectively trained to be competent in using computers for classroom instruction (Clark, 2000). Further, it may be difficult to find appropriate software specifically designed to complement curriculum goals. It is crucial that future teachers be prepared to use computers effectively, and imperative that the teachers' education programs explore ways to prepare pre-service teachers to use computer technology.

One obstacle to computer technology use in the classroom is that of teachers finding the time and resources to implement technology (Iding et al., 2002). The research on teachers' beliefs and practices using computer technology indicates that a large number of teachers never use this technology for a wide range of activities, largely from their inability to properly evaluate and select software.

A 1998 national survey funded by a grant from the National Science Foundation's Division of Education and Human Resources analyzed responses from 4,000 U.S. teachers concerning their beliefs and practices, use of computers, pedagogies, and school context (Becker, 2000a). One important finding was that teachers who place a high value on sharing their knowledge with their colleagues were quite different from teachers who have little or no engagement in professional dialog or activities. Unfortunately, it is likely that many teachers do not have knowledge-sharing incorporated into their work schedules and job descriptions. It could be considered unfair to expect teachers to do work-related activities outside of the schedules of work they are paid for. Teachers who share knowledge tend to be constructivist in their beliefs and teaching and use computer technology for teaching and learning. Not all evidence, however, is positive about computer use in the classroom enhancing learning and motivation.

Some studies indicate that more traditional methods of teaching are more effective than computer technology (Forsyth & Archer, 1997). The main body of research, however, shows inconsistent findings varying from no effect on academic performance to moderate effectiveness. Cuban and Kirkpatrick (1998) state that current research on the efficacy of computer technology in the classroom does not have a clear focus. They identify three primary bodies of research on the efficacy of computers in education which are single studies, meta-analyses, and critical reviews, all of which have positive, negative, or mixed findings. Further, little research has been done on distance learning or technological applications for disabled students.

The above literature has shown that while computer use in the classroom has a positive influence on student learning and engagement, there are predictors for a teacher's computer use in the classroom. Literature reveals the need for more in-depth studies introducing practical software solutions for teachers. This study explored the practical application of an online biology museum designed to help teachers overcome factors that could hinder computer use in the classroom. Computer technology used with the learning cycle approach may bridge the gap between learning and the integration of technology in the curricula. The Internet was not designed to foster inquiry learning. Educational software is not always based firmly on any particular educational theory. The web-based software used in this case study was specifically designed to incorporate the ideals of inquiry learning in the form of the learning cycle described below.

THE LEARNING CYCLE

The learning cycle is a three-phase inquiry approach for teaching science. The learning cycle evolved from the developmental theory of Piaget (Piaget, 1970). This learning cycle is a strategy that employs a three-phase sequence: exploration, concept development, and application. Figure 1 illustrates the learning cycle model.

The National Science Foundation sponsored research in the learning cycle in the1960s as part of the Science Curriculum Improvement Study (SCIS). It was used first in elementary schools, but later was implemented in middle schools and high schools (Beisenherz & Dantonio, 1996). The *Museum Explorer* online biology website was designed with this learning cycle approach in mind.

The learning cycle has been the focus of many hundreds of studies to assess its effectiveness. Guzzetti (1993) conducted a meta-analysis of learning cycle-based studies and found positive results. Some research (Kyle & Bonnstetter, 1992) has shown that students of teachers who use the learning cycle have greater achievement and success in science, and are more motivated to learn science than students whose teachers use more traditional methods of science teaching (Marek & Cavallo, 1997).

FIGURE 1.   The Learning Cycle. Source: Teaching and Learning to
Standards: Science, 2002-2003

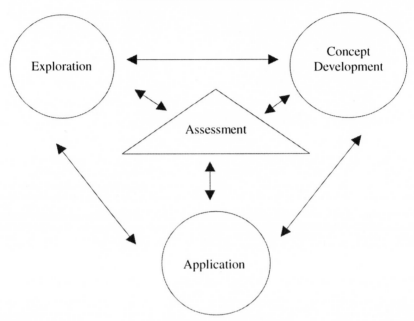

Lawson (2001) states that the learning cycle is an effective approach both to help students construct concepts and conceptual systems as well as develop effective reasoning patterns. Lawson identifies three types of learning cycle approaches: (a) descriptive, (b) empirical-inductive, and (c) hypothetical-deductive. The hypothetical-deductive and the empirical-inductive approaches are more complex than the descriptive approach. The descriptive learning cycle approach requires basic skills such as observation, communication, measurement, inferences, and predictions (Barnum & Kotar, 1989). The basic assumption of the learning cycle strategy is that learning will be more effective if students have concrete experiences and are encouraged to explore in activities that are open-ended and inquiry-based. This should lead the students to develop skills of fluent application of new ideas into a new context (Beisenherz & Dantonio, 1996).

SUMMARY

This section focused on the areas relevant to the case study. The need for more research studies on the effect of computer technology use on student engagement and learning in middle school science classrooms implemented through partnerships warrants investigation. The aspects explored in this background were the following: (a) the body of research in the historical background of museums in education has indicated that the educational function of museums should be to provide alternative educational experiences for their communities, (b) partnerships with schools are a practical avenue to provide these experiences, yet the literature has shown that seldom are these partnerships sustained, (c) student engagement is a critical intervening variable in determining if positive learning outcomes are attained, (d) computer technology in the science classroom has wonderful possibilities when used correctly. Research reveals that computer technology in the science classroom can be a viable enhancement to learning, (e) although there are a number of commonly accepted predictors of computer use in the classroom, further in-depth research needs to be conducted, and (f) the use of the learning cycle is an effective approach to help students construct concepts and conceptual systems. The basic assumption is that learning could be more effective when students have concrete experiences and are encouraged to explore in activities that are open-ended and inquiry-based. Such activities may be found in interactive online virtual biology museums used in conjunction with university biology museums.

Computer technology implemented through museum / school partnerships gives a glimpse of large and untapped possibilities. This study offers insight into important implications of new educational strategies. More small-scale innovations studied longitudinally over time are needed so the efficiency and success may be measured with accuracy.

CHAPTER THREE

METHODS, CONTEXT, AND PROCEDURES

This chapter will address the research design, the instruments that were employed, describe in greater detail the context of the case study, and describe the intervention that was evaluated in this study. The first section, however, will review the purpose of the research and restate the research questions of interest. The second section will discuss the research design. In the third, the research participants and setting, *Museum Explorer* online biology museum, and participating university will be described. Finally, the schedule of study tasks, as well as procedures and data collection strategies, including the instruments that were used, will be discussed.

PURPOSE AND RESEARCH QUESTIONS

The purpose of all research is to understand the world we live in. The purpose of this case study was to examine the effect of an interactive online biology museum website, designed by the researcher and called *Museum Explorer,* on middle school students' content knowledge and learning engagement.

In this case study student engagement is defined as positive attitude and interest in the subject. Engaged students using computers are actively involved in their own learning and actively participate and show increased interest as they interact with the computer software (see "computer learning engagement" definition in Chapter One).

Specific goals of the study were to: (a) identify the learning content effect of a virtual biology museum implemented through a museum / school partnership with the Portland State University biology museum on middle school students, (b) examine the learning engagement of students using *Museum Explorer*, an online digital biology museum designed for middle school students, and (c) determine what further engagement is generated by field trips to the museum and communication with a university assistant curator through email correspondence.

The nature of the research questions drives the choice of methodology (Creswell, 1998). Careful examination of relevant literature in light of the specific goals outlined above lead to the following three research questions:

1. What is the effect of *Museum Explorer* (a virtual biology museum used in conjunction with a museum / school partnership) on middle school students' content knowledge?
2. What is the effect of *Museum Explorer* on middle school students' learning engagement?
3. What further engagement is generated by field trips to the Portland State University biology museum and communication with the assistant curator via email?

Answers to each of these research questions were sought by funneling the analysis for that question through a set of measurement instruments. Each instrument set was the result of careful research design aimed at using quantitative and qualitative research tools to produce an answer to that research question. For example, research question one was answered by evaluating the measurement outputs of three testing instruments: (1) pre-test of biology content knowledge, (2) post-test of biology content knowledge, (3) a teacher open-ended questionnaire, and (4) notebook assignment. Figure 2 depicts a model that could describe this process.

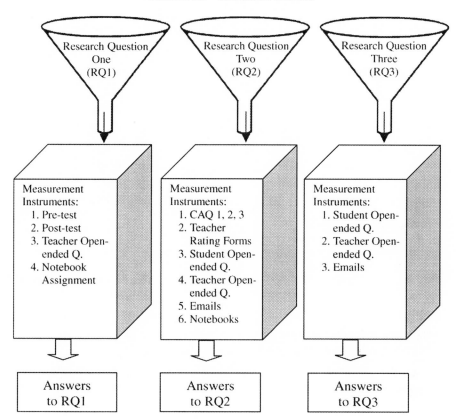

FIGURE 2.   Research Model

METHODOLOGY AND RESEARCH DESIGN

The research design issue in this study was which type of research best elicits correlational relationships in the biology classroom. A number of factors suggested that a case study approach would be the best way to address these research questions. First, Patton (2002) states that the power of purposeful (non-random) sampling lies in the selection of information-rich cases for in-depth study. The classroom setting for this study was such an information-rich environment. In particular, extensive measurements were available within the context of a science class where content knowledge was regularly measured. Second, Yin (1993) identifies a case study as a more empirical inquiry that investigates a phenomenon within its real-life context, when the boundaries between phenomenon and context are not clearly evident, and in which multiple sources of evidence are used. The classroom setting in this study was a real-life context in which various testing instruments were regularly used. Third, according to Janesick (1994), case study research is used to offer a framework that provides a detailed examination of one setting. In this case study, two science classrooms in a single middle school provided one such setting. Therefore, this study used the case study approach to examine how students are affected using a virtual biology museum as a vehicle of learning in conjunction with an university biology museum. The remaining issue was whether to use quantitative, purely qualitative or mixed method research design in eliciting correlational relationships.

Quantitative versus Qualitative Research Design

Quantitative methods statistically analyze numbers, such as scores on knowledge tests, and groups of numbers to determine those causal relationships. The main purpose of quantitative research is to detect causal relationships (Borg & Gall, 1989). However, the random selection often required in quantitative research prevents quantitative methods from being a viable option in situations where such selection is prohibited. For example, research within a classroom environment may not be allowed to assign a group of students for control group purposes.

Creswell (1998) identifies several compelling reasons for a researcher to undertake a qualitative study instead. These reasons include: (a) the nature of the research questions, (b) when the topic needs to be explored, (c) when there is a need to present a detailed view of the topic, and (d) when there is a need to study the individuals in their natural setting. Although less generalizable than experimental results because the data are unique to the context of the study, qualitative researchers can also make predictions based on that particular perspective. The great value in the qualitative method is the openness to rethinking and finding new themes that explain the subject's experiences. In fact, qualitative research methods do collect information from exactly the type of attitude questionnaires, notebook entries, and other observations available in this study. Such information can also be used to formulate a particular paradigm or perspective. The inclusion of qualitative design is a necessary element as it relates to insight, discovery, and interpretation of the phenomena or "the case" that is under consideration (Merriam, 1990). This study sought a holistic description and explanation.

Finally, Marshall and Rossman (1999) identify the need for qualitative research when studying a little-known innovative system. The online museum developed by the researcher in this case was a unique and innovative supplement for science curricula. As this supplement was a little-known innovative system, more than just quantitative data was needed. Furthermore, qualitative research methods are particularly important for studies where the participants' experiences are outside of a societal norm, such as Latino students in middle school biology classes, whose primary language is not English. Qualitative research allows the researcher to understand the meanings of the lives of the students unfiltered by external standards of what is "normal" (Janesick, 1994).

Some of those favoring quantitative methods may insist that qualitative methods are not as good as quantitative methods at generalizing or describing correlational relationships. However, there is also truth in the proposition that qualitative research enriches quantitative research. In addition, purely quantitative research designs can at times be logistically or economically difficult. Research data for this kind of case study is richer and more comprehensive with qualitative and quantitative research methods employed.

Mixed Method Research Design

Particularly in the field of education where complex and interacting factors of causation are hard to isolate, scholars recognize that each method tells us different things about the same world (Stanovich, 2000). Clearly, quantitative research and qualitative research answer different questions. However, the context of the research questions guides the selection and the appropriateness of design and methodology. In this case, the context of Latino middle school students in biology classes lent itself to qualitative observation. Therefore, the strengths of both qualitative and quantitative research were combined, and the data was gathered utilizing a mixed methodology research design. The study provided an information-rich case for a mixed methodology design.

Several additional features of the study identified it to be well suited for a case study using a mixed method design. First, the "case" was identified as two middle school classrooms at one specific school, where the effect of an intervention of an online computer-based biology learning application on the students' knowledge and engagement was studied. Second, the case was a "bounded system." It was bounded in time because the duration was ten weeks, and it was bounded in place because its context was a single middle school. Third, as the previous outline of measuring instruments suggested, multiple sources of information were available to provide an in-depth picture of the students' responses to the intervention. These consisted of student pre- and post-tests, student computer attitude questionnaires, open-ended questionnaires at the end of the study for both students and teacher, rating forms filled out by the teacher on student engagement, student notebooks, and email correspondence.

Mixed Method Data Collection Instruments

Biology content knowledge was evaluated with knowledge tests, student attitudes with questionnaires, and student engagement with open-ended questionnaires, teacher rating forms, and the examination of various student assignments. The measuring instruments included pre-tests, post-tests, questionnaires, teacher rating forms, student notebooks, and emails. These instruments are described in more detail below:

1. Administration of a knowledge test (pre-test and post-test) on the first and fifth weeks covered the biology content of the online museum. The pre-test measured content knowledge before the intervention of the *Museum Explorer*, and the post-test measured any changes in content knowledge after the intervention (see Appendix D). Although both tests were substantively the same, the post-test answer choices were scrambled to prevent students from sharing answers. Quantitative examination of these knowledge tests helped answer research question one.

2. Administration of a computer attitude questionnaires (CAQ) (Knezek, Christensen, & Miyashita, 1999) to the students in the first, fifth, and tenth weeks of the study (see Appendix A). The first computer attitude questionnaire measured the students' attitudes, and the second and third questionnaires measured any changes in students' attitudes after the intervention. Frequencies, percentages, means, standard deviations, and cross tabulations were used to quantitatively examine changes in students' attitude, thus reflecting engagement. These results helped to answer research question two.

3. Administration of open-ended questionnaires to the students and teacher following the administration of the computer attitude questionnaire in the fifth week (see Appendices B & C). The open-ended questionnaires were based on a modified version of a study developed by William Beeland (2003). The teacher questionnaire helped measure the effect of the intervention on student content knowledge and engagement. The student questionnaire further measured the effect on student engagement.

4. Teacher rating of students' engagement. The teacher rating forms were filled out during the three weeks in the computer lab and contributed to the understanding of student engagement (see Appendix E). The teacher rating form was developed from the Robert Bangert-Drowns and Curtis Pyke (2002) study on teacher ratings of student engagement with educational software. Engagement of the student was categorized into various forms or levels, the most basic of which were disengagement, unsystematic engagement, and frustrated engagement. Quantitative examination of the frequencies, means, and standard deviations helped to answer research question two.

5. Notebooks. All students were given Mead notebooks to use during the three-weeks in the computer labs. Examining the number of notebook entries of each student helped to quantitatively measure student engagement and answered research question two.

6. Emails. Students had opportunity to contact the assistant curator at the Portland State University biology museum. Question types were qualitatively examined as well as differences in pre- and post-test

scores of email users compared to non-email users and helped answer research question three.

These measuring instruments were designed to evaluate the effectiveness of an online digital biology museum to transfer knowledge and increase engagement of middle school students. The resulting data was used to explore both whether the introduction of the *Museum Explorer* influenced learning engagement and content knowledge as well as those factors associated with that influence. It also addressed further engagement that may have been generated by the field trip and correspondence with the assistant curator at Portland State University using email.

As this study dealt with both the contemporary issue of computer technology use in the science classroom and the unique intervention of an online biology museum integrated into the middle school science curricula, it was well suited for empirical study within such a context. Further, this case study relied on multiple sources of evidence from several instruments, and thus established a clear chain of evidence (Yin, 1993). Therefore, this study was well suited for using quantitative as well as qualitative methodologies in a case study.

Table 1 summarizes the areas of inquiry and the data collection methods that were used to investigate each area.

The first research question, "What is the learning effect of *Museum Explorer* on middle school students' content knowledge?" was answered using pre-tests and post-tests, the science teacher's responses on the open-ended questionnaires, and the notebook assignment. The data was analyzed quantitatively using Statistical Package for Social Sciences (SPSS, 2003) data management software. The function of this computer program was to create spreadsheet data sets for statistical analysis from textual responses, which were coded and analyzed quantitatively.

The assessment of learning was measured from the differences in the average score for the group before and after the intervention. The limitations were that the full effect of the intervention of *Museum Explorer* could not be compared to no intervention at all. The new experience mid-year for the students could explain some variations. Also, variables such as prior knowledge gained during the first part of the school year as well as differences

TABLE 1.   Data Collection Methods and Research Questions

Research Questions	Pre-/Post-Tests	Student Questionnaires	Teacher Questionnaire	Teacher Rating Forms	Notebooks & Emails
1. What is the effect of *Museum Explorer* on middle school students' content knowledge?	√		√		√
2. What is the effect of *Museum Explorer* on middle school students' learning engagement?		√	√	√	
3. What further engagement *is* generated by field trips to the PSU biology museum and communication with a graduate assistant curator via email?		√	√		√

in instruction between the two classes may have influenced learning. Yet, as a case study, this information provides valuable insights into a real-life context of computer use and knowledge gained in the classroom.

The second research question, "What is the effect of *Museum Explorer* on student learning engagement?" was answered through student computer attitude questionnaires, the teacher ratings of student engagement, open-ended questionnaires, and student notebooks. The computer attitude questionnaire instrument was adapted from the computer attitude questionnaire developed by Knezek, Christensen, and Miyashita (1999). This questionnaire was adapted for the middle school grades and has been validated for more than eight years by researchers in numerous state, national, and international studies. The indices or categories selected from the questionnaire to help answer the research questions regarding engagement were computer importance, computer enjoyment, motivation / persistence, and computer email use. Sixteen questions from the original questionnaire were selected by the researcher to best measure student learning engagement. Four additional demographic questions were added to the questionnaire for relevant information such as gender, age, and computer and Internet access at home. The questionnaire consisted of 16 Likert-type self-report questions at four levels: strongly disagree, disagree, agree, and strongly agree.

The teacher rating form that was used to help measure student engagement was developed from Bangert-Drowns and Pyke's (2002) study on teacher ratings of student engagement with educational software. Their study involved the use of a seven-level scale of engagement aimed at determining the extent to which students are enthusiastic and persistent as they interact with software. The researchers categorized engagement of the student into various forms or levels, the most basic of which were disengagement, unsystematic engagement, and frustrated engagement.

The third research question, "What further engagement is generated by field trips to the Portland State University biology museum and communication with an assistant curator via email?" was answered through examination of the open-ended questionnaires as well as the data gathered on the email users and non-email users.

Table 2 illustrates the indicators of engagement and the items in the instruments that match these indicators and helped to answer the research questions.

TABLE 2.   Indicators of Engagement and Matching Instrument Items

Indicators of Engagement	Instrument	Items in Instrument that Test Indicators
Computer Importance	• Computer Attitude Questionnaire (CAQ)	3, 5, 7
Computer Enjoyment	• Computer Attitude Questionnaire	1, 2, 4, 6, 8, 9, 10
	• Student Open-ended Questionnaire	1, 4, 5
	• Teacher Open-ended Questionnaire	1, 3, 6
	• Teacher Rating Forms	4, 5, 6, 7
Motivation / Persistence	• Computer Attitude Questionnaire	11, 12, 13, 14, 15
	• Student Open-ended Questionnaire	3
	• Teacher Open-ended Questionnaire	3, 6
	• Teacher Rating Forms	4, 5, 6, 7
Email Usage	• Computer Attitude Questionnaire	16
	• Student Open-ended Questionnaire	5
	• Teacher Open-ended Questionnaire	6

RESEARCH SETTING

Background: Site Selection

Edgeview Middle School (pseudonym), located in a rural district in Oregon, was selected for this study. The school district is composed of four elementary schools, two middle schools, and one high school. Nearly 500 students attend Edgeview Middle School. Nearly 65% of all the students in the school's district are considered learners of English as a second language. More than 41% of the district's staff members are bilingual (English-Spanish or English-Russian). The overall rating for academic achievement for Edgeview is low, with over 63% of the students in ESL programs.

The school's mission statement is to "engage and inspire all students to achieve challenging goals and aspirations, and contribute to a diverse world." Computer technology is a big part of this school's mission. While 99% of the nation's public schools have access to the Internet, high poverty schools have fewer rooms with Internet access (National Center for Education Statistics, 2003). Edgeview is newly built and takes its place among the better-equipped public schools in Oregon. The school is equipped with several large computer labs with a total of 186 computers, broadband Internet connections, and the teachers encourage their students to use these labs. Further, one teacher at Edgeview had a technology class responsible for designing web pages for the teachers. After the web page was designed and posted on the Internet, the student responsible for that project kept it up-dated. Many of the teachers have had their own websites. There are two computer labs as well as a computer annex at the middle school where students use computers during class time and after school.

The participants in this study were students in two middle school science classes within Edgeview, with one male science teacher for both classes. The combined classes consisted of 49 students. All 49 of these middle school students were of Latino descent. While all students participated in the activities, data was gathered only from those who returned their parental consent forms.

The decision to do this study at Edgewood originated from contact with a science teacher from Edgeview at an Oregon Science Teachers' Association (OSTA) conference in the fall of 2001 where the researcher had an exhibit. Several hundred science teachers attended this event. The exhibit had specimens from the museum on a table as well as two different videos playing that showed different aspects of the museum. The purpose of the exhibit was to meet science teachers and generate interest in participating in the case study. Previously the Oregon Department of Education School Finance and Data Analysis Department had introduced the researcher to several teachers who had shown interest in the upcoming study. These teachers, although innovative in many of their teaching approaches, did not have the computer technology necessary for this study in their classrooms.

The science teacher whom the researcher met at the OSTA conference had taught science and math at Edgeview for more than 10 years. He spent time discussing the museum and asked questions about my upcoming research project. He seemed interested in the proposed study and suggested using two of his own science classes. After the conference he and the researcher corresponded via email. Further, the researcher observed his science classes on two occasions. The researcher selected his classes for the study. Among all the schools considered in Portland, Oregon, and the surrounding area, only Edgeview was technologically capable of supporting an online museum with a science teacher interested in his students participating in the case study.

FIGURE 3.   Units of Analysis

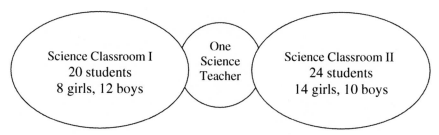

Units of Analysis

One male science teacher and two of his science classes were the units of analysis as shown in Figure 3.

The students in Class II were described by the science teacher as needing more support in academic work than the students in Class I. The effects of *Museum Explorer* were measured through computer attitude questionnaires, knowledge tests, open-ended questionnaires, teacher rating forms, student notebooks, and emails. The teacher filled out only the teacher open-ended questionnaire.

Participants

The science teacher

The science teacher had been a teacher / leader among his colleagues in the school district for over 10 years. As an example, he diligently campaigned along with his students to get the field adjacent to the school designated as a natural habitat, which it eventually was. He conducted outdoor school classes at Edgeview, and the local newspapers often reported on his activities. The researcher first met him at the Oregon Science Teachers Association conference in 2001. There was opportunity to tell him about the upcoming case study, and he expressed interest in his science classes participating.

He taught math, science, and reading in one large classroom in the west wing of Edgeview Middle School. He was in his middle or late thirties and had an excellent connection with his students. He was skilled in computer use and encouraged his students to use the computer lab.

The science teacher expected that the instructional material in *Museum Explorer* would cover areas in the state science standards. He emailed the researcher the Life Science projected plan for the sixth grade. He also explained that not all the life science benchmarks were included in his email attachment because 7th and 8th grades each have their own share of the pie. He said that not all districts would do it the way described in the projected science plan. The list included the main concepts for April-June such as: (a) organisms adapt to their habitat and life requirements, (b) an organism's structures are related to their function, and (c) organisms can be studied and described in terms of cells, tissues, and organs. Everything on the list, he continued, is found within the state standards for middle schools.

The students

Students from two 6th grade science classes participated in the case study. There were a total of 49 students in the two science classes. The science teacher had decided that the students in the two classes would participate in all activities of the case study as part of their regular science classroom study. Therefore, all 49 students participated in the case study activities whether or not all students returned their parental consent forms. However, data from students who failed to bring in the parental consent forms were eliminated from the analysis.

The class that met first in the science classroom consisted of 23 students (Class I), and the class that met later in the morning consisted of 26 students (Class II). Class I had 15 boys and 8 girls with a total of 23 students. Class II had 12 boys and 14 girls with a total of 26 students. All 49 students participated in the activities.

Following is a description of the class composition that the science teacher emailed to the researcher:

> My 6th grade science classes are enrolled in a bilingual maintenance program. Many of these students have been enrolled in bilingual classes since kindergarten, starting mostly in their mother tongue, Spanish, and transitioning gradually to a mostly English program. But our district has decided in the last couple of years that we want to maintain

bilingual literacy skills through high school. My students receive social studies instruction in Spanish, but all other subjects are in English. They are unusual in that they have maintained native language skills. But they are also unusual in that their academic skills have been generally high in all their classes. We expect a lot of them.

The second of my classes are kids who seem to need support in English to achieve well in all classes. Their skills are not as high. But the general literacy level of both classes is pretty good. They are all readers in English. Sixty-two percent of kids in this district hear another language spoken at home. For this reason, we are working to assure that all classes are taught with attentiveness to language, while keeping academic standards high.

This email alerted the researcher to the potential differences and academic needs the students from the two classes might have. During the final development of the *Museum Explorer* website, particular care was given to help those students who were somewhat behind in their English skills, such as adding the voice reading of the text.

The participant observer

Throughout the study the researcher was a participant-observer. According to Marshall and Rossman (1999), participant observation demands first-hand involvement in the social world chosen for the study and is basic to all qualitative studies. Yin (1993) suggests that the investigator may take a variety of roles within the case study situation and may actually participate in the events being studied. In this case study, not only was the researcher engaged in managing the events, but also had designed and created the website. Participant-observation may have problems dealing with potential biases (1993). Some of these potential problems were dealt with by having a variety of measuring instruments to help answer the research questions.

The researcher was more than a physical presence throughout the study, and both the science teacher and researcher were kept busy throughout the study. During the first, fifth, and tenth weeks of the administration of the questionnaire and pre- and post-tests, the students had questions that needed further explanations. Furthermore, since the questionnaires and tests were given the same day, and with the involvement of the preparations of specimens for the pre- and post-tests while class was in progress, considerable synchronization of timing was required. After each session with the classes, the researcher took time to write field notes about what had transpired and notations on the students' responses.

The School Context

Edgeview Middle School and Meridian Elementary School. Edgeview Middle School and Meridian Elementary School (pseudonyms) are both in the heart of Oregon's heavily agricultural Willamette Valley. The town has a population of more than 20,000 and has a rich cultural base of Anglos, Latinos, Mennonites, Russians, and senior citizens. The school district has the highest percentage of Spanish-speaking students in the state, with nearly 65% of all students in the district learners of English as a second language. More than 41% of the district's staff members are bilingual English-Spanish or bilingual English-Russian.

The October 2003, Edgeview District School enrollment showed the student body to be composed of 69% Latino, 16% Russian, and 15% Anglo. Edgeview Middle School and Meridian Elementary School are located at the same site and share resources. The computer lab for this study is located in the elementary school. More than 1000 students attend these two schools. Both schools have computer labs where the students have computers to work on. The students from the two science classes would spend time working in these labs occasionally. The combined schools have a total of 307 computers.

There are nearly 500 students who attend Edgeview Middle School and 600 students who attend Meridian Elementary School. The students in the science teacher's two classes who participated in this case study were of Latino heritage. The school recognizes its unique characteristic of diverse cultures as shown by the school's motto, "diverse in culture: unified in mission."

Edgeview is located one mile outside the town. The descriptions from the researcher's field notes described the faculty, staff, and students as friendly and well dressed. The school structure itself was immaculate and modern. The school culture could best be characterized as being upbeat. The researcher's experience with the students on the two visits before the study was that they were well behaved and friendly. The nicely prepared samples of student work displayed on the walls outside each classroom gave the impression of highly motivated students and teachers. The Meridian Elementary School students, as they moved from classroom to classroom, followed quietly in single file behind an adult. Edgeview Middle School students, however, visited with each other animatedly as they went to their classrooms. The administrative offices for both schools are behind glass walls with couches for students to sit at when they wait for a parent, or take "time-out" from the classroom for misbehaving.

The science classroom

The science classroom was in a large room in the west wing of Edgeview. It had enough tables and chairs for the students to be comfortable with plenty of room to move about. There were four sections in the room where two or three large tables were placed together, and five or six students sat at each section. The teacher had assigned the sitting arrangements at the beginning of the school year, and each day the students sat at the same seat. The first, fifth, and tenth weeks of the study were conducted in this room, as well as one day in the tenth week for the follow-up computer attitude questionnaire. There were many science projects the students had created in their science or math classes occupying every available counter, wall, or cabinet face.

The computer lab

Meridian Elementary School is part of the same building complex as Edgeview Middle School. Two cafeterias for the schools separate the elementary school from the middle school. The computer lab available to the science teacher and the two classes for the duration of the study is located in Meridian Elementary School, and was used for weeks two, three, and four of the study. The science teacher had hoped to obtain use of the best computer lab, but another teacher reserved this lab at the beginning of the year. It was important for the students to have headphones for sound, and only the lab in the elementary school was fully equipped. Except for the long walk from the home science classroom to the computer lab at the far end of the elementary school building, the lab was suitable for the case study.

The students from the two classes came to the science classroom at different times. During the three weeks in the computer lab, the students from Class I arrived at the lab at 12:00 and left at 1:00. Students from Class II arrived at the computer lab at 2:15 and left at 3:15.

Meridian Elementary School also has a library with 12 PCs and an annex lab with 25 Pentium III computers. The computer lab used for the two classes at Meridian Elementary has 30 Pentium III computers, each with 1.7GHz, 128 MB RAM, and 20 GB hard drives. The building has a single T-1 broadband connection to share between both schools. The routing of connection was from Meridian Elementary School to Salem to open Internet, and then to Portland State University where the *Museum Explorer* website was hosted.

Intervention

The* Museum Explorer *website. The purpose of this research was, in part, to determine if there is any noticeable positive relationship between biology learning and the use of interactive computer-based materials. In particular, the case study aimed to identify a relationship between student learning and engagement and the use of dynamic and interactive computer-based media. The goal was to create such a dynamic and interactive computer-based learning environment and see if it increased students' engagement and understanding of basic biology facts. Attention was focused on designing an environment that would engage students of middle school age in an interactive way, motivate learning, and increase interest in biology.

Studies have shown (Mayer & Moreno, 1998) that students better understand an explanation when corresponding words and pictures are presented at the same time. Also, auditory narration may be better than on-screen text when giving explanations. Therefore, the aim of the *Museum Explorer* was to use the economy and potential of Internet Technology to give students a learning experience that used varied multimedia such as video, sound, 3D images, and the accumulated store of facts on northwest vertebrates.

It was designed to contain joint textual, visual, and auditory information about mammals. The students viewed images of the specimens housed in the museum, but also accessed further information regarding the species. This innovative use of Internet Technology enabled the *Museum Explorer* to give students an opportunity to view videos of the living species, hear sounds the living animals make, see habitat and biotic province maps, view rotations of skulls, listen to short lectures, take quizzes to test their understanding, and much more.

With the above goals in mind, the *Museum Explorer* (www.museum-explorer.org) was specifically designed for this research project as an interactive online computer-based biology learning application. The application was created by the researcher for this study, and development was guided by five requirements: economy, scalability, easy administration, modular design, and support for multimedia. Meeting the economy requirement would allow the project to get done and the application to be maintained on a limited budget. The scalability requirement would allow the application to be later expanded to meet the growing needs of a biology museum without fundamental changes to application architecture. The easy administration requirement would allow for any museum staffer to update the application with information from the latest specimen without any specialized knowledge in programming or software design. The modular design requirement would allow the application to be easily expanded and altered through modules to meet changing needs of teachers and curators. Finally, the multimedia requirement would ensure the continued support for the addition of the multimedia content identified in the study as enhancing the student content knowledge and contributing to student engagement.

Three specific open source software tools were identified as the most viable options to realizing these requirements of economy, scalability, easy administration, modular design, and multimedia support: (1) Apache web server (httpd.apache.org), (2) MySQL database server (www.mysql.com), and (3) PHP hypertext pre-processing language (www.php.net). Apache web server was used because it was the server platform Portland State University's Office of Information Technology provided access to for this project. Second, MySQL database server was selected because it was supported on the Apache web servers provided for the study by Portland State University; and because it was widely considered the world's most popular open source database. Third, PHP scripts were used both because Portland State University's servers supported PHP scripts and because PHP scripts provided a web interface to the potentially large database of biology specimen records used in this research project (see Appendix L).

Although it was under the researcher's direction and control, the *Museum Explorer* was hosted temporarily for the duration of the research project in a website folder made available for the study by Portland State University's Office of Information Technology. It was developed using freely available Open Source software (see Appendix L). Graphics and other multimedia content were obtained, with permissions, from various sources that included images and videos of specimens taken within the Portland State University biology museum, archived media from faculty, and public domain media available for not-for-profit use by other teaching institutions and websites. Hereafter it will be referred to as "*Museum Explorer*," or simply the "website."

The Learning Approach of Museum Explorer

The *Museum Explorer* was intended to be used in conjunction with the three-phase learning cycle approach noted previously in the background. Table 3 displays this learning cycle approach.

The plan was for the science teacher to implement the three phases of the learning cycle approach during the three weeks his students used the website. The three-phase learning cycle approach includes: (a) exploration, (b) concept development, and (3) application. *Museum Explorer* followed the three-phase learning cycle approach as discussed in the background.

- *Exploration Phase*: During the exploration phase, the students learned through their own actions and reactions as they explored new ideas (Lawson, 2001). As the students explored the website, motivation was expected to be heightened before the concept was introduced. Students in this study were expected to be particularly interested in the videos, and the interactive quizzes and games. During the exploration phase, students had opportunity to explore the website in an interactive and open-ended manner. Such exploration raised questions,

TABLE 3.   Learning Cycle Approach

Exploration Phase
Students learn through their own actions and reactions as they explore new ideas and materials on the website. They are encouraged to write down questions in their notebooks or email the curator in the museum.

Concept Development Phase
Students focus on content and terms they discovered during the exploration phase. Students discuss interactively with others. Teacher takes more active role during this phase, largely in the science classroom. Students read emails from assistant curator and discuss answers with the teacher.

Application Phase
Students reinforce and expand their interest and knowledge. Students are given new examples to problems. Material in the website advances incrementally to help students learn concepts in a variety of ways. Students use the knowledge gained from the website in assignments given by the teacher in the classroom

complexities, or contradictions. The students were encouraged to email the assistant curator at the university museum any questions that had arisen during the explorations of the website. Further, the students were encouraged to keep a record of these questions that arose in their notebooks.

• *Concept Development Phase*: The concept development phase was a time to focus on content and terms the students discovered during the exploration phase. This phase built on the students' discoveries, inquiries, and curiosity. The students wrote down in their notebooks the new terms and concepts learned each day. Further, they used these new terms in homework assignments given by the teacher in the science classroom.

- *Application Phase*: The concepts were reinforced or expanded in the application phase, and the students had more time with the website. Some pages in the website were designed for exploration, others for concept development, and still others for application. The activities for the students included writing in their notebooks and sending emails to the curator of the biology museum. During the application phase the students were given new examples of problems that reinforced the concept they had learned. This phase gives time and opportunities for students to incorporate the concepts into their own thinking.

Oregon State Standards

Since this research project was conducted within the Oregon public school system, the schedule of learning concepts were designed around the main concepts in the state standards in Oregon for the duration of the case study. While there are no benchmarks for the sixth grade, it was helpful to examine the benchmarks for the fifth grade, especially since the students in the study are ESL (English as a Second Language) learners. In 1996, the school district in which the case study was conducted transformed its educational program for English language learners. The English Transition Program Mission was started in 1996 whose mission is to develop English proficiency among English language learners and assist them in achieving the high academic standards which are required of all students. Because of this it was important to keep standards high, yet attainable. After review and consultation with the science teacher, a few of the Oregon benchmarks for the fifth grade were identified that were appropriate for the case study. These were:

- Group or classify organisms based on a variety of characteristics.
- Describe basic plant and animal structures and their functions.
- Associate specific structures with their functions in the survival of the organism.
- Describe the relationship between characteristics of specific habitats and the organisms that live there.

- Use drawings or models to represent a series of food chains for specific habitats.
- Identify the producers, consumers, and decomposers in a given habitat.
- Describe how adaptations help a species survive.
- Make observations. Ask questions or form hypotheses based on those observations, which can be explored through scientific investigations.

One concept the Oregon state standards require, and which the science teacher had requested the *Museum Explorer* to introduce, was how organisms adapt to their habitat and life requirements. Therefore, the website was designed so that students could study organism adaptation on several of the web pages. General information about mammals was yet another concept incorporated into the teaching materials on the website. Behavior and habitat maps were introduced. Table 4 lists the concepts covered, the web pages within the *Museum Explorer* where concepts were discussed, and the questions on the pre-test and post-test that related to the concepts. Students

Table 4. Oregon Science Standards Covered in Web Pages and Pre- and Post-Tests

Concept	Web Page	Question #
1. Group organisms based on a variety of characteristics.	About Mammals, Overview, Skeleton,	2, 4, 5, 6
2. Describe basic plant and animal structures and their functions.	About Mammals, Skeleton / Teeth / Skulls	1, 2, 3, 5, 7, 8
3. Associate specific structures with their functions in the survival of the organism.	About Mammals, Skeleton / Teeth, Skulls	2, 4, 5, 6, 12
4. Describe the relationship between characteristics of specific habitats and the organisms that live there.	Overview, Habitat, Behavior	2, 4, 11
5. Use drawings or models to represent a series of food chains for specific habitats.	Overview, Habitat, Skeleton	9
6. Identify the producers, consumers, and decomposers in a given habitat.	Overview, Habitat	9
7. Describe how adaptations help a species survive.	Overview, Behavior, Skeleton / Teeth	3, 6
8. Make observations. Ask questions or form hypotheses based on those observations.	Behavior	10

learned about these concepts not only from the text, but also from the many videos in the web site.

The teacher found the *Museum Explorer* to be a good fit for April's science concepts and used what the students learned in the website as a launch pad for further discussions in more detail in his science classroom. This was a continuation of the concept development phase of the learning cycle.

Detailed Description of Museum Explorer

The *Museum Explorer* website was designed with graphics and moving objects that would hold a student's interest. Even the beginning page had a variety of multimedia and interactive activities to pursue as shown in Figure 4.

FIGURE 4.   Main Web Page in *Museum Explorer,* 2004©

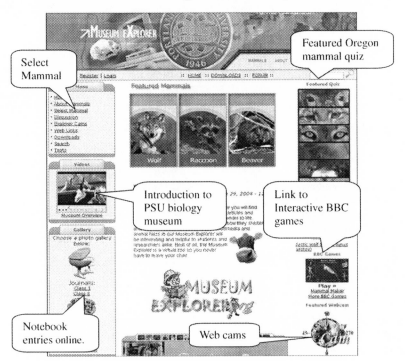

The students could visit the animal web cam links, play interactive animal games, or listen to a professor of biology at Portland State University introduce the physical museum. The menu at the upper left of the website main page included a Select Mammal menu item. Selecting this item took the viewer to a circular menu of mammals included for the study (see Figure 5). Since the time frame of this project was limited, students were unable to explore all animals in depth. However, materials covered sufficiently met the three-phase learning approach, state standards, as well as the particular learning objectives of the study.

Mammal Overview web page. Five basic categories of information were presented for each mammal: overview, skeleton, habitat, behavior, and maps. Each of these pages in turn included printouts, videos, text, audio, quizzes, and other subtopics in that category's own submenu. Selecting a mammal in the menu shown below took the student to the Overview page. Each of

FIGURE 5.   Select Mammal Menu Web Page in *Museum Explorer,* 2004©

these detail pages had five selectable tabs at the top of the page corresponding to five categories of details about that mammal (see Figure 6).

Since the students in this case study were Latino, the website was designed with the option for them to listen along in English as they read each paragraph. All paragraphs of text had an audio button so that the student could both read and listen to the narration read aloud by a voice actor. A few vocabulary words for each page were highlighted and were presented in a vocabulary box to the lower left of each page. The student could click on each word to read the definition of that word, as well as listen to the audio

FIGURE 6.   Cougar Overview Web Page in *Museum Explorer,* 2004©

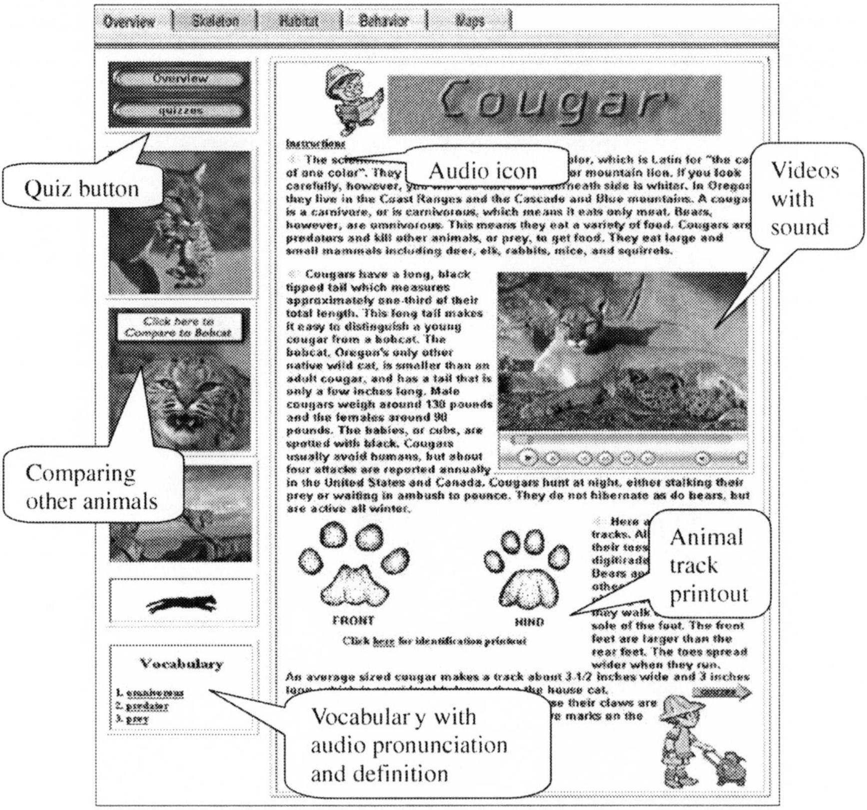

pronunciation. Ideally, a Spanish-English dictionary with audio pronunciation would be added to the web site.

Each of the tabbed mammal detail pages had a menu that linked to a sub-page containing interactive quizzes (Figure 7). These pages were designed as part of the application phase in the learning cycle where students could reinforce what they had just learned. Students were instructed to proceed through all these quizzes.

The interactive quizzes were made with a test-creating software tool readily available on the Internet which can be used free of charge by those working for government or non-profit institutions (http://web.uvic.ca/hrd/hotpot/). The types of interactive quizzes included multiple choice, short-answer, jumbled-sentence, crossword, matching / ordering, and gap-fill exercises.

FIGURE 7.   Quiz Menu Web Page in *Museum Explorer*, 2004©

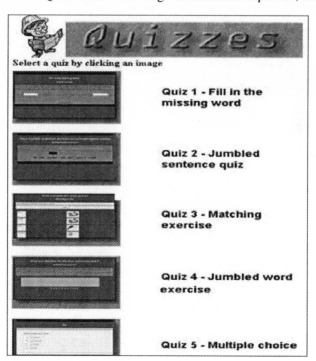

Mammal Skeleton web page. Following the Overview page was the Skeleton page (see Figure 8). Here the students listened to the assistant curator of the biology museum discuss the skull or bones of the animal. The page was designed to complement the Oregon state standards and concepts. These can be viewed in Table 4 and are concepts 1, 2, and 3. The Skulls and Bones pages had interactive rotations of skulls and videos about bones. Again, these pages each had interactive quizzes.

Figure 8.   Skulls and Bones Web Page in *Museum Explorer*, 2004©

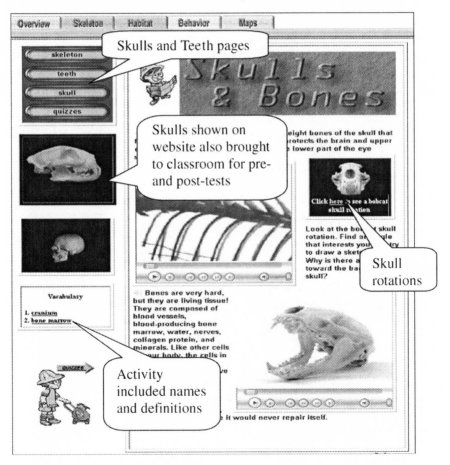

Mammal Habitat web page. The Habitat page provided an opportunity for students to learn about biomes with the specific climate and life forms that live there (see Figure 9).

This page was designed to follow the concepts in the Oregon science standards requirements. These concepts are listed as concepts 4, 5, and 6 in Table 4.

FIGURE 9.   Habitat Web Page in *Museum Explorer*, 2004©

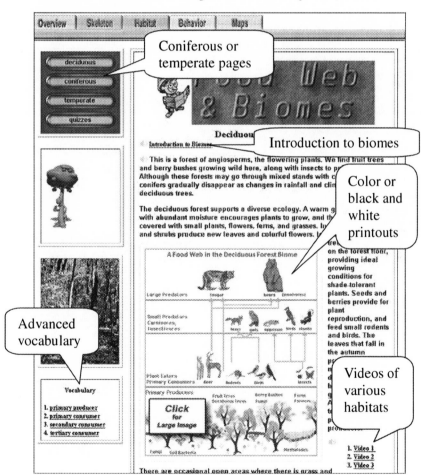

Mammal Behavior web page. The Behavior page (see Figure 10) was designed to complement the Oregon science standards concepts that are listed as concepts 7 and 8 in Table 4.

Several things made this page more interactive than the other pages. There were more sounds the animal makes on this page, more videos, and an assignment to pretend they are field biologists studying an animal. Students were encouraged to select one of the videos and write about what

Figure 10.   Behavior Web Page in *Museum Explorer,* 2004©

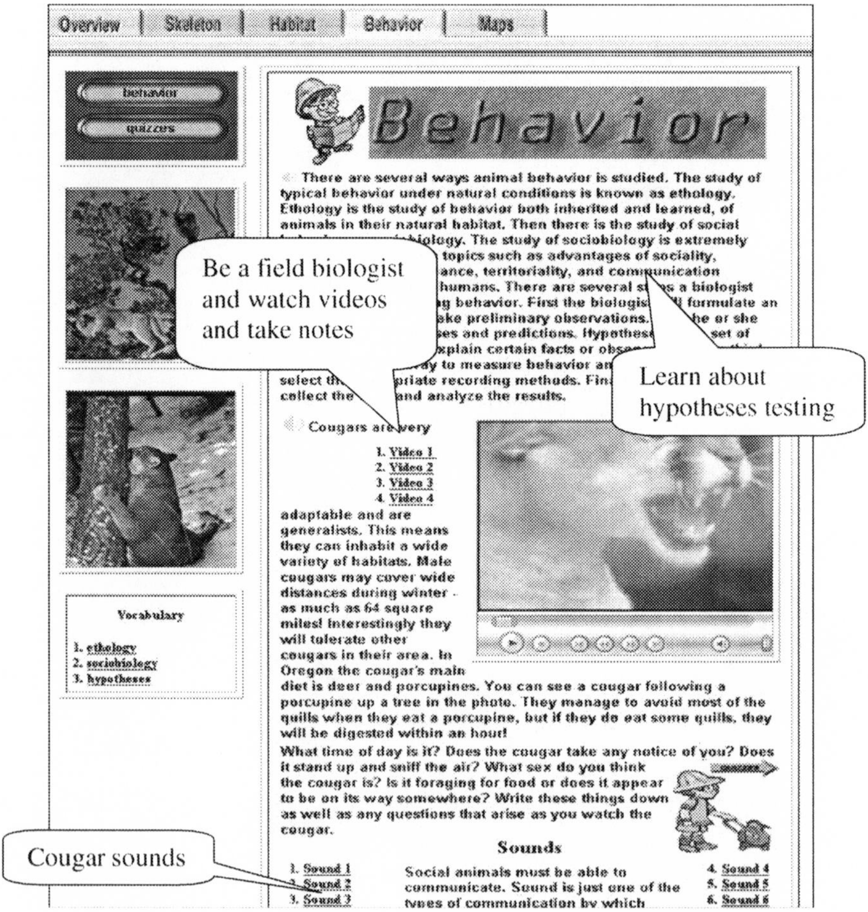

they think was happening. The students then drew pictures in the notebooks as a field biologist would do.

Mammal Maps web page. The Maps page was the final page for the students to explore. Students searched for information about the county they live in and if any of the mammals they studied in *Museum Explorer* live in their county (see Figure 11).

FIGURE 11.   Maps Web Page in *Museum Explorer,* 2004©

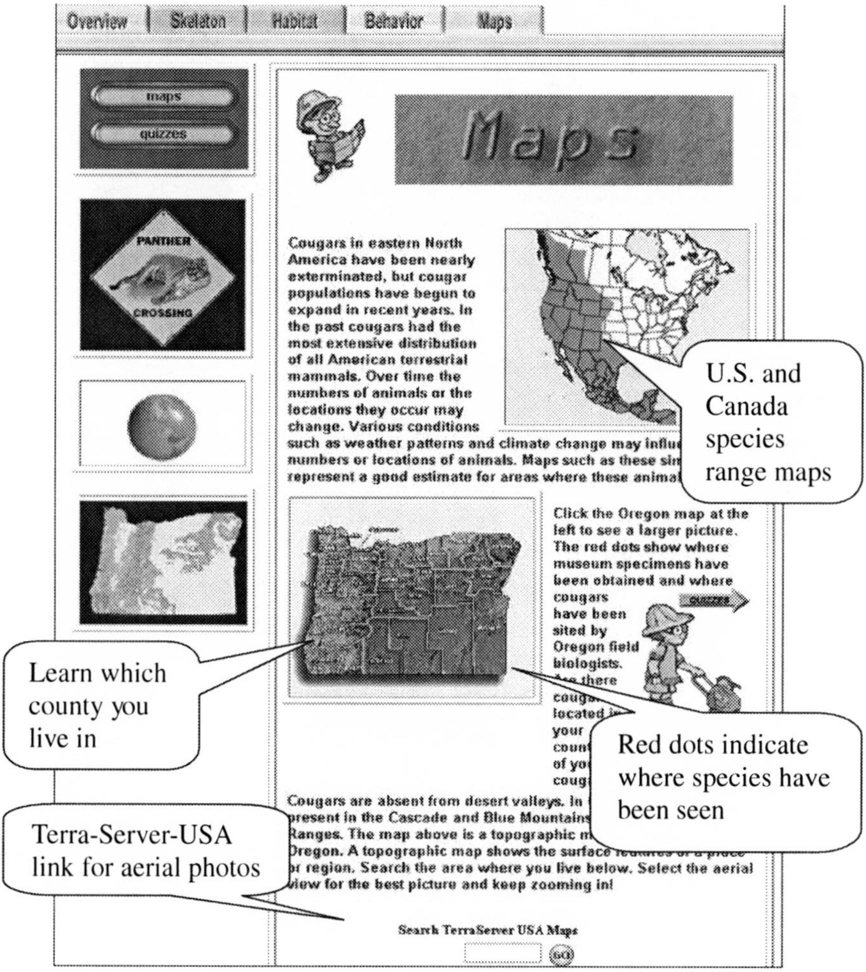

Museum / School Partnership

This study marked the potential beginning stage of development for a new university museum / school partnership to develop through the use of a virtual biology museum at Portland State University. Dr. Luis Ruedas, Professor of Biology at Portland State University, served as the PSU liaison to the collaborative. He authorized the use of primary museum resources as needed and made arrangements for the graduate biology assistant curator to connect with the middle school students.

For a number of years, the researcher developed and designed a computerized database of the museum's specimen collections under the direction of the biology department, specifically Dr. Richard Forbes. The researcher and Dr. Forbes realized the great potential of making these resources available to non-university classrooms through Internet connections. Fortunately, the PSU biology department supported making the comprehensive information on each of the museum's 10,000 specimens available to area classrooms. Developing an engaging interactive multimedia virtual biology museum seemed to offer a unique integration of science, education, and high computer technology.

The Portland State University biology museum was known in the early 1960s as the Portland State College Collection of Vertebrates. Professor George Fisler and his students developed a basic collection of study specimens of fishes, amphibians, reptiles, birds, and mammals. Most were from northwestern Oregon, but some specimens collected by Professor Fisler in the northern Neotropics were also included.

Beginning in 1964, through donations of specimens, mutually beneficial exchanges with other institutions, and collections by Dr. Richard Forbes and students under his direction, the museum's holdings increased substantially both in numbers and geographic range of specimens represented.

Since the arrival of Dr. Deborah Duffield, and under her leadership in the Marine Mammals Stranding Program, many significant specimens of marine mammals have been added to the collection. Also of special importance is the growing collection of assembled and mounted skeletons, prepared by students under the direction of Dr. Forbes, Dr. Duffield, and Dr. Stan Hillman, of a wide variety of terrestrial and marine birds and mammals. The collection of vertebrates was given its current name in 1998.

Currently, the museum contains nearly 10,000 specimens. Specimens housed in the museum serve the scientific community in several ways. They are available to PSU classes and for examination by visiting scientists, artists, agency personnel, and school groups at all levels. However, few local schools are aware of the existence of this valuable educational resource. Further, there may be those who may not know how to utilize it even if they knew it was available. Access to an online virtual biology museum in connection with the university could introduce more educators to this powerful learning interface. While the Oregon Department of Education does have a section on virtual tours on its website, none originates from local educational institutions.

STUDY PROCEDURES

Schedule of Events

The study was designed to begin during the spring of 2004 and continue for ten weeks, which included the follow-up questionnaire after the first five weeks. The students took part in the study as an extension of their regular science curriculum. A total of 10 weeks were spent at the Edgeview Middle School and Meridian Elementary School where the computer lab is located. Students were told that although they are required to participate in the study as part of their daily science class schedule, the data gathered from their participation would be withheld from the study if they so chose. Again, the students' participation in the 10-week study did not affect their grades.

The researcher visited the school and science classroom twice before the study began. The first visit to Edgeview provided an opportunity to meet with the principal. The principal, a biologist, had already visited with the science teacher and was interested in the possibility of one or two of the science classes participating in the case study. The science teacher and researcher corresponded through email many times on details about the upcoming case study. The second visit was two months before the study began in order to meet the students from the two classes who were to participate in the study. Details were discussed over the phone several times. Information from the science teacher was gathered to make the necessary revisions of the instruments used in the study. The preparations for the study with the science teacher consisted of two visits to his science classroom, emails, and phone conversations. During the design of the website it had been an important element to receive input from the science teacher and follow as much as possible the suggestions he would make.

The science teacher participated throughout the duration of the study and took one open-ended questionnaire based on a modified version of a study developed by William Beeland (2003). This questionnaire asked questions on the perceived engagement of the students (see Appendix C). The teacher also came on the field trip and remained with the students each class period, so the answers for the open-ended questionnaire came from first-hand observations of his students during the study.

The case study unit was scheduled to extend over a 10-week period, and the schedule of events was organized into first week tasks, second through fourth week tasks, fifth week tasks, and tenth week follow-up tasks.

Week one consisted of some teacher training time when there was an opportunity outside of class time for the science teacher to try *Museum Explorer* online and go over the schedule for the next several weeks. The pre-test and a computer attitude questionnaire were administered to the two classes on a single day in their science classroom. The second, third, and fourth weeks were spent in the computer lab where the students worked on the *Museum Explorer* website. The main portion of the study was conducted during these three weeks in the computer lab in Meridian Elementary School where the students, teacher, and researcher met three days each week for 60 minutes per day.

During the fifth week the students took a field trip to the university biology museum. The following day the post-test, the second computer attitude questionnaire, and an open-ended questionnaire were administered. The science teacher at this time filled out the open-ended questionnaire. Plans were in place if it became necessary to postpone the field trip to a later date. The tenth week, or five weeks following the day the students took the second round of tests, the students took a third computer attitude questionnaire in the science classroom. This questionnaire was identical to the previous two that were administered during the first and fifth weeks. Figure 12 illustrates the project timeline for the case study.

FIGURE 12. *Museum Explorer* Projected Timeline

Task	Week #1	Week #2	Week #3	Week #4	Week #5	Week #10
Teacher Training	Friday					
Implementation of *Museum Explorer*		3 Days (180 min. total)	3 Days (180 min. total)	3 Days (180 min. total)		
Teacher Questionnaire					Friday	Friday
Student Questionnaires	Friday				Friday	Friday
Pre- and Post-Tests	Friday				Friday	Friday
Field Trip					Thursday	

As this timeline suggests, most of the case study fieldwork time was done in the computer lab during weeks two, three, and four. During these peak weeks of the study, the students came to the computer lab for one hour each Tuesday, Wednesday, and Thursday. During these weeks the researcher saw the students only at the computer lab. The students worked directly with the website during the second, third, and fourth weeks in the computer lab. The students put entries in their notebooks every day in the lab as they worked on the website. The students used the main computer in the lab to email the assistant curator of the university biology museum. They used the science teacher's email account to send the emails since they did not have their own email accounts.

Students also kept a daily notebook of questions that occurred to them in the course of the class that day, what they thought the answer might be, and communicated with the assistant curator via email for help. As the students already used notebooks for science and math classes, no formal instructions in taking notes were needed. Directions were given to keep notes on interesting facts, write down questions that came to mind as they explored the online museum, and used the pages for drawing pictures. Periodically the students checked in to see what the assistant curator had emailed in reply, and shared this with the other students.

The students progressed through the web pages at their own pace, although they were told at the beginning of each class what pages to start with. The pages had several activities to explore, including vocabulary words from the text, videos, printouts, and quizzes. Each page had more material than might be covered in the sixty minutes in the computer lab. If they had not finished a page the previous day, they were allowed to finish up the next day while others went ahead with the topic for the day. Table 5 illustrates the topics covered each week. All pages had five or six interactive quizzes. Each quiz had information that could be found on the page they were studying. The students were directed not to go to another animal until they had read all information on the page, watched the videos, looked up the vocabulary words, and had taken all the quizzes on the quiz page.

The last Thursday of the fourth week ended the computer lab sessions. Week five consisted of a field trip on Thursday to the Oregon Zoo and Portland State University biology museum. The teacher had decided to include the trip to the Oregon Zoo on the same day the students came to the museum. In the morning they visited the zoo and in the afternoon they visited the university biology museum.

The following day the students took the post-test, filled out the open-ended questionnaires, and took the computer attitude questionnaire a second time. The format of this questionnaire was identical to the first questionnaire. The students first took the post-test. This was identical to the pre-test with the exception of two specimens. The pre-test and post-test will be discussed in more detail in Chapter Four. The post-test had the multiple-choice answers scrambled for half of the tests to prevent sharing answers. The students from both classes spent approximately 30 minutes on the

TABLE 5. Schedule of Topics Covered During Study

	Week One	Week Two	Week Three
	About Mammals		
Tuesday	Mammal Overview	Teeth and Skulls	Habitat / Behavior
Wednesday	Mammal Overview	Teeth and Skulls	Behavior / Maps
Thursday	Skeleton	Habitat / Behavior	Maps

post-test. Following the post-test the students spent 10 or 15 minutes taking the computer attitude questionnaire. Next they took the open-ended response questionnaire.

The follow-up computer attitude questionnaire was given on the 10th week after the start of the study. This questionnaire was administered to see if there were attitude changes during the last five weeks. The follow-up questionnaire was identical to the previous two questionnaires. The students spent 10 to 15 minutes to fill out the questionnaire.

Overall, the students using *Museum Explorer* gained experience in the identification of the distinguishing characteristics of animals and in recognizing adaptations of mammals. They learned about the food chains in an ecosystem, learned form and function of bone structure of mammals, and learned about Oregon counties. Assessment took place throughout the learning cycle experience. The students took daily interactive quizzes on the website to monitor their own progress and put the scores in their notebooks.

Participation in this project was voluntary and involved no unusual risks to the participants. The parents could change their decision to allow their child to participate at any time during the project with no negative consequences. Although the students were required to participate in the activities, any student at any time could have requested that data from his / her participation be removed with no negative consequences. This means that no responses from that student would be entered into the data analysis.

Sampling Strategies and Data Collection

This study used several instruments to collect the information necessary to answer the case study's three research questions. The last day of the first week the students took the first computer attitude questionnaire. This computer attitude questionnaire measured the students' attitude, and the second and third questionnaires measured any changes in students' attitudes after the intervention. The questionnaires took approximately 30 minutes to complete.

Following the administration of the computer attitude questionnaire, the students took a pre-test on simple biology facts that took around 40 minutes to complete. The pre-test measured content knowledge before the intervention of the *Museum Explorer*, and the post-test taken the fifth week measured any changes in content knowledge after the intervention (see Appendix D). The instrument section gives a more detailed account of the pre-test and post-test. The purpose of the pre-test was to determine the students' level of basic biology understanding relevant to the topics covered in this study.

Weeks two through four, which made up most of the treatment of the study, consisted of student computer time in the lab for 60 minutes each day. During this time the science teacher and researcher were in the lab with the students to direct and collect various qualitative data. Students worked on *Museum Explorer* and took the online quizzes. They were encouraged to write notes about what they learned in the Mead notebooks. Students also used their notebooks to write questions or problems that they had during the three weeks, or simply drew pictures they liked on the website. Students were encouraged by the science teacher to email the assistant curator at the university museum when they had questions as they explored the website. The teacher filled out several of the teacher rating forms during weeks two through four. The teacher rating form was a seven-question rating of student engagement based on the engagement scale developed by Bangert-Drowns and Pyke (2002). The teacher rated a certain percentage of the students on their engagement with the online museum. During week five, the day following the field trip to the Portland State University biology museum, the post-test, computer attitude questionnaire, and the open-ended questionnaires were administered in the science classroom at Edgeview Middle School.

Throughout this data collection, confidentiality was assured by strict adherence to coded format of pre-test, post-test, questionnaires, and teacher rating forms. Consent forms were obtained from the science teacher, the students' parents, the students themselves, and the school principal (see Appendices).

Measurement Instruments

Knowledge test

A knowledge test (pre- and post-tests) was developed to cover the biology content of the curriculum (see Appendix D). It helped answer the research question "What is the effect of *Museum Explorer* on middle school students' content knowledge?". The purpose of the test was to help establish the respondents' biology knowledge base in the first week and again at the fifth week after exploring the virtual biology museum and taking the field trip. The pre- and post-tests were composed of questions on the content found in *Museum Explorer* and took approximately 40 minutes to complete. Both tests were the same. All questions fell within the Science Content Standards (Oregon Department of Education, 2003). These standards included describing the characteristics, structures, and function of organisms and explaining the behavior and interdependence of organisms in their natural environments.

The science room was large with enough tables and chairs for the students to be comfortable with plenty of room to move about. Two or three tables were placed together to make separate sections, and around five or six students sat at each section. The teacher had assigned these sitting arrangements at the beginning of the school year, and each day the students sat at the same spot. The arrangements for the pre- and post-tests were that three extra tables had two or three physical specimens from the museum such as skins, skulls, or skeletons. At the time of the tests four or five students were assigned to each of the three tables with the specimens.

While questions one through eight had corresponding skulls, skeletons, skins, mounted specimens, bones, and teeth, questions nine through twelve had no specimens to which the questions referred, but rather multiple-choice questions. The four questions with no corresponding specimens were answered at two tables where the students sat. The remainder of the students sat at their own tables to answer these four questions. When the groups at the tables were finished, the teacher called out for the students to rotate to the next table. The students had about six minutes at each table. The post-test had two different forms with the multiple choices for each question in a different order. Once the students were standing in front of the tables, these tests were alternately given to the students. When the tests were completed, the teacher or one of the students who had completed the test collected them.

Student computer attitude questionnaires

The computer attitude questionnaire was given the first, fifth, and tenth weeks and helped to answer the research questions on engagement. The questionnaire instrument (see Appendix A) was adapted from the Computer Attitude Questionnaire (Knezek, Christensen, & Miyashita, 1999). It has been developed and validated for more than eight years by researchers in numerous state, national, and international studies (1999). The categories selected from the computer attitude questionnaire helped answer the research questions regarding engagement were computer importance, computer enjoyment, computer motivation / persistence, and computer email use. The constructs measured by the questionnaire were defined by the meanings commonly used for these terms in standard English. Computer importance for this study is defined as the perceived value or significance of knowing how to use computers. Computer enjoyment is defined as the amount of pleasure derived from using computers. Motivation and persistence is defined as unceasing effort and positive attitudes while working with computers. The questionnaire for this case study was modified to a 16-item questionnaire consisting of Likert-type self-report questions. There were four additional questions regarding demographics such as age, gender, and home computer and Internet access. The responses were on a four-point scale of strongly disagree, disagree, agree, and strongly agree.

The questionnaires collected demographic information about each student. The students were asked to indicate personal information regarding gender, age, language status, and computer and Internet access at home. The computer attitude questionnaire was administered during the fifth week and was the same as the previous questionnaire.

Follow-up questionnaire

A follow-up computer attitude questionnaire was given to the students the tenth week, or five weeks after the completion of the first five weeks of the study. This follow-up questionnaire was given to determine if there were changes in attitude regarding computers during the four weeks of no intervention.

Student notebooks

Students were given Mead notebooks in which they entered notes on various things they learned from the website. They also were encouraged to draw pictures of interesting things they found on the website. They brought these notebooks with them from the science classroom when they came to the lab each day, and took them to the science classroom after the lab session. They also wrote down their scores on the online quizzes. These notebooks offered some insight into student engagement. The number of pages of text written or pictures drawn was used as an indicator of student engagement.

Email correspondence

Email correspondence helped determine the comfort level and engagement of students in the use of this type of communication and the students' ability to investigate topics of interest to them. The assistant curator from the university biology museum not only corresponded with the students using email, but was seen by the students on the website as he discussed skulls and skeletons. Further, he met with them when they went on the field trip to the biology museum.

Teacher and student open-ended questionnaires

There were open-ended questionnaires (see Appendices B & C) that allowed the students and teacher to voice their opinions regarding their experiences using *Museum Explorer* and the field trip to the museum. These questions that were analyzed qualitatively, added a dimension to the measurement of engagement not identified through the computer attitude questionnaire. The open-ended questionnaires for the teacher and students were modified from a previous study on student engagement in which the researchers examined both students' and teachers' attitudes on technology use in the classroom (Beeland, 2003). Because the teacher knew his students on a day-to-day basis, his perceived beliefs about the students' engagement revealed important factors unavailable through the students' questionnaires.

Teacher rating forms

The teacher rating form (see Appendix E) was developed from the Robert Bangert-Drowns and Curtis Pyke (2002) study on student engagement using educational software. Their study concluded that students are often enthusiastic and persistent as they interact with software. These observations can be categorized into modes of behavior. The seven modes and the descriptions are listed in Table 6.

This taxonomy on a seven-mode rating scale was used. Engagement of the student was categorized into various forms or levels, the most basic of which were disengagement, unsystematic engagement, and frustrated engagement. Further information on this teacher rating form can be found in the results section of Chapter Four.

In this case study 15 students from the two classes were randomly targeted for such observation using the teacher rating forms. Each computer lab session lasted sixty minutes. This gave the teacher time to observe approximately three or four target students each day (with each day having

TABLE 6.   Modes of Student Engagement with Educational Software

Name of mode	Description
Disengagement	Student avoids or discontinues software interaction; sometimes inattentive, purposeless, uninterested tinkering with software elements.
Unsystematic engagement	Student shows no higher-order goals with software; moves from one activity to another without apparent reason.
Frustrated engagement	Student attempts to achieve specific software goals unsuccessfully.
Structure-dependent engagement	Student navigates and operates the software competently to pursue goals communicated by the software or teacher.
Self-regulated interest	Student adjusts software features to sustain deeply involved, interesting, or challenging interactions for personally defined purposes.
Critical engagement	Student manipulates software to test personal understanding or operational or content-related limitations of software representations.
Literate thinking	Student explores software from multiple, personally meaningful perspectives; uses perspective-sensitive interpretations to reflect on personal values or experience.

Source: Bangert-Drowns and Pyke, 2002.

ITEM ON HOLD

Title: Virtual destinations and
              student learning in middle
              school : a case study of a
              biology museum online / Mindi
              Donaldson.
Author: Donaldson, Mindi.
Call Number:QH315 .D642006
Enumeration:
Chronology:
Copy: 1
Item Barcode*31611003069835*

Item Being H

Patron: Jessica Lee Dale
Patron Barco*2251000732677*
Patron Phone309-472-5665

Hold Expires10/22/2009
Pickup At: .ARUCirculation Desk

a different group of target students). Prior to the lab session the teacher reminded the students that there will be some rating forms filled out and to continue working. The teacher casually stood behind the targeted student to watch the interaction with the software for around five minutes as the form was filled out.

Data Analysis

Data from the questionnaires were analyzed quantitatively using SPSS (Statistical Package for the Social Sciences, 2003) data management software, and the data was manually keyed in. Relations between variables such as gender were analyzed and graphed quantitatively using cross tabulations and descriptive statistics. Item and multi-item scale reliability on the computer attitude questionnaire provided evidence that the three categories of computer importance, computer enjoyment, and motivation / persistence were reliable measurements or indicators of student engagement. The open-ended questionnaires were coded and analyzed qualitatively for emerging patterns. The questions and answers were printed out and then categorized according to specific words used in the answers. In this manner the similarities and differences in data were retrieved and themes and patterns emerged.

One critical issue was to maintain the internal validity of the study and account for factors that may contaminate measurement. Campbell and Stanley (1963) discuss many of these factors, often considered threats to internal validity. These include intervening events, testing effects, instrumentation, group selection, and statistical regression (outlier movement towards the mean). Potential differences between the two classes were identified early on in the study to be of value for the case study because of the description on class composition from the science teacher. Students from Class II were described as needing more academic support and having lower English language skills than students from Class I. The construct validity in this case study was met by using a variety of instruments and measures. Using a detailed protocol for data collection strengthened the reliability as well as the internal validity of the study. Further, such detailed protocol enhanced the potential for the study to be replicated (Merriam, 1990). Lincoln and Guba (1985) suggest that external validity may be enhanced if the researcher provides a rich, thick description for others who may be interested in the generalizability of the study.

Research question One

The first research question, "What is the effect of *Museum Explorer* on middle school students' content knowledge?" was answered using pre- and post-tests (see Appendix D) and the teacher open-ended questionnaire. The effect of *Museum Explorer* is defined as changes in students' content knowledge. Content knowledge is the level of basic biology understanding. The instruments chosen to detect and measure these changes were the content knowledge pre-test and post-tests (see Appendix D) and two questions in the teacher open-ended questionnaire. The pre-test measured content knowledge before the intervention of the *Museum Explorer*, and the post-test measured any changes in content knowledge after the intervention. Data were analyzed quantitatively using descriptive statistics, means and standard deviations, and correlations using SPSS (2003). The open-ended questionnaires were coded and analyzed qualitatively for emerging patterns. The assessment of learning was measured from the differences in the average score for the group before and after the intervention. The limitation of this was that the full effect of the intervention of *Museum Explorer* can not be compared to no intervention at all. The new experience mid-year for these students could explain some variations.

Research question Two

The second research question, "What is the effect of *Museum Explorer* on student learning engagement?" was answered using descriptive statistics, frequencies, inferential statistics such as cross tabulations, and qualitative analysis. The data gathered helped measure the effect of *Museum Explorer* on students' engagement. The effect of *Museum Explorer* is defined as changes in student engagement. Increased positive attitudes in this case study were interpreted as increased student engagement. The instruments chosen to detect and measure student engagement were three computer attitude questionnaires–qualitative examination of open-ended response questionnaires for students and teacher, the teacher rating forms, student notebooks, and email use. The administration of the first computer attitude questionnaire was designed to measure students' attitudes, and the administration of the second and third questionnaires was designed to measure any changes in students' attitudes after the intervention.

The open-ended response questionnaires for the teacher and students were given after the three weeks in the computer lab, or on the fifth week (see Appendices B & C). The questionnaires for the students and the teacher were different. The questions in the students' open-ended questionnaire asked them to relate their experiences and feelings while exploring the website, corresponding with the assistant curator, and visiting the university biology museum. The questions in the teacher's open-ended questionnaire asked for observations of students' engagement and content learning from a more pedagogical and experienced viewpoint. The questions in both open-ended questionnaires helped in answering the research question on the effect of *Museum Explorer* on student engagement.

The teacher rating forms (see Appendix E) were filled out during the three weeks in the computer lab and contributed to understanding the effects of the website on student engagement.

The individual student notebooks were used during the three weeks in the computer lab. The sums of individual pages, filled with either notes or drawings, helped measure student engagement.

Research question Three

The third research question, "What further engagement is generated by a field trip to the Portland State University biology museum and communication with an assistant curator via email?" was answered using quantitative descriptive statistics, frequencies, means and standard deviations for the closed-ended items, and qualitative examination of the open-ended questionnaire responses. The email correspondence the students sent the assistant curator of the Portland State University biology museum were used to help answer research question three. The responses of the email users to question 5 in the open-ended questionnaire and question 6 in the teacher open-ended questionnaire were also qualitatively analyzed. Finally, the differences between email and non-email users in the computer attitude questionnaires and pre- and post-tests also were examined to help answer research question three.

Ethical Issues

As a graduate research project at a federally funded institution of higher learning that involves human subjects, ethical standards were an important element in the success of this study. The review and approval of Portland State University's Human Subjects Research Review Committee (HSRRC) were obtained before the study began. HSRRC is empowered to review and approve, reject, postpone, or modify all proposals for research with human subjects. In this case, the first step was to procure permission for the study to be conducted at Edgeview from the Human Subjects Research Review Committee at Portland State University (see Appendix J). Next, permission from the principal of the middle school was obtained (see Appendix H). Following this, the participants were informed of the purpose and objective of this study. Consent forms from the participants, whom in this case study were the students, the students' parents, and the science teacher were distributed, signed, and returned (see Appendices F, G, and I). The confidentiality of the participants in the final report was ensured. Further, removing any content that could identify the subjects was of vital importance.

The uniqueness of the study may prevent extrapolation. However, because this research project was new, with a paucity of similar research projects to compare it with, it may still be theoretically generalizable and of value to educators and policy-makers. The construct validity in this case study was met by the use of a variety of instruments and measures to obtain the objectives of the research. Obvious differences between the classes and genders were noted. Although randomization and control group designs were not feasible in this study, comparing differences between classes and genders offered some explanations for variance in the data. Using a detailed protocol for data collection strengthened the reliability issue.

Summary

The methods, context, and procedures of this case study were designed to reveal the ways in which a virtual biology museum combined with a museum / school partnership could enhance the classroom science learning experience. *Museum Explorer* was designed to allow students to pursue topics of interest to them within the framework of a larger unit.

CHAPTER FOUR

RESEARCH FINDINGS

The purpose of this case study was to answer three research questions: (1) what is the effect of *Museum Explorer* on middle school students' content knowledge, (2) what is the effect of *Museum Explorer* on student learning engagement, and (3) what further engagement is generated by a field trip to the Portland State University biology museum and communication with an assistant curator via email. The study aimed to identify a relationship between student learning and engagement and the use of dynamic and interactive computer-based media. While the previous chapter described the research design, context, methods, and procedures, this chapter addresses the data gathered and results.

The context of this study made it difficult to do solely quantitative or experimental research because there was no control group and the study took place in a natural classroom setting. Thus it would have been difficult to control variables. Therefore, an alternative mixed method approach was chosen. This approach collects quantitative and qualitative data at the same time and gives equal priority to both. Although outside the purely quantitative paradigm, and admittedly maybe not resulting in the desired combination of qualitative and quantitative data, this mixed method approach was the most feasible for this study.

The approval of Portland State University's Human Subjects Research Review Committee (HSRRC) was obtained. The consent forms from the participants, whom in this case study were the students, the students' parents, and the science teacher were also obtained. Permission for the study at Edgeview was granted by the principal one month before the study began.

The data were collected from computer attitude questionnaires, a pre-test and post-test, teacher rating forms, student and teacher open-ended questionnaires, student notebooks, and emails sent to the assistant curator of the Portland State University biology museum. The table below summarizes the areas of inquiry and the data collection methods used to investigate each area. Note the sources of evidence for the areas of inquiry that were selected to facilitate triangulation of data.

RESEARCH IMPLEMENTATION

The science teacher decided that the students would participate in all the activities in the case study. The researcher and science teacher corresponded through email 26 times after obtaining permission from the Human Subjects Research Review Committee (see Appendix J) to conduct the study.

Five of the students did not return their parental consent forms. Therefore, data collected from these students were eliminated before any statistical procedure was conducted. The data that were included in the study were from 22 boys and 22 girls. Three students from Class I failed to bring back the parental consent forms. Data from 12 boys and 8 girls were included in the analysis. Two students from Class II failed to bring back the parental consent forms. Data from 10 boys and 14 girls from Class II, or a total of 24 students,

TABLE 7.   Data Collection Methods and Research Questions

Research Questions	Pre- / Post-Tests	Student Questionnaires	Teacher Questionnaire	Teacher Rating Forms	Notebooks & Emails
# 1	√		√		√
# 2		√	√	√	√
# 3		√	√		√

were included in the analysis. Data were gathered from the 44 students, (22 boys and 22 girls) who brought in the parental consent forms.

The combined classrooms had 27 (55%) male students and 22 (45%) female students who participated in the activities. The majority of the students (64%) were 12 years of age. A smaller number (27%) of the students were 11 years of age. Four students (8%) were 13 years of age. All students were of Latino origin. There were three sets of twins in the two classes. Two sets were boys and one set were girls.

The students from the two classes who participated in the study came to the science classroom at different times. During the three weeks in the computer lab the students from Class I arrived at the lab at 12:00 and left at 1:00. The students from Class II arrived at the computer lab at 2:15 and left at 3:15.

The computer lab used for the two classes was in Meridian Elementary School which is located at the same building site as the middle school. The lab has 30 Pentium III computers, each with 1.7GHz, 128 MB RAM, and 20 GB hard drives. With a bandwidth requirement limit of 256k per workstation, the T-1 had enough bandwidth for a maximum of 12 computers. However, this was not enough bandwidth to handle the heavy multimedia traffic on the *Museum Explorer* website. In addition, the computers in the lab had in place the safety measure of Internet filters which prohibited initial use of the multimedia viewing software on computers in the lab. The first day of the study in the computer lab the videos on *Museum Explorer* did not play. The computer technician spent time after the first session and turned off the security filters so the video software players would work. The last day of week four in the computer lab, the Internet connection failed altogether and the classes were dismissed after only 10 or 15 minutes.

The *Museum Explorer* website was created in conjunction with the three-phase learning cycle approach. The plan was to implement the three phases of learning and imbed this learning cycle approach within the website. The three phase learning cycle approach includes: (a) exploration, (b) concept development, and (c) application. The students were encouraged during the exploration phase to contact the assistant curator of the biology museum if they had questions. Further, they were encouraged to keep a record of these questions in their notebooks. The concept development phase was a time for students to focus on content and terms discovered during the exploration phase. It had been hoped that the science teacher would take a more active role in presenting concepts and would use their questions as a launch pad for more explorations. During the application phase the students expanded their interest and knowledge. Students assessed themselves during this phase when they took the daily online quizzes. However, due to time and scheduling constraints, the learning cycle was used only loosely during the study.

RESULTS: RESEARCH QUESTION ONE

Research question one: What is the effect of Museum Explorer (a virtual biology museum used in conjunction with a museum / school partnership) on middle school students' content knowledge?

The effect of *Museum Explorer* was defined as changes in students' content knowledge. Content knowledge is the level of basic biology understanding. The instruments chosen to detect and measure these changes were the content knowledge pre-test and post-tests (see Appendix D), two questions in the teacher open-ended questionnaire, and the notebook assignment.

The pre-test measured content knowledge before the intervention of the *Museum Explorer* and the post-test measured any changes in content knowledge after the intervention. Although both tests were substantively the same, half of the post-test answer choices were scrambled to prevent students from sharing answers.

This research question was investigated using frequencies and descriptive statistics to measure the differences in the scores in the pre-test and post-test. Further, the responses from two of the questions in the teacher open-ended questionnaire were analyzed, as well as the notebook assignment. It should be noted that the limitations of this research design would be that the full effect of the intervention of *Museum Explorer* could not be compared to no intervention at all. The study was conducted within a public school setting where school administration delegated decisions regarding the study to the participating science teacher. The science teacher insisted that both classes participate fully, and therefore was unwilling to approve of removing intervention from one class for use as a control group. Although this hampered the final analysis of the effect on content knowledge, sufficient identifiable characteristics were detected to proceed with the data analysis.

Potential problems with this study and barriers to research validity should be briefly addressed here before describing and attempting to interpret the results. Of course it is desirable to draw correct and generalizable conclusions about the reality observed in this case study. Merriam's (1990) advice was followed and several strategies were used to help ensure internal validity. First, methodological triangulation was used to balance the advantages and disadvantages of various measurement instruments. Second, data were gathered over time using the same questionnaires to measure changes that had occurred. Third, the study involved participants in all phases of the research. Also, the researcher's biases and assumptions were taken into consideration throughout the case study.

The unique participant characteristics of the Latino students in this case may have hampered extrapolation. Also, students trying harder or otherwise reacting on the post-test and other second measurements may have reduced the accuracy of the later measurements.

Finally, the choice of non-experimental research design may have been more susceptible to threats of validity. Many scholars consider randomized experimental designs like the pre-test post-test control group design to be the best way to eliminate threats to validity. However, randomization and control group designs were not feasible in this study. Therefore, the non-experimental one-group pre-test / post-test design was chosen. Using a detailed protocol for data collection strengthened the reliability as well as the internal validity of the study. Further, such detailed protocol improved the potential for the study to be replicated (Merriam, 1990). Lincoln and Guba (1985) suggest that external validity may be enhanced if the researcher provides a rich, thick description for others who may be interested in the generalizability of the study.

Pre-test and Post-test

The pre-test and post-test used the same test questions and testing format. Before the pre-test was handed out the students were allowed to walk around and briefly look at the specimens. They particularly enjoyed the bobcat skin and would pet it as they would a living cat.

The questions in the pre-test and post-test (see Appendix D) were:

1. What animal did this skull come from? (pre-test bear, post-test wolf)
2. Look at the teeth of this animal. What do you think it eats? (deer teeth)
3. Here is a cat skeleton. What one item is not a function of the skeleton?
4. Here is a skin of an animal that lives in Oregon. What do you think it is? (pre-test bobcat, post-test raccoon)
5. Each of these skulls has been given a number. Which number is a rodent? (skulls of beaver, bobcat, wolf, bear)
6. Look at the webbed back feet of this beaver. This helps it swim and is a good example of: (answer: adaptation, skin of beaver)
7. Look at these teeth. You will see a tag on one of the teeth. What is this tooth called? (answer: canine, wolf skull)
8. These bones are called (answer: vertebrae, specimen of vertebrae)
9. Deer eat plants. What words best describe its role in the food web? (primary consumer)
10. There are many counties in Oregon. Which county is your school in?
11. When people formulate or make an hypothesis, they are making: (a set of theories intended to explain certain facts)
12. What is not true about mammals? (mammals don't nurse their babies)

Administration

The pre-test had two tables available to place the specimens on for questions 1 through 8. Questions 9 through 12 had no corresponding specimens and the students were directed to return to their seats to answer these questions. No students from either class left any blank answers on the pre-test. Four students were absent from Class I, which left 16 students, and none were absent from Class II for the pre-test, which left 24 students. The teacher and researcher had planned for the time at each table to be no more than five minutes, but this plan was abandoned when we realized some students needed more time. Ten minutes were spent at each of the two specimen tables, with another ten minutes to answer questions 9 through 12. When the students finished answering the questions at one table they stood and waited until all had finished and then the teacher called out to rotate to the next table as a group. A total of 30 minutes was spent on the pre-test.

The post-test, given four weeks after the pre-test, was conducted in a similar manner. Two students were absent from Class I for the post-test, which left 18 students, and one student was absent from Class II for the post-test, which left 23 students. The teacher and students had cleared off the various student projects on the long back counter for the post-test. This allowed room for each specimen with the corresponding question to be separated by three feet and made it easier to monitor the students. There was no time limit and the students spent two to three minutes per question. However, if a student stood too long at one question, the teacher directed them to move to the next question and specimen.

Eight students were lined up at the back counter in front of each specimen that had the corresponding question number on a green index card. Two other tables had questions 9 and 10, or 11 and 12. There were enough chairs at these tables for three students each. The remaining students sat at their own desks to answer these questions. The student who was started at question 8 and had not answered questions 1 through 7 went to the tables with questions 9 through 12. Then this student returned to the counter to answer questions 1 through 7. There was some confusion in the rotations, but the teacher and researcher managed to keep the test going without too much distraction. Three students from Class II left a few answers blank and no student from Class I left an answer blank. A total of 30 minutes was spent on the post-test. The day of the post-test included the open-ended response questionnaires and computer attitude questionnaires. Following is the report on the findings from the pre-test and post-test.

Frequency distributions

Analysis begins with frequency distributions of the data and other descriptive statistics. Frequency distributions for the pre-test results show that questions 4, 5, 6, 9, and 12 had the greatest increases in correct answers. While there were no correct answers on the pre-test for question 1, the post-test had 10% correct answers on question 1. Question 5 had the largest gain in correct answers, ranging from 2 correct answers on the pre-test to 20 correct answers on the post-test. This was a remarkable 44% point gain in correct answers. The second highest gain in correct answers was on question 4 with a 40% point gain. Question 7 showed no increase at all. This question asked, "Look at these teeth. You will see a tag on one of the teeth. What is this tooth called?" Although there were many opportunities to learn about teeth in the website, the information may have been inadequately presented.

The percentages of correct answers for the pre-test and post-test, as well as the summary of the overall change in correct answers, are presented in Table 8. The percentage point gains of over 20 points are shaded for easy viewing.

These data illustrate the increases in content learning for questions 4, 5, 6, 9, and 12, although all other questions except question 7 showed increases. Questions 2, 3, 7, and 8 showed the least amount of increases in correct answers. Although at first it may not be clear why some questions had greater increases in correct answers, looking at the change in pre-test and post-test scores by gender revealed declining scores for boys on some questions and declining scores for girls on others. The graph in Figure 13 illustrates the results of the two tests more visually.

TABLE 8.   Changes in Correct Answers from Pre-Test to Post-Test

Question	Pre % (count)	Post % (count)	Gain / Loss % Points
1	0 (0)	9.8 (4)	9.8 (4)
2	17.5 (7)	22.0 (9)	4.5 (2)
3	37.5 (15)	41.5 (17)	4.0 (2)
4	55.0 (22)	95.1 (39)	40.1 (17)
5	5.0 (2)	48.8 (20)	43.8 (18)
6	45.0 (18)	73.2 (30)	28.2 (12)
7	35.0 (14)	34.2 (14)	–.8 (0)
8	46.2 (18)	53.7 (22)	7.5 (4)
9	12.5 (5)	48.0 (19)	35.5 (14)
10	62.5 (25)	75.0 (30)	12.5 (5)
11	30.0 (12)	53.0 (21)	23.0 (9)
12	17.5 (7)	51.3 (20)	33.8 (13)
Average	30.3 (12)	50.5 (20)	20.2 (8)

(N = 40 pre-test, N = 41 post-test)

Gender differences

Christie (2004) states that studies on gender and computers conducted between 1984 and 2004 present an overall picture of male dominance. Boys used computers more than the girls and three times as many boys as girls participated in summer computer camps. Using a constructivist approach in mathematics, science, and technology is particularly important for girls to

FIGURE 13.   Percentages of Correct and Incorrect Answers from Pre-Test and Post-Test. (pre-test N = 40, post-test N = 41)

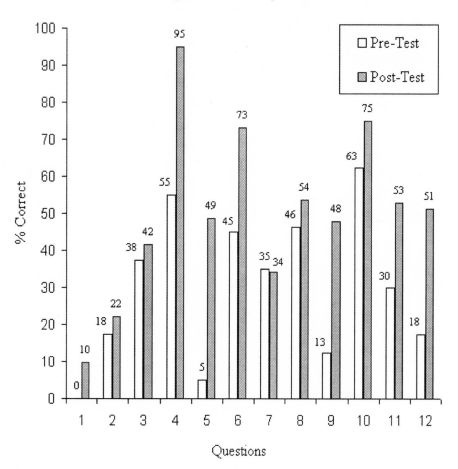

help bridge this gap (Ross, 1993). Because the intervention of the web site used constructivist approaches to learning, the researcher decided to calculate if such differences were seen in this study.

There were significant differences between genders in pre-test and post-test scores. Table 9 shows the differences in correct answers of the genders as well as the increased correct percentages.

This table illustrates the differences in correct answers of the genders, particularly in questions 2, 4, 5, 6, 7, 11, and 12. Percentage point gains of more than 20 points are shaded for easy viewing. Data for the girls showed the greatest gains in questions 4, 5, 6, 9, 10, 11, and 12. Three of these gains were greater than 30 points. However, there were also decreases in question 2. The boys showed the greatest increases in questions 4, 5, 6, 9 and 12. The boys had three questions with percentage point gains over 30. Results for the boys showed increases in correct answers for all questions but question 7. Questions 1, 2, 3, 7, 8, and 10

TABLE 9.   Gender Comparison of Changes in Correct Answers

	Boys			Girls		
Question	Pre-test Correct %	Post-test Correct %	Gain / Loss % Points	Pre-test Correct %	Post-test Correct %	Gain / Loss % Points
1	0	10.5	10.5	0	9.5	9.5
2	14.3	26.3	12.0	26.3	19.0	–7.3
3	28.6	31.6	3.0	47.4	52.4	5.0
4	57.4	86.4	29.0	52.6	90.5	37.9
5	9.5	42.1	32.6	0	52.4	52.4
6	47.6	68.4	20.8	42.1	76.2	34.1
7	38.1	21.1	–17.0	31.6	42.9	11.3
8	42.1	52.6	10.5	47.4	57.1	9.7
9	19.0	55.6	36.6	10.5	38.1	27.6
10	66.7	83.3	16.6	52.6	66.7	14.1
11	38.1	55.6	17.5	21.1	47.6	26.5
12	14.3	61.1	46.8	15.8	40.0	24.2
Average			18.2			20.4

(N = 22 boys and 22 girls)

had the least increases in correct answers for both genders. It may be that the questions were not articulated in a manner appropriate for this study or that the combination of the questions and information found in the website was inadequate.

Neither the boys nor the girls were able to answer question one on the pre-test, but there was nearly the same increase of correct answers for both genders on the post-test. Figure 14 illustrates the gender differences. Question 2 showed a gain of 12 points for the boys. The girls, however, showed a decrease of 7.3 points. The girls showed an increase of correct answers on the post-test for question 3 and the boys showed a slight rise of 3% points.

FIGURE 14.   Gender Increases and Decreases Between Pre-Test / Post-Test Scores. (pre-test number = 40, post-test number = 41)

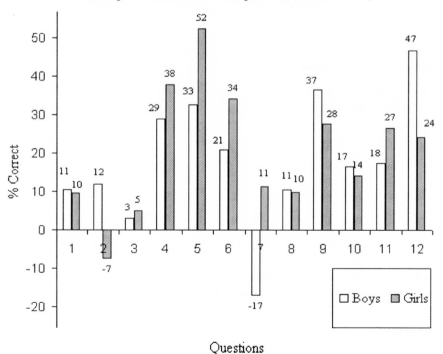

Figure 13 also shows both genders increasing in correct answers on Question 4, with the girls showing 37.9% points gained, and the boys showing 29% points gained. Question 5 showed strong gains of correct answers in both genders. The girls, however, had the greatest gains. They had gone from 0% in correct answers on the pre-test to 52.4% correct answers on the post-test. The boys showed a gain of 32.6% points in correct answers on question 5. Question 7 showed the boys dropping from a 38.1% at the pre-test down to 21.1% at the post-test, or a 17% decline in percentage points. The girls showed 11.3% points gained.

It is unclear why the boys had a more difficult time on this question regarding teeth. The website may not have covered the topic in a way that both the boys and the girls could understand. Both genders had percentages in the 30s at the time of the pre-test. Question 8 showed only a small gain in correct answers. Question 9 had good gains in correct answers for both genders. The boys showed higher gains of correct answers for question 10 than the girls. Question 12 showed that the boys had their greatest gain (46.8% points), going from a 14.3% at the pre-test to a 61.1% at the post-test. Question 5 showed that the girls had their greatest percentage point gains in correct answers, going from 0 correct answers on the pre-test to 52.4% correct answers on the post-test.

The effect of *Museum Explorer* on content learning was only somewhat greater for the girls than for the boys. Overall, the girls had only slight gains of correct answers with 20.4 average percentage points gained. The boys had an average percentage point gain of 18.2 in correct answers.

Differences Between Classes I and II

Gender differences were not the only interesting differences noted in the pre-test and post-test results. Clear differences in the scores of the first and second classes did show up in the research results and are illustrated in Table 10. Potential differences between the two classes were identified early on in the study to be of value for the case study because of the description on class composition from the science teacher. Students from Class II were described as needing more academic support and having lower English language skills than students from Class I.

TABLE 10.   Class Changes in Correct Answers on Pre-Test and Post-Test

Question	Class I			Class II		
	Pre-test Correct%	Post-test Correct%	Gain / Loss Points	Pre-test Correct%	Post-test Correct%	Gain / Loss Points
1	0	15.8	15.8	0	4.5	4.5
2	15.0	31.6	16.6	20.0	13.6	–6.4
3	15.0	21.1	6.1	60.0	59.1	.9
4	85.0	94.7	9.7	25.0	95.5	70.5
5	5.0	31.6	26.6	5.0	63.6	58.5
6	45.0	73.7	28.7	45.0	72.7	27.7
7	50.0	31.6	–18.4	20.0	36.4	16.4
8	30.0	52.6	22.6	63.2	54.5	–8.7
9	15.0	50.0	35.0	10.0	45.5	35.5
10	50.0	66.7	16.7	75.0	81.8	6.8
11	40.0	55.6	15.6	20.0	50.0	30.0
12	0	41.2	41.2	35.0	59.1	24.1
Average			18.0			21.7

Class I: $N = 20$; Class II: $N = 24$.

Percentage point gains greater than 20 points for both classes are shaded in Table 9 for easier viewing. The results show that Class II had higher percentage points gained with the greatest gain being 70.5 points on question 4. The greatest percentage point gain in correct answers for Class I was 41.2 points on question 9.

In questions 2 and 8, Class II had decreased correct answers, but Class I increased in questions 2 and 8. Class I decreased only in question 7. For this class the pre-test total in correct answers for question 7 was 50%, whereas the pre-test total percentages for Class II were 20% with a percentage point gain of 16.4 points on the post-test. Question 4 showed 85% of the students from Class I on the pre-test having correct answers, yet their percentage point gain on the post-test was only 9.7 points. Class II had a remarkable percentage point gain on question 4 from only 25% at the pre-test to 95.5% at the post-test, or a percentage point gain of 70.5 points.

The effect of *Museum Explorer* on the students' increased content knowledge was greater for students in Class II, with an average percentage point gain in correct answers of 21.7 points. Class I had an average percentage point gain of 18 points. The greater percentage point gains in correct answers for the students in Class II, the students who needed more academic support, may reveal that because of lower English language proficiency, the experiences using the website during the three weeks in the lab allowed for increased content knowledge. Comparing achievement scores with the results from this study may have helped in the analysis, but such scores were unavailable to the researcher. The graphics incorporated into all aspects of the website, plus the daily interactive quizzes may have also contributed to student learning. Following is a report on the two questions in the open-ended teacher questionnaire that helped answer research question one.

Teacher Open-Ended Questionnaire

The teacher open-ended questionnaire had a total of 6 questions for the teacher to answer. Questions 4 and 5 helped to answer the first research question on the effect of *Museum Explorer* on student content knowledge. Questions 1 through 3 helped to answer research question 3 regarding engagement. Question 4 asked, "Do you believe the use of *Museum Explorer* contributes to student learning? Why or why not?" The teacher responded:

> Yes, I'm sure that *Museum Explorer* contributes to student learning. I overheard conversations that indicated learning, and watching kids take the quizzes showed me that they were mastering some of the material at the time. Coupled with other learning experiences, I believe *Museum Explorer* can help develop learning that is retained over time, encourages kids to seek and comprehend more learning about our North American native mammals, and to be better informed about the concept of adaptation and the role of the physical environment in shaping animal adaptations.

The teacher mentioned several important learning modes such as self-guided learning, mastery, and increased engagement leading to inquiry. It should be noted that the teacher indicated the need for these learning modes to be coupled with other learning experiences. Anecdotally, the teacher had mentioned a conversation he had with one of his students. This student, a boy, had more difficulty with his English skills than any other student in the two classes and needed more academic support. The teacher was sitting with him one lunch hour and they were discussing *Museum Explorer*. The teacher asked him if he knew the scientific name for the cougar. The boy smiled and immediately said "Felis concolor!" The teacher was surprised and pleased.

Question 5, "In what ways, if any, did the interaction with *Museum Explorer* address the three modalities of learning: visual, auditory, and tactile?" helped answer the research question on the effect of the website on student content knowledge. The teacher responded:

> Certainly *Museum Explorer* employs visual, auditory and tactile modes of response, as all of these are employed by the students interacting with the program. The visual and auditory are the richest modes employed, the tactile being solely a function of computer manipulation. The visual and auditory information presented is rich and complex and abundant, much more so than, say, reading a book or text would be, or hearing a teacher explain and show concepts. That is the power of this medium. For more extended studies, books could be used for deepening the concepts.
> However, it is to be remembered that the interactions are still between students and *representations* of reality, and that the more reality the teacher can provide, the better. The provision of skeletons, and especially the stories that the researcher told about her work with articulating skeletons in the past, the trip to the zoo and the PSU lecture room, added rich dimensions to the student's experience.

The teacher noted one of the more important elements of this case study - the partnership that connects reality (the biology museum and specimens) to the classroom using representations of reality (the website). The use of email in contacting the museum personnel also offers this connecting link between representations and reality. The teacher responded that the power of the multimedia was rich and complex. Multimedia may have its drawbacks. It has been suggested that using both visual and auditory modes may cause a "split-attention" effect, and the students divide their attention across multiple inputs (Mousavi, Low, & Sweller, 1995). Nonetheless, the teacher felt that the effect of the multimedia website did increase student content knowledge.

Notebook Assignment

A notebook assignment was an additional measuring instrument with research data that may also address research question one. The science teacher gave the students an assignment during the third and final week in the computer lab. The science teacher had asked the students to write their assignments in their notebooks. He had not mentioned this, so the researcher was unaware of the assignment until the researcher collected the notebooks to photocopy during the fifth week. Results from this assignment seem to also reveal another aspect of the effect of the website on student learning. As this was not a designed instrument for measuring content knowledge, it will only be mentioned briefly. The teacher assignment was:

> Write an essay on one or both of the following topics, using your notebook from *Museum Explorer*. Explain how the differences in body structures (parts) of two mammals are related to differences in their habitats and life requirements. Choose two mammals you studied in the *Museum Explorer* website. Using examples from the *Museum Explorer* show how a mammal's body structures (parts) are matched to their functions (the jobs they have to do for that animal). For example, the beak (a *structure*) of a hummingbird is very long and thin, so that it can slide deep into a flower to drink the nectar inside (its *function*).

The students made a title page in their notebooks called homework assignment. Most of the students took one or two pages to write out their assignment and these were included in the notebook analysis as part of the entries. Figure 15 displays a typical entry for the notebook assignment. Many students selected the wolf to discuss various adaptations. The post-test indicated there were 28% point increases in correct answers on question 6 that asked about adaptations, with the girls having more gains in correct answers than boys.

FIGURE 15. Notebook Assignment: Drawing of Wolf Adaptations

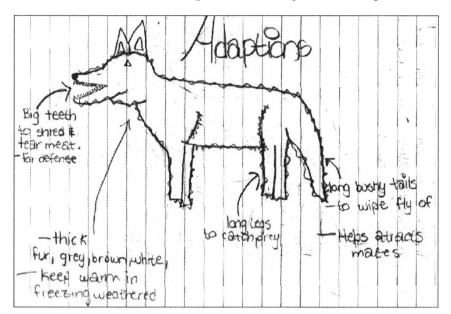

The entry depicted in Figure 15 was drawn by one of the girls and reflects the information she gathered from both the website as well as from class discussions in the science classroom. Figure 16 shows another example.

The example depicted in Figure 16 is from the boy who was identified by the teacher as having the lowest English skills and who has lived in America only a short time. He did an exceptional job in using his own words in this report, rather than simply copying the words from the website.

Such essays and pictures drawn for their notebook assignment demonstrated that they were learning about adaptations and used the contents of *Museum Explorer* as a guide. They also were gathering information from discussions with the teacher in the science classroom, because some of their responses included information not found on the webpage. The students had drawn pictures of the wolf with arrows to point to adaptations of the wolf, such as heavy fur to keep the wolf warm and a bushy tail that is used to signal to other wolves.

FIGURE 16.   Notebook Assignment: Report on the Wolf

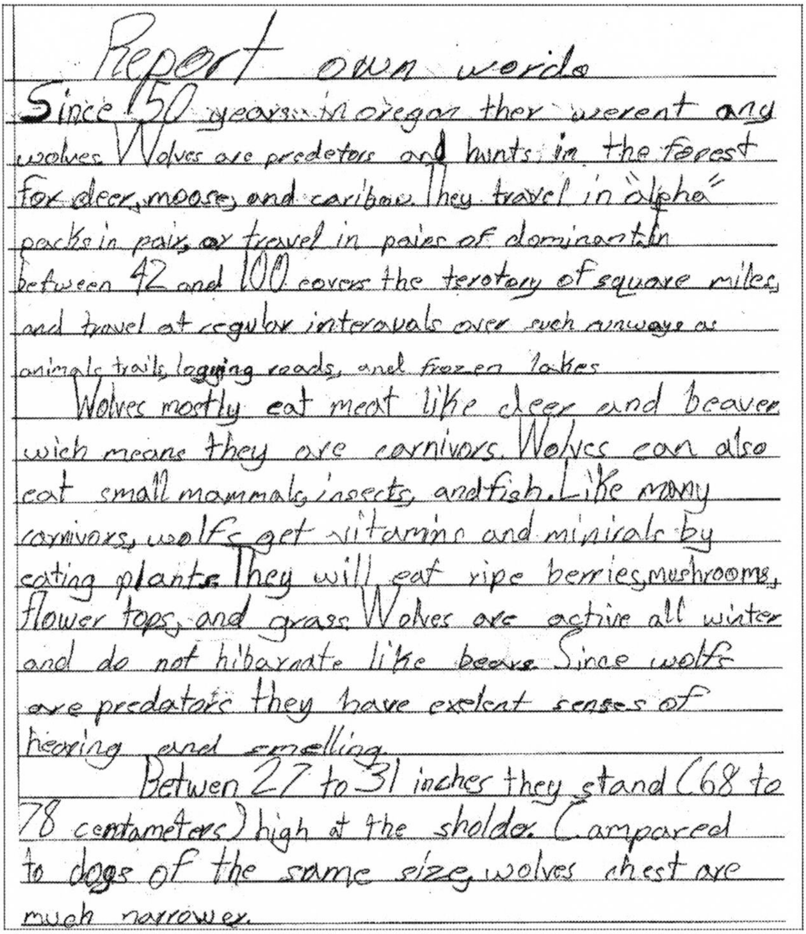

> Report own words
>
> Since 150 years in oregon ther werent any wolves. Wolves are predeters and hunts in the forest for deer, moose, and caribow. They travel in alpha packs in pairs or travel in pairs of dominant In between 42 and 100 covers the terotory of square miles, and travel at regular interavals over such runways or animals trails logging roads, and frozen lakes.
>
>   Wolves mostly eat meat like deer and beaver wich means they are carnivors. Wolves can also eat small mammals, insects, and fish. Like many carnivors, wolfs get vitamins and minirals by eating plants. They will eat ripe berries, mushrooms, flower tops, and grass. Wolves are active all winter and do not hibarnate like bears. Since wolfs are predators they have exelent senses of hearing and smelling.
>
>   Betwen 27 to 31 inches they stand (68 to 78 centameters) high at the sholder. Compared to dogs of the same size, wolves chest are much narrower.

Summary of Results for Research Question One

The pre-test, post-test, teacher open-ended questionnaire, and the notebook assignment all gave clear evidence that the website did have a positive effect on student content knowledge. The combined classes averaged 20 percentage points more in increased correct answers on the post-test. The effect of *Museum Explorer* on student content knowledge was greater for the girls than the boys, and greater on Class II than on Class I. While the pre-test had measured content knowledge before the intervention of *Museum Explorer*, the post-test measured increased positive changes in content knowledge after the intervention. Although extraneous variables could skew the results one way or another, the changes in knowledge that occurred from the time of the pre-test to the post-test were positive. Further discussion regarding this research question will be in Chapter Five.

RESULTS: RESEARCH QUESTION TWO

Research question two: What is the effect of Museum Explorer on student learning engagement?

This section reports on the results gathered from the instruments used to answer research question two and measure the effect of *Museum Explorer* on student engagement. The effect of *Museum Explorer* was defined as changes in student engagement. Engagement was defined as positive attitudes and interest in the subject. Increased positive attitudes in this case study are interpreted as increased student engagement. The instruments chosen to detect and measure student engagement were three computer attitude questionnaires, open-ended response questionnaires for students and teacher, teacher rating forms, student notebooks, and email use.

The first computer attitude questionnaire given the first week of the study measured students' attitudes, and the second and third questionnaires given the fifth and tenth weeks measured any changes in students' attitudes after the intervention.

The open-ended response questionnaires for the teacher and students were given after the three weeks in the computer lab, or on the fifth week (see Appendices B & C). The questionnaires for the students and the teacher were different. The questions in both open-ended questionnaires helped to answer the research question on the effect of *Museum Explorer* on student engagement.

The teacher rating forms (see Appendix E) were filled out during the three weeks in the computer lab and contribute to understanding the effects of the website on student engagement. The female teacher who substituted during the third week of the study filled out the forms that were used in this study.

The individual student notebooks (Mead composition notebooks) were used during the three weeks in the computer lab. Only two students expressed their own attitudes or feelings in the notebooks. After the study the teacher commented that he wished he had encouraged the students to express their attitudes more in the notebooks. However, they did take many notes from the website and drew pictures. The sums of individual pages filled out with either notes or drawings were used to help measure student engagement. These pages included the one or two pages used for the teacher notebook assignment on the third week in the lab.

Emails were used by 27% of the students. The questions were emailed to the assistant curator of the university biology museum and were mostly why, how, or what questions. The students had watched and listened to videos of the assistant curator discussing various aspects of bones and skulls, so they at least could picture in their minds the person they were writing to. The assistant curator was faithful to promptly reply to their questions by the following day. The students were using the teacher's email account for the correspondence. He chose to print out the replies on his own printer in the science classroom. Therefore, there was little discussion of the correspondence between the curator and the students in the computer lab in the researcher's presence. Occasionally the students told the researcher that the teacher had not yet printed out their answers, and they were disappointed.

Results from each of these instruments will be reported. Where applicable, descriptive statistics, frequency distributions, means and standard deviations, cross tabulations, correlations, and qualitative analysis were used to analyze the results from these measurement instruments and identify causal relationships between *Museum Explorer* and students' engagement. First, results from the computer attitude questionnaire will be reported. Next, results from the teacher rating forms will be reported on, followed by examination of the student notebooks. A discussion on the outcome of the student and teacher open-ended questionnaires is also included. Finally, the use of email will be discussed.

Computer Attitude Questionnaire (CAQ)

The computer attitude questionnaire used in this case study was adapted and modified from a study by Knezek, Christensen, and Miyashita, (1999).

The instrument was developed as an extension of the Young Children's Computer Inventory (YCCI) during 1993–95 with middle school students targeted. The computer attitude questionnaire measured prevailing attitudes rather than achievement. The questionnaire was a 62-item, Likert-type self-report questionnaire and was intended for use in the middle school environment (1999).

The researchers (1999) had developed and validated the indices of computer importance, computer enjoyment, computer motivation and persistence, and email usage. The constructs measured by the questionnaire are assumed to be defined by the meanings commonly used for these terms in standard English. The Knezek model of engagement was adopted for this study. Table 11 lists the four categories of engagement defined and measured with this model and defines the meanings assigned to each category.

For this study, Knezek's computer attitude questionnaire was modified to 20 items that were determined to best answer research question two. Questions 17 through 20 are of demographic nature. It was necessary to ensure that negative wording did not skew scores, so items 2, 8, 9, 10, and 11 were reversed. The students were given the following choices of four levels of responses: (1) strongly disagree, (2) disagree, (3) agree, and (4) strongly agree. These four levels of responses were chosen to avoid neutral responses.

Administration

All students who took the three computer attitude questionnaires were assigned codes to protect anonymity. The researcher was the only one who knew whom the codes represented. The responses from the questionnaires

TABLE 11. Knezek's Engagement Categories and Meanings*

Category	Meanings
Computer Importance	Perceived value or significance of knowing how to use computers
Computer Enjoyment	Amount of pleasure derived from using computers
Motivation / Persistence	The psychological feature that arouses a person to action toward a desired goal. Unceasing effort.
Email Use	Students transmitting messages electronically using computers

*Categories and meanings derived from Knezek's Computer Attitude Questionnaire, 1999.

administered three separate times were encoded using SPSS (Statistical Package for the Social Sciences, 2003). The responses were entered into the SPSS database using manual data entry. The accuracy of the data entries was ensured by examining each cell twice for any incorrect numeric codes. Further, five questionnaires were randomly selected and compared to the database entries to check for errors. No errors were found.

The computer attitude questionnaire was given in the first week of the study, in the fifth week, and again five weeks later in the tenth week of the study. There was no variation in text format in the three questionnaires.

In the first week there were four students absent from Class I. When the questionnaire was administered in the fifth week of the study there were two students absent from Class I. The follow-up questionnaire had two students absent and again these students were also from Class I. Class II had all students present for the three questionnaires.

The fundamental ideas of the categories of computer importance, computer enjoyment, computer motivation / persistence and computer email use are described in Table 12. The category of computer importance includes items 3, 5, and 7. The category of computer enjoyment includes items 1, 2, 4, 6, 8, 9, and 10. The category of computer motivation / persistence includes items 11, 12, 13, 14, and 15. Finally, the category of email use includes item 16.

These categories and associated questionnaire items were adopted for evaluating the computer attitude questionnaire administered in this study. The following list shows how items within these categories were organized and analyzed. The five items with reverse-codes are in brackets. From this point forward all reversed coding will be shown without brackets.

Items that measured computer importance:

3. I will be able to get a good job if I learn how to use a computer.
5. I learn many new things when I use a computer.
7. I believe that it is very important for me to learn how to use a computer.

Items that measured computer enjoyment:

1. I like using a computer.
2. I am [not] tired of using a computer.

TABLE 12.   Computer Attitude Questionnaire*: Item Numbers and
Variables Measured

Categories**	Items	Total Scores	Fundamental Idea of Categories
Computer importance	3, 5, 7	12	Perceived VALUE or significance of knowing how to use computers
Computer enjoyment	1, 2, 4, 6, 8, 9, 10	28	Amount of pleasure derived from using computers
Computer motivation & persistence	11, 12, 13, 14, 15	20	The psychological feature that arouses a person to action toward a desired goal. Unceasing effort.
Email usage	16	4	Using electronic mail to send messages

Note: 4 point scale system from 1 (strongly disagree) to 4 (strongly agree).
*Adapted from Knezek's Computer Attitude Questionnaire, 1999.
**Categories derived from Knezek's Computer Attitude questionnaire, 1999.

4.   I enjoy computer games very much.
6.   I enjoy lessons on the computer.
8.   Working with a computer [does not] make me nervous.
9.   Using a computer is [not] hard for me.
10.   Computers are [not] difficult to use.

Items that measured computer motivation and persistence:

11.   I can [not] learn more from books than from a computer.
12.   I try to finish whatever I begin.
13.   I enjoy working on a difficult problem.
14.   I do my homework.
15.   I study hard.

Item that measured engagement related to email usage:

16.   The use of email helps me learn more.

Items that measured engagement from computer and Internet access at home and how many hours student spent on home computer each week:

17. I have a computer at home.
18. My computer has Internet access.
19. If you have a computer at home, how many hours a week do you use it?
      0 – 2 hours _____
      2 – 4 hours _____
      4 – 6 hours _____
      more than 6 hours _____

Items regarding demographic and ethnic information:

20. I am a girl _____ I am a boy_____
      I am ____years old
      I am Latino _____
      I am Russian _____
      I am both Latino and Russian _____

Results from the computer attitude questionnaires (CAQ)

This section reports the findings of the data gathered from the three computer attitude questionnaires administered to the students. First, there will be a report on the results of the reliability testing that was conducted. Next, there will be reports on the findings from the data gathered from both classes as a whole unit, the genders, and the differences between the two classes. In conclusion, there will be a short discussion on the data from the 12 students who emailed the assistant curator of the Portland State University biology museum. Data were analyzed using frequencies, descriptive statistics, cross tabulations, and correlations.

Reliability Estimates: Each item was evaluated using the Scale Reliability Analysis in SPSS. This tested my assumption that items 3, 5, and 7 on computer importance correlate, that the items 1, 2, 4, 6, 8, 9, and 10 on computer enjoyment correlate, and that the items 11, 12, 13, 14, and 15 on computer motivation / persistence correlate. Table 13 presents the results.

TABLE 13.   Computer Attitude Questionnaire Item Analysis Reliability

Computer Attitude Questionnaire*		Categories**		
		Computer Importance	Computer Enjoyment	Motivation / Persistence
	Items	3, 5, 7	1,2,4,6,8,9,10	11,12,13,14,15
CAQ#1 (Week 1)		a = .56	a = .69	a = .61
CAQ#2 (Week 5)	alphas	a = .69	a = .46	a = .64
CAQ#3 (Week 10)		a = .79	a = .72	a = .66

*Adapted from Knezek's Computer Attitude Questionnaire, 1999.
**Categories derived from Knezek's Computer Attitude Questionnaire, 1999.

An alpha of .6 > 1 is a precursor to accepting the item and moving on to create multi-item scales. Computer attitude questionnaires 1 and 2 have alphas below the set value of .6 > 1. However, if item 3 in Computer Importance were deleted in computer attitude questionnaire 1, the .56 alpha would have been .61, an acceptable alpha. That would leave only one alpha on Computer Enjoyment from computer attitude questionnaire two with an unacceptable alpha of .46. The lower alphas in Table 12 reflect the problems when a smaller item questionnaire is used, and in this revised questionnaire only sixteen items were used. This was not enough to have a true measurement of item reliability. However, considering the low item questionnaire, it was decided to leave in item 3 in the first questionnaire in the data analysis and move on to a multi-item scale analysis using the reliability analysis in SPSS.

Student engagement, like many variables social scientists desire to measure, is impossible to assess explicitly or directly. Instead, researchers ask a series of questions they think correlate closely to the desired variable and combine the answers into a single numerical value. However, for items to be used to form a new scale they need to have internal consistency and measure the same thing, in this case ensuring that they do in fact correlate and are in fact reliable measures of student engagement. The coefficient commonly used for assessing internal consistency is Cronbach's alpha (α). Alpha indicates the probability of rejecting the statistical hypothesis that each student engagement category does in fact measure engagement, when that hypothesis is true. In simpler terms, it represents reliability in terms of the ratio of true score variance to observed score variance. The stronger the relationship between true score and observed score, the closer alpha will be to 1.0.

This study assumes that the alpha may be less for scales with fewer items. Although Knezek, whose computer attitude questionnaire this research questionnaire was adapted from, considers alpha's between .60 and .65 undesirable and an alpha above .65 acceptable, there were fewer items in this study than in Knezek's (Knezek, Christensen, & Miyashita, 2000). Therefore, this study assumes that alpha values of 0.6 to 0.8 are regarded as satisfactory.

The next step was to examine the alpha values for the categories of computer importance, computer enjoyment, and computer motivation / persistence and determine if these could measure student engagement. Table 14 presents the alphas for the multi-item scale reliability conducted using SPSS.

The alpha values depicted in Table 14 are acceptable alphas of .60 or more. This is evidence that the three categories of computer importance, computer enjoyment, and computer motivation / persistence were sufficiently reliable measurements or indicators of student engagement. This means that the categories in the first computer attitude questionnaire measured engagement with 60% reliability. The second computer attitude questionnaire had 68% reliability. The third computer attitude questionnaire had 69% reliability. Again, the small number of items caused the researcher to feel that if the numbers of items were greater these alphas would have been higher. Therefore, it was decided to retain all items and all categories. Given that the categories were sufficiently reliable measurements or

TABLE 14.   Multi-Item Scale Analysis

Categories*	CAQ*1	CAQ*2	CAQ*3
Computer importance, computer enjoyment, and motivation / persistence	$a = .60$	$a = .68$	$a = .69$

*Categories derived from Knezek's Computer Attitude Questionnaire, 1999

indicators of student engagement, the next section looks at the result to identify different levels of student engagement with computers by demographic characteristics.

Results by Demographics: Results from the computer attitude questionnaires begin with items 17 through 19. These items asked information regarding computer access at home, Internet access at home, and how many hours a week they spend on the home computers.

When asked, "I have a computer at home," 70.5% responded yes and 29.5% responded no. When asked, "My computer has Internet access," 43.2% responded yes and 56.8% responded no. More boys than girls reported that they did not have a computer at home. Four of the 12 students who used email for correspondence in the study reported that they did not have computers at home. At the time of the third computer attitude questionnaire 53.8% of those students who reported that they have no computers at home strongly agreed to item 3, "I will be able to get a good job if I learn how to use a computer." However, only 34.5% of those students with computers at home strongly agreed in response to this item. This is nearly a 20 percentage point difference. On item 5, "I learn many new things when I use a computer," 37.9% of the students who reported that they have a computer at home strongly agreed on the third questionnaire, whereas 76.9% of those students with no computer at home strongly agreed that they learn many new things when they use a computer. There will be further discussion of this in Chapter Five. Item 19 asked, "If you have a computer at home, how many hours a week do you use it?" There was an increased percentage of students using the computer 0 – 2 hours five weeks from 51.6% at the start of the study to 73.5% at the time of the third questionnaire ten weeks later. This increase may be due to increased use of computers for homework assignments.

Following is a discussion of the data from the combined classes. Next there will follow a discussion of data on genders, and finally there will be a discussion on the data on the two separate classes.

Combined Classes: Frequencies, percentages, means, standard deviations, and cross tabulations of each item were used to describe the students' attitudes about computers. Table 15 presents the results on items 1 through 16.

Table 15. Frequencies and Percentages of Student Attitudes Towards Computers

Item	Response	CAQ*1 (Week 1)		CAQ*2 (Week 5)		CAQ*3 (Week 10)	
		f	%	f	%	f	%
1. I like using a computer.	Strongly disagree						
	Disagree						
	Agree	10	25.0	14	33.3	12	28.6
	Strongly agree	30	75.0	28	66.7	30	71.4
2. I am not tired of using	Strongly disagree	1	2.5				
a computer.	Disagree	2	5.0	1	2.4		
	Agree	7	17.5	7	16.7	10	23.8
	Strongly agree	30	75.0	34	81.0	32	76.2
3. I will be able to get a good job	Strongly disagree	1	2.5				
if I learn how to use	Disagree	2	5.0	1	2.4	2	4.8
a computer.	Agree	22	55.0	19	45.2	23	54.8
	Strongly agree	15	37.5	22	52.4	17	40.5
4. I enjoy computer games	Strongly disagree	2	5.0	1	2.4		
very much.	Disagree			1	2.4	3	7.1
	Agree	8	20.0	12	28.6	7	16.7
	Strongly agree	30	75.0	28	66.7	32	76.2
5. I learn many new things when	Strongly disagree						
I use a computer.	Disagree	1	2.5	2	4.8	1	2.4
	Agree	19	47.5	20	47.6	20	47.6
	Strongly agree	20	50.0	20	47.6	21	50.0
6. I enjoy lessons on the	Strongly disagree	3	7.5	1	2.4	1	2.4
computer.	Disagree	2	5.0	5	11.9	8	19.0
	Agree	20	50.0	19	45.2	17	40.5
	Strongly agree	15	37.5	17	40.5	16	38.1
7. I believe that it is very	Strongly disagree	1	2.6				
important for me to learn	Disagree	1	2.6	1	2.4	1	2.4
how to use a computer.	Agree	11	28.2	19	45.2	19	45.2
	Strongly agree	26	66.7	22	52.4	22	52.4
8. Working with a computer does	Strongly disagree						
not make me nervous.	Disagree	4	10.0	1	2.4	2	4.9
	Agree	8	20.0	13	31.0	9	22.0
	Strongly agree	28	70	28	66.7	30	73.2

(Continued)

TABLE 15.   (*Continued*)

Item	Response	CAQ*1 (Week 1)		CAQ*2 (Week 5)		CAQ*3 (Week 10)	
		f	%	f	%	f	%
9. Using a computer is not hard for me.	Strongly disagree	1	2.6	1	2.4		
	Disagree	4	10.5	5	12.2	3	7.1
	Agree	13	34.2	12	29.3	14	33.3
	Strongly agree	20	52.6	23	56.1	25	59.5
10. Computers are not difficult to use.	Strongly disagree			4	9.8	1	2.4
	Disagree	9	23.1	2	4.9	3	7.1
	Agree	13	33.3	13	31.7	14	33.3
	Strongly agree	17	43.6	22	53.7	24	57.1
11. I can not learn more from books than from a computer.	Strongly disagree	4	10.0	3	7.5	2	4.8
	Disagree	4	10.0	9	22.5	4	9.5
	Agree	14	35.0	15	37.5	21	50.0
	Strongly agree	18	45.0	13	32.5	15	35.7
12. I try to finish whatever I begin.	Strongly disagree						
	Disagree			1	2.4	4	9.5
	Agree	23	57.5	18	43.9	19	45.2
	Strongly agree	17	42.5	22	53.7	19	45.2
13. I enjoy working on a difficult problem.	Strongly disagree	6	15.4	3	7.1	8	19.0
	Disagree	9	23.1	12	28.6	10	23.8
	Agree	16	41	18	42.9	17	40.5
	Strongly agree	8	20.5	9	21.4	7	16.7
14. I do my homework	Strongly disagree	4	10.3	1	2.4	2	4.8
	Disagree	4	10.3	5	11.9	8	19.0
	Agree	16	41	18	42.9	16	38.1
	Strongly agree	15	38.5	18	42.9	16	38.1
15. I study hard.	Strongly disagree	2	5.3	1	2.4	3	7.1
	Disagree	3	7.9	8	19.0	6	14.3
	Agree	14	36.8	18	42.9	14	33.3
	Strongly agree	19	50.0	15	35.7	19	45.2
16. The use of email helps me learn more.	Strongly disagree	9	22.5	13	31.0	13	31.0
	Disagree	14	35.0	16	38.1	16	38.1
	Agree	13	32.5	9	21.4	8	19.0
	Strongly agree	3	7.5	4	9.5	5	11.9
			N = 40		*N* = 40		*N* = 42

Note: 4 point scale system from 1 (strongly disagree) to 4 (strongly agree).
*Adapted from Knezek's Computer Attitude questionnaire, 1999.

The greatest increase in questions 1 through 16 in the strongly agree response from the time of the first questionnaire to the follow-up questionnaire was on item 10, "Computers are not difficult to use." The response at the first questionnaire was 43.6% who strongly agreed and increased at the follow-up questionnaire to 57.1%. This was a 14 percentage point gain in strong agreement. The greatest increase (14.9 points) in attitude change in the strongly agree response from the time of the first questionnaire (37.5%) to the second questionnaire (52.4%) was on item 3, "I will be able to get a good job if I learn how to use a computer." The greatest decline (14.3 points) in strong agreement from the first questionnaire (66.7%) to the third questionnaire (52.4%) was on item 7, "I believe that it is very important for me to learn how to use a computer." However, it is important to note that student responses often stayed within the positive responses of either agree or strongly agree. This indicated only slight increased or decreased percentages in attitude changes. Therefore, the negative responses and the positive responses were combined to further examine overall attitude changes. These results are listed in the category sections of computer importance, computer enjoyment, computer motivation / persistence, and email usage.

As this study looked for signs of positive changes in attitudes about using computers, the researcher first looked at the highest means. Item 2, "I am not tired of using computers," ($M = 3.79$, $SD = .48$), shows the highest mean. The second highest mean ($M = 3.75$, $SD = .44$) was item 1, "I like using a computer." Next, the researcher looked for the greatest positive changes in mean scores. Item 9, "I enjoy lessons on the computer," showed the greatest increase in mean scores (.15%). Item 16, "The use of email helps me learn more," ($M = 2.07$, $SD = .97$), shows the lowest mean score. This item and item 15, "I study hard," had the lowest mean scores. Table 16 displays these means and standard deviations for the three computer attitude questionnaires.

Computer Importance: This procedure only examined the first and third questionnaires. There were 66.7% of students who disagreed on computer importance category at the first questionnaire and changed to agree on the second questionnaire. Further, 27.5% of students who agreed on computer importance at the first questionnaire showed increased attitude changes

TABLE 16.   Means and Standard Deviations of Student Attitudes

	CAQ*1 (Week 1)		CAQ*2 (Week 5)		CAQ*3 (Week 10)	
	M	*SD*	*M*	*SD*	*M*	*SD*
1) I like using a computer.	3.75	.44	3.67	.48	3.71	.46
2) I am not tired of using a computer.	3.65	.70	3.79	.48	3.76	.43
3) I will be able to get a good job if I learn to use a computer.	3.28	.68	3.52	.55	3.36	.58
4) I enjoy computer games very much.	3.65	.74	3.60	.66	3.69	.60
5) I learn many new things when I use a computer.	3.48	.55	3.45	.48	3.48	.55
6) I enjoy lessons on the computer.	3.18	.84	3.21	.78	3.14	.81
7) I believe that it is very important for me to learn how to use a computer.	3.59	.68	3.50	.55	3.50	.55
8) Working with a computer does not make me nervous.	3.60	.67	3.62	.54	3.68	.57
9) Using a computer is not hard for me.	3.37	.79	3.39	.80	3.52	.63
10) Computers are not difficult to use.	3.21	.80	3.29	.96	3.45	.74
11) I can not learn more from books than from a computer.	3.2	.98	3.0	.93	3.2	.79
12) I try to finish whatever I begin.	3.43	.50	3.41	.77	3.36	.66
13) I enjoy working on a difficult problem.	2.67	.98	2.71	.97	2.55	.99
14) I do my homework.	3.08	.96	3.19	.83	3.10	.88
15) I study hard.	3.32	.84	3.05	.85	3.17	.93
16) The use of email helps me learn more.	2.30	.94	2.07	.97	2.12	.99
Total	*N = 40*		*N = 42*		*N = 42*	

Note: 4 point scale system from 1 (strongly disagree) to 4 (strongly agree).
*Adapted from Knezek's Computer Attitude Questionnaire, 1999.

to strong agreement at the third questionnaire. Table 17 displays these results from the cross-tabulation procedure performed on the category of computer importance.

Note, however, that the 32.8% who responded with strong agreement at the first questionnaire changed to merely agree at the follow-up questionnaire. These results are statistically significant because the chi-square test statistic and associated p-value are well below the standard cut-off for statistical significance of .05. This means that the probability of getting

Table 17.   Changes in Attitude Toward Computer
Importance Over Duration of Study

| | | | (Week 10) Computer Attitude Questionnaire* 3 | | | |
		Response	Disagree	Agree	Strongly agree	Total
(Week 1) Computer Attitude Questionnaire* 1		Strongly disagree			100%	100%
		Disagree	33.3%	66.7%		100%
		Agree	5.9%	66.7%	27.5%	100%
		Strongly agree		32.8%	67.2%	100%

$\chi^2 = 29.2$ ($p \leq 0.05$).
Note: 4 point scale system from 1 (strongly disagree) to 4 (strongly agree).
*Adapted from Knezek's Computer Attitude Questionnaire, 1999.

these numbers by chance is less than 5%. Following is a report on the combined negative responses and combined positive responses for the category of computer importance.

Combined Computer Importance: Combining the two negative responses and the two positive responses gives a clearer look at the general tendencies in attitudes of the students. Table 18 displays these combined tendencies in percentages. The category of computer importance included items 3, 5, and 7. Notice the shaded right column that lists the changes from the first to the last questionnaire.

These results reveal a slight increase in positive attitudes in items 3, 5, and 7. The results of the category of computer importance across the three questionnaires indicated that items 3 and 7 had increased from the first questionnaire to the second questionnaire and question five dropped from the first questionnaire to the second questionnaire, but then rose again on the follow-up questionnaire. The students began with high positive attitudes on all three items when they started the case study. Therefore, major positive increased changes could not be expected.

Computer Enjoyment: The category of computer enjoyment included items 1, 2, 4, 6, 8, 9, and 10. Table 19 displays the results from the cross-tabulation procedure performed on the category of computer enjoyment.

Fifty-seven percent of those who strongly disagreed on the first questionnaire changed at the third questionnaire to merely disagree. 21 percent of those who

TABLE 18. Combined Response Percentages for Category** of Computer Importance

Computer Importance Items	CAQ*1 (Week 1)		CAQ*2 (Week 5)		CAQ*3 (Week 10)		Change from caq1 to caq3
	strongly disagree / disagree	strongly agree / agree	strongly disagree / disagree	strongly agree / agree	strongly disagree / disagree	strongly agree / agree	
3. I will be able to get a good job if I learn to use a computer.	7.5%	92.0%	2.4%	97.6%	4.8%	95.3%	+3.3
5. I learn many new things when I use a computer.	2.5%	97.5%	4.8%	95.2%	2.4%	97.6%	+.1
7. I believe that it is very important for me to learn how to use a computer.	5.2%	94.9%	2.4%	97.6%	2.4%	97.6%	+2.7
Total	N = 40		N = 42		N = 42		

*Adapted from Knezek's Computer Attitude Questionnaire, 1999.
**Category derived from Knezek's Computer Attitude Questionnaire, 1999.

TABLE 19. Change in Attitude About Computer Enjoyment
(CAQ Category** Items 1, 2, 4, 6, 8, 9, and 10)

| | Response | (Week 10) Computer Attitude Questionnaire* 3 | | | | |
		Strongly disagree	Disagree	Agree	Strongly agree	Total
(Week 1) Computer Attitude Questionnaire*1	Strongly disagree	14.3%	57.1%	28.6%	0%	100%
	Disagree	0%	10.5%	21.1%	68.4%	100%
	Agree	0%	11.8%	46.8%	42.9%	100%
	Strongly agree	.7%	2.2%	19.1%	80.1%	100%

χ^2= 87.6 (p-value = ≤ .05) 4 point scale system from 1 (strongly disagree) to 4 (strongly agree).
*Adapted from Knezek's Computer Attitude Questionnaire, 1999.
**Categories derived from Knezek's Computer Attitude Questionnaire, 1999.

disagreed on the first questionnaire changed to agree on the third questionnaire. Notice that 28.6% of the students who responded in the first computer attitude questionnaire that they strongly disagreed changed to agree on the third questionnaire.

Even more remarkable is the fact that 68.4% of the students who responded in the first computer attitude questionnaire that they disagreed changed their responses to strongly agree on the third computer attitude questionnaire. Further, 42.9% of those who agreed on the first questionnaire changed to strongly agree on the third questionnaire. These results are statistically significant because the chi-square test statistic and associated p-value are well below the standard cut-off for statistical significance of .05. This means that the probability of getting these numbers by chance is less than 5%.

Combined Computer Enjoyment: Combining the negative attitudes and the positive attitudes gives a clearer picture of the trends in attitudes of the students on computer enjoyment. Table 19 displays these results. The results of the multi-item scale of computer enjoyment indicated that items 2, 8, 9, and 10 had increased positive percentages in computer enjoyment. Only item 4, "I enjoy computer games very much," and 6, "I enjoy lessons on the computer," showed decreasing percentages.

The responses to item 1, "I like using a computer," indicate that 100% of the students agreed or strongly agreed across all three questionnaires. This indicates that the positive attitudes about liking to use computers did not change across the three questionnaires. Item 2, "I am (not) tired of using a computer," shows an increased agreement or strong agreement from 92.5% on the first questionnaire, up to 97.7% on the second questionnaire, and finally 100% on the final questionnaire. The 7.5 percentage point gain in increased positive attitudes indicates computer enjoyment. Table 20 displays the combined responses for the category of computer enjoyment.

Item 4, "I enjoy computer games very much," showed a slight decrease in positive attitude from the first questionnaire (95.0%) and second questionnaires (95.3%) and then declined to 92.9% on the third questionnaire. This indicated the declining enjoyment of computer games.

Item 6, "I enjoy lessons on the computer," displays decreasing percentages across the three questionnaires. The first questionnaire shows a positive attitude of 87.5% followed by a drop to 85.7% on the second questionnaire. The third questionnaire revealed an even larger drop to 78.6% in positive attitudes.

Item 8, "Working with a computer does not make me nervous," shows increased positive attitudes. Ninety percent of the students responded that they have positive attitudes about not feeling nervous working with computers. There was a gain at the second questionnaire with 97.7% who responded that they are not nervous. The third questionnaire showed a drop down to 95.2% but this is still a 5.2 percentage point gain from the first to the third questionnaire.

Item 9, "Using a computer is not hard for me," shows a 6 percentage point increase in positive attitudes from the first questionnaire to the follow-up questionnaire. This indicated an increase in their confidence about using computers.

Item 10, "Computers are not difficult to use," shows the greatest increase of changes in positive attitudes. There were 76.9% of the students with positive attitudes at the first questionnaire, but this increased to 90.4% at the follow-up questionnaire. This was a 13.5 percentage point gain in positive attitudes. Items 9 and 10 are very similar and deal with the students' levels of confidence and enjoyment using computers.

TABLE 20. Combined Response Percentages for Category** of Computer Enjoyment

Enjoyment Items	CAQ*1 (Week 1)		CAQ*2 (Week 5)		CAQ*3 (Week 10)		Change from caq1 to caq3
	strongly disagree / disagree	strongly agree / agree	strongly disagree / disagree	strongly agree / agree	strongly disagree / disagree	strongly agree / agree	
1. I like using a computer.		100%		100%		100%	+0
2. I am not tired of using a computer.	7.5%	92.5%	2.4%	97.7%		100%	+7.5
4. I enjoy computer games...	5.0%	95.0%	4.8%	95.3%	7.1%	92.9%	−2.1
6. I enjoy lessons on the computer.	12.5%	87.5%	14.3%	85.7%	21.4%	78.6%	−8.9
8. Working with a computer does not make me nervous.	10.0%	90.0%	2.4%	97.7%	4.9%	95.2%	+5.2
9. Using a computer is not hard...	13.1%	86.8%	14.6%	85.4%	7.1%	92.8%	+6.0
10. Computers are not difficult to use.	23.1%	76.9%	14.7%	85.4%	9.5%	90.4%	+13.5
Total	N = 40		N = 42		N = 42		

*Adapted from Knezek's Computer Attitude Questionnaire. 1999.
**Category derived from Knezek's Computer Attitude Questionnaire. 1999.

Computer Motivation / Persistence: While questions 12 through 15 do not directly deal with students' interaction with computers, the element of motivation could have been a factor effecting student engagement. Beeland, (2003) notes that engagement is critical to student motivation during the learning process. Further, he states that the effective use of technology can be used to create a motivational classroom environment. Therefore, these four questions were included in the questionnaire to be analyzed. Fifty-five percent of those who strongly disagreed in the first questionnaire that using computers made them more motivated and persistent felt the same in the third computer attitude at the end of the study (see Table 21).

Only 10.3% of those who strongly disagreed at the first of the study changed at the end to agree. Sixty-three percent of those students who disagreed in the first questionnaire that using computers made them more motivated and persistent, felt the same in the third questionnaire. Thirty percent of those who disagreed at the first questionnaire dropped to strongly disagree by the end of the study. Only 6.7% of those who disagreed changed to agree by the third questionnaire. Nearly 21% of those who agreed at the first questionnaire changed to strongly agree at the third questionnaire. Only 6.9% of those who strongly disagreed on the first of the study showed a major change at the end by responding that they now strongly agree. These

TABLE 21.   Change in Attitude on Motivation / Persistence Over Duration of Study (CAQ Category** Items 11, 12, 13, 14, and 15)

	(Week 10) Computer Attitude Questionnaire* 3				
Response	**Strongly disagree**	**Disagree**	**Agree**	**Strongly agree**	**Total**
Strongly disagree	55.2%	27.6%	10.3%	6.9%	100%
Disagree	30.0%	63.3%	6.7%		100%
Agree	1.4%	16.7%	61.1%	20.8%	100%
Strongly agree	3.2%	4.8%	20.6%	71.4%	100%

(row label, left axis: (Week 1) Computer Attitude Questionnaire* 1)*

χ^2= 79.4 ($p \leq 0.05$).
Note: 4 point scale system from 1 (strongly disagree) to 4 (strongly agree).
*Adapted from Knezek's Computer Attitude Questionnaire, 1999.
**Category derived from Knezek's Computer Attitude Questionnaire, 1999.

results are statistically significant because the chi-square test statistic and associated p-value are well below the standard cut-off for statistical significance of .05. This means that the probability of getting these numbers by chance is less than 5%.

Combined Motivation / Persistence: The negative and the positive attitudes combined give a clearer picture of the trends in attitudes of the students on computer motivation and persistence. Table 22 displays these results.

Most items in the category of computer motivation / persistence show decreased attitudes across time. Only item 11 had increased positive attitudes. At the time of the first questionnaire there were 77.5% of the students who had positive attitudes that they could learn more from computers than from a book. At the time of the third questionnaire these attitudes had increased to 85.7%. This was an 8.2% point gain in positive attitudes. The extraneous variables such as the case study being conducted toward the end of the school year, unknown experiences in home life or school, or the technical problems of the Internet not

TABLE 22.   Combined Response Percentages for Motivation /
Persistence (CAQ Category** Items 11, 12, 13, 14, and 15)

Motivation / Persistence Items	CAQ*1 (Week 1)		CAQ*3 (Week 10)		
	strongly disagree / disagree	strongly agree / agree	strongly disagree / disagree	strongly agree / agree	Change from caq1 to caq3
11. I can not learn more from books than from a computer.	22.5%	77.5%	19.1%	85.7%	+8.2
12. I try to finish whatever begin.		100%	9.5%	90.4%	–9.6
13. I enjoy working on a difficult problem.	38.5%	61.5%	42.8%	57.2%	–4.2
14. I do my homework.	20.6%	79.5%	23.8%	76.2%	–3.3
15. I study hard.	13.2%	86.8%	21.4%	78.5%	–8.3
Total	N = 40		N = 42		

*Adapted from Knezek's Computer Attitude Questionnaire, 1999.
**Derived from Knezek's Computer Attitude Questionnaire, 1999.

working in the lab may have influenced their attitudes about computer motivation or persistence. Following is a short report on the category of email use.

Email Use: The category of email use only had one item, "The use of email helps me learn more." Table 23 shows the results from the cross-tabulation conducted on the category of email use.

Only 15% of those who responded with agree on the first questionnaire changed to strongly agree on the third questionnaire. There was a strong drop in attitudes with 39% of those students who disagreed at the first questionnaire changing their responses to strongly disagree on the third questionnaire. Sixty seven percent of those who strongly disagreed at the first questionnaire changed to merely disagree on the third questionnaire. The chi-square test has a p-value of .098.

Combined Email Attitude: Finally, examining the combined negative and positive responses helps to clarify the trends in attitudes about using email to help them learn more (see Table 24).

Item 16, "The use of email helps me learn more," had surprising results because nearly 27.3% of the students elected to use email during the course of the case study. The first questionnaire shows that only 40% of the students felt a positive attitude about email helping them learn more. However,

TABLE 23.   Change in Attitude About Computer Email Use Over Duration of Study (CAQ Category** Item 16)

		(Week 10) Computer Attitude Questionnaire* 3				
	Response	Strongly disagree	Disagree	Agree	Strongly agree	Total
(Week 1) Computer Attitude Questionnaire* 1	**Strongly disagree**	55.6%	33.3%	0%	11.1%	100%
	Disagree	38.5%	46.2%	7.7%	7.7%	100%
	Agree	15.4%	23.1%	46.2%	15.4%	100%
	Strongly agree	0%	66.7%	0%	33.3%	100%

χ^2= 18.6 (*p*-value =.098), 4 point scale system from 1 (strongly disagree) to 4 (strongly agree).
*Adapted from Knezek's Computer Attitude Questionnaire, 1999.
**Category Derived from Knezek's Computer Attitude Questionnaire, 1999.

after using email in the case study, that percentage declined to 30.9% and remained the same on the third questionnaire. This was a 9.1% point drop from the first questionnaire to the third questionnaire. Later, there will be a discussion of the 12 students who used email during the study. Although both the email and non-email users declined in positive attitudes on item 16, the responses in positive attitudes at the end of the study were still much higher than non-email users.

In conclusion, the results of the computer attitude questionnaires for the combined classes show that the items with increased positive attitudes between the first questionnaire and the follow-up questionnaire are 1, 2, 3, 7, 8, 9, 10, and 11. Items 4, 6, 12, 13, 14, 15, and 16 indicated decreased positive attitudes between the first questionnaire and the follow-up questionnaire. The greatest increase was item 10 with a 12 percentage point gain. The lowest decrease was item 16 with a 12% decline in positive attitudes. The next section will examine the results from the data of the two genders.

Gender differences

This section looks at the changes in computer attitudes of the genders across time. Cross tabulations were performed on the three categories of

TABLE 24.　Combined Response Percentages for Email Use

Email Items	CAQ*1 (First Week)		CAQ*2 (Fifth Week)		CAQ*3 (Tenth Week)		Change from caq1 to caq3
	strongly disagree / disagree	strongly agree / agree	strongly disagree / disagree	strongly agree / agree	strongly disagree / disagree	strongly agree / agree	
16. The use of email helps me learn more.	57.5%	40.0%	69.1%	30.9%	69.1%	30.9%	−9.1
Total	N = 40		N = 42		N = 42		

*Adapted from Knezek's Computer Attitude Questionnaire, 1999.

computer importance, computer enjoyment, and computer motivation / persistence. The first and third questionnaires were examined.

Computer Importance: Fifty percent of the boys who indicated disagreement on computer importance on the first questionnaire had no change in attitude on the third questionnaire as presented in Table 25 on the following page. However, another 50% of those who disagreed on the first questionnaire changed to agree on the third questionnaire. Twenty-four percent of the boys who strongly agreed about computer importance at the first questionnaire changed to merely agree on the third questionnaire. Table 25 displays these results.

Nearly 21% of the boys who agreed at the first questionnaire changed to strongly agree on the third questionnaire. These results are statistically significant because the chi-square test statistic and associated p-value are well below the standard cut-off for statistical significance of .05. This means that the probability of getting these numbers by chance is less than 5%.

The data from the girls' cross tabulation showed more increased positive changes across time than the boys (see Table 26). Nearly 35% of those girls who agreed at the first questionnaire changed to strongly agree on the second questionnaire.

One hundred percent of the girls who strongly disagreed on the first questionnaire changed to agree on the second questionnaire. However, nearly 38% of the girls who strongly agreed at the time of the first questionnaire

TABLE 25.   Attitude Changes in Boys on Computer Importance
(CAQ Category** Items 3, 5, and 7)

(Week 1) Computer Attitude Questionnaire* 1 Responses	(Week 10) Computer Attitude Questionnaire* 3			
	Disagree	Agree	Strongly agree	Total
Disagree	50.0%	50.0%		100%
Agree	8.3%	70.8%	20.8%	100%
Strongly agree		24.2%	75.8%	100%

$\chi^2 = 31.7$ ($p \leq 0.05$) $N = 22$, 4 point scale system from 1 (strongly disagree) to 4 (strongly agree).
*Adapted from Knezek's Computer Attitude Questionnaire, 1999.
**Derived from Knezek's Computer Attitude Questionnaire, 1999.

changed to merely agree on the second questionnaire. These results are statistically significant because the chi-square test statistic and associated p-value are well below the standard cut-off for statistical significance of .05. This means that the probability of getting these numbers by chance is less than 5%.

Computer Enjoyment: Next, cross tabulations were performed on the category of computer enjoyment (see Table 27). First, the data from the girls will be reported on. Fifty-one percent of the girls who agreed about computer enjoyment at the first questionnaire changed to strongly agree on the third questionnaire. Note the strong change of 57.1% of the girls who disagreed at the time of the first questionnaire changed to strongly agree at the third questionnaire. Nearly 43% of those who disagreed at the first questionnaire changed to agree at the third questionnaire.

Only 16.7% of those who strongly agreed at the first questionnaire changed to merely agree at the third questionnaire. Once again, these results are statistically significant because the chi-square test statistic and associated p-value are well below the standard cut-off for statistical significance of .05. This means that the probability of getting these numbers by chance is less than 5%.

Table 28 shows the changes in boys' attitudes on this category. Nearly 67% of the boys who strongly disagreed at the first questionnaire merely

TABLE 26.   Attitude Changes in Girls on Computer Importance (CAQ Category** Items 3, 5, and 7)

(Week 1) Computer Attitude Questionnaire* 1	Responses	(Week 5) Computer Attitude Questionnaire* 2			
		Disagree	Agree	Strongly agree	Total
	Strongly disagree		100%		100%
	Disagree	100%			
	Agree	65.4%	34.6%		100%
	Strongly agree	3.4%	37.9%	58.6%	100%

$\chi^2 = 33.2$ ($p \leq 0.05$) $N = 22$, 4 point scale system from 1 (strongly disagree) to 4 (strongly agree).
*Adapted from Knezek's Computer Attitude Questionnaire, 1999.
**Category derived from Knezek's Computer Attitude Questionnaire, 1999.

TABLE 27. Attitude Changes in Girls on
Computer Enjoyment (CAQ Category** Items
1, 2, 4, 6, 8, 9, and 10)

		(Week 10) Computer Attitude Questionnaire* 3			
	Responses	Disagree	Agree	Strongly agree	Total
(Week 1) Computer Attitude Questionnaire* 1	Disagree		42.9%	57.1%	100%
	Agree	8.9%	40.0%	51.1%	100%
	Strongly agree		16.7%	83.3%	100%

$\chi^2 = 18.7$ ($p \leq 0.05$) $N = 22$, 4 point scale system from 1 (strongly disagree) to 4 (strongly agree).
*Adapted from Knezek's Computer Attitude Questionnaire, 1999.
**Category derived from Knezek's Computer Attitude Questionnaire, 1999.

disagreed at the third questionnaire. Thirty-three percent of the boys who strongly disagreed changed to agree on the third questionnaire.

Thirty percent (30.8%) who disagreed at the first questionnaire changed to agree at the time of the third questionnaire. More remarkable is that 53.8% of those boys who disagreed at the first questionnaire changed to strongly agree on the third questionnaire. These changes in attitudes reflect the positive effect that *Museum Explorer* had on the boys' computer enjoyment. Again, these results are statistically significant because the chi-square test statistic and associated p-value are well below the standard cut-off for statistical significance of .05.

Both boys and girls showed increased positive attitude changes over time, thus reflecting on the positive effects of enjoyment with *Museum Explorer*.

Finally, cross tabulations were performed on the category of computer motivation and persistence. First, the data from the cross tabulations of the boys will be looked at (see Table 29).

The majority of the boys retained the same attitude over time, regarding computers being a motivating factor. Only 14.6% of those who agreed at the first questionnaire changed to disagree at the third questionnaire. Twenty-six (26.8%) of those who agreed at the first questionnaire changed to strongly agree at the third questionnaire. Twenty-five percent of those

Table 28. Attitude Changes in Boys on Computer
Enjoyment (CAQ Category** Items 1, 2, 4, 6, 8, 9, and 10)

		(Week 10) Computer Attitude Questionnaire* 3				
	Responses	Strongly disagree	Disagree	Agree	Strongly agree	Total
(Week 1) Computer Attitude Questionnaire* 1	Strongly disagree		66.7%	33.3%		100%
	Disagree		15.4%	30.8%	53.8%	100%
	Agree		17.2%	62.1%	20.7%	100%
	Strongly agree	1.1%	2.2%	12.0%	84.8%	100%

χ^2 = 78.1 ($p \leq 0.05$). 4 point scale system from 1 (strongly disagree) to 4 (strongly agree).
*Adapted from Knezek's Computer Attitude Questionnaire, 1999.
**Category derived from Knezek's Computer Attitude Questionnaire, 1999.

who disagreed at the first questionnaire changed to agree on the third questionnaire. These results are statistically significant because the chi-square test statistic and associated p-value are well below the standard cut-off for statistical significance of .05.

Table 30 displays the data on attitude changes of the girls.

Thirty-three percent of those girls who strongly disagreed at the first questionnaire changed to merely disagree at the third questionnaire. However, another 33.3% of the girls who strongly disagreed at the first questionnaire changed to agree at the third questionnaire. Nearly 27% of those who agreed at the first questionnaire changed to strongly agree at the third questionnaire. This data revealed that girls had slightly more positive changes in attitude about computer motivation and persistence than did the boys. The results are statistically significant because the chi-square test statistic and associated p-value are well below the standard cut-off for statistical significance of .05.

Following is a short discussion on gender differences on items 1, 3, 11, and 16.

General attitudes about computers

Item One—I like using a computer: Frequencies and percentages were used to calculate the tendencies of the genders on item 1. These three items were selected because the researcher felt that they were general and could

TABLE 29.   Attitude Changes in Boys on Computer
Motivation / Persistence (CAQ Category** Items 11, 12, 13, 14, and 15)

(Week 1) Computer Attitude Questionnaire* 1 Responses	(Week 10) Computer Attitude Questionnaire* 3				
	Strongly disagree	Disagree	Agree	Strongly agree	Total
Strongly disagree	50.0%	33.3%	8.3%	8.3%	100%
Disagree	12.5%	62.5%	25.0%		100%
Agree		14.6%	58.5%	26.8%	100%
Strongly agree		5.3%	23.7%	71.1%	100%

χ^2 = 79.4 ($p \leq 0.05$), 4 point scale system from 1 (strongly disagree) to 4 (strongly agree).
*Adapted from Knezek's Computer Attitude Questionnaire, 1999.
**Category derived from Knezek's Computer Attitude Questionnaire, 1999.

TABLE 30.   Attitude Changes in Girls on Computer Motivation /
Persistence (CAQ Category** Items 11, 12, 13, 14, and 15)

(Week 1) Computer Attitude Questionnaire* 1 Responses	(Week 10) Computer Attitude Questionnaire* 3				
	Strongly disagree	Disagree	Agree	Strongly agree	Total
Strongly disagree	33.3%	33.3%	33.3%		100%
Disagree	36.4%	36.4%	18.2%	9.1%	100%
Agree		9.8%	63.4%	26.8%	100%
Strongly agree	5.0%	2.5%	20.0%	72.5%	100%

χ^2 = 25.5 ($p \leq 0.05$), 4 point scale system from 1 (strongly disagree) to 4 (strongly agree).
*Adapted from Knezek's Computer Attitude Questionnaire, 1999.
**Category derived from Knezek's Computer Attitude Questionnaire, 1999.

possibly reveal more differences between the genders than other items.
Table 31 illustrates the attitudes of the genders on liking computers. Item 1
had no negative responses from the boys or girls.

There were a greater percentage of boys than girls on the first two
questionnaires who strongly agreed. However, on the third questionnaire
a higher percentage (81%) of the girls had stronger agreement in liking
to use computers than the boys. The boys started with 81% who strongly
agreed that they liked using computers at the first questionnaire, yet dipped

down to 66.7%, which was a 14.3% point drop after the three weeks using *Museum Explorer*.

The girls started with 73.7% who strongly agreed that they liked computers at the first questionnaire and then dropped down to 63.6%, a 10% point drop after using *Museum Explorer* for three weeks. However, there was a significant rise in the girls at the third questionnaire to 81%. This was a 17% point increase from the time of the second questionnaire to the third questionnaire. The boys had steady decreases in strong agreement across time, whereas the girls decreased at the second questionnaire but then sharply increased at the third questionnaire. The reasons for these patterns may be due to the fact that the last day in the lab the Internet connection was down and students, teacher, and researcher experienced quite a bit of frustration this day in both classes. It is reasonable to assume that, had the Internet connection worked the last day in the computer lab, both genders may have had better attitudes the following day when they took the test. This is one of the extraneous variables that could affect the outcomes as well as outcomes to other items in the questionnaire.

Item Three—I will be able to get a good job if I learn how to use a computer: Table 32 displays the gender differences on item three. The boys did not show as much increased strong positive changes as the girls. The strong agreement declined from 47.6% at the first questionnaire down to 42.9% in the last questionnaire, whereas the girls started with 26.3% strong agreement and increased to 42.9% at the last questionnaire. More boys disagreed than girls. The effect of *Museum Explorer* reflects positive increased strong

TABLE 31.   Relationship Between Student Gender and Item #1

Item#1 I like using computers	Response	CAQ*1 (Week 1)		CAQ*2 (Week 5)		CAQ*3 (Week 10)	
		Boys	Girls	Boys	Girls	Boys	Girls
	Agree	19.0%	26.3%	26.3%	36.4%	33.3%	19.0%
	Strongly agree	81.0%	73.7%	73.7%	63.6%	66.7%	81.0%
(Number of Cases)		(21)	(19)	(20)	(19)	(22)	(21)

N = 44.

Note: 4 point scale system from 1 (strongly disagree) to 4 (strongly agree).

*Adapted from Knezek's Computer Attitude Questionnaire, 1999.

attitudes over time for the girls and increased moderate agreement for the boys over time.

Item Eleven—I can not learn more from books than from a computer: The results from item 11 show interesting data that offer insights into gender attitudes about the value of computers as a learning tool as compared to books. The girls showed a strong decline from strong agreement at the first questionnaire (42.1%) down to 23.8% on the next two questionnaires. The girls showed a strong increase in agreement from the first questionnaire to the third questionnaire, which was nearly a 20% point increase in changed attitudes. The boys showed the same strong agreement at the first and third questionnaires. There was only a 10% point increase in agreement from the first questionnaire to the third questionnaire. Table 33 displays these differences.

There was an increase in the response of disagree at the time of the first questionnaire to the second questionnaire (28.6%). There was an 18% point decline in the girls' negative attitudes from the time of the second questionnaire to the third questionnaire (9.5%). Again, the Internet not

TABLE 32.   Relationship Between Student Gender and Item #3

		Student Gender					
		Boys			Girls		
	Response	CAQ*1 Week 1	CAQ*2 Week 5	CAQ*3 Week 10	CAQ*1 Week 1	CAQ*2 Week 5	CAQ*3 Week 10
Item #3 I will be able to get a good job if I learn how to use the computer	Strongly disagree	0%	0%	0%	5.30%	0%	0%
	Disagree	9.5%	5.3%	4.8%	0%	0%	4.8%
	Agree	42.9%	42.1%	52.4%	68.4%	45.5%	52.4%
	Strongly agree	47.6%	52.6%	42.9%	26.3%	54.5%	42.9%
Total			100%			100%	
(Number of Cases)		(21)	(19)	(21)	(19)	(22)	(21)

N = 44.

Note: 4 point scale system from 1 (strongly disagree) to 4 (strongly agree).

*Adapted from Knezek's Computer Attitude Questionnaire, 1999.

working the last day in the lab may have affected the girls at the time of the second questionnaire more than the boys.

Combining the negatives and positives again gives a clearer picture of the tendencies. Table 34 illustrates these attitude tendencies that combines the strongly disagree and disagree; and the strongly agree and agree.

The boys had higher positive increased percentages going from 76.2% on the first questionnaire up to 85.7% on the third questionnaire. The girls started with 84.2% in positive agreement up to 85.7% on the third questionnaire, which reflects only a slight change. A larger percentage of the girls increased in negative attitudes, going from only 15.8% up to 28.6% at the second questionnaire, but then declined to 14.3% in negative attitudes. This combined data of positive and negative attitudes reflects that boys had greater degrees of changes in positive attitudes by the end of the study than did the girls.

Item Sixteen—The use of email helps me learn more: Students throughout the three weeks in the computer lab were encouraged to email the assistant

TABLE 33. Relationship Between Student's Gender and Item #11

		Student's Gender					
		Boys			Girls		
	Response	CAQ*1 Week 1	CAQ*2 Week 5	CAQ*3 Week 10	CAQ*1 Week 1	CAQ* Week 5	CAQ*3 Week 10
Item #11 I cannot learn more from books than from a computer	Strongly disagree	19.0%	11.1%	4.8%	0%	0%	4.8%
	Disagree	4.8%	11.1%	9.5%	15.8%	28.6%	9.5%
	Agree	23.8%	27.8%	33.3%	42.1%	47.6%	61.9%
	Strongly agree	52.4%	50.0%	52.4%	42.1%	23.8%	23.8%
Total			100%			100%	
(Number of Cases)		(21)	(18)	(21)	(19)	(21)	(22)

N = 22.

Note: 4 point scale system from 1 (strongly disagree) to 4 (strongly agree).

*Adapted from Knezek's Computer Attitude Questionnaire, 1999.

TABLE 34. Combined Responses for Item #11

| Item #11 | CAQ*1 (Week 1) | | CAQ*2 (Week 5) | | CAQ*3 (Week 10) | |
I cannot learn more from books than from a computer	strongly disagree / disagree	strongly agree / agree	strongly disagree / disagree	strongly agree / agree	strongly disagree / disagree	strongly agree / agree
Boys	23.8%	76.2%	22.2%	77.8%	14.3%	85.7%
Girls	15.8%	84.2%	28.6%	71.4%	14.3%	85.7%

N = 44.
*Adapted from Knezek's Computer Attitude Questionnaire, 1999.

curator of the Portland State University biology museum. Twelve students took advantage of the opportunity. Table 35 shows the data gathered from Item 16 "The use of email helps me learn more."

The first questionnaire shows that more boys than girls strongly disagreed with the statement that email helps them learn more, but a higher percentage of boys strongly agreed (14.3%) than did the girls (5.3%) on the first questionnaire. The second questionnaire shows the same tendencies of the two genders on strong agreement and strong disagreement. However, on the third questionnaire there was a change in attitude with a higher percentage of girls (38.1%) who strongly disagreed than boys (19.0%). This may reflect that the girls' attitudes regarding email use in learning are more negative than the boys' attitudes.

Combining the positive responses of strongly agree and agree and the negative responses of strongly disagree and disagree is useful to understand the general tendencies of the genders as shown in Table 36. The boys started with higher percentages (47.6%) than the girls (42.1%) in the response of strongly agree, and at the third questionnaire they again had higher percentages (38%) in the responses of strongly agree.

The male students had a 21.6% point increase in negative attitudes about the use of email, to help them learn more from the time of the first questionnaire to the second questionnaire. However, the percentages decreased down to 61.9% at the third questionnaire. There was a total of a 9.5% point increase in negative attitudes of the boys from the first questionnaire to the follow-up questionnaire. There was a decrease in

TABLE 35.   Relationship Between Student Gender and Item #16

	Response	Student's Gender					
		Boys			Girls		
		CAQ*1 Week 1	CAQ*2 Week 5	CAQ*3 Week 10	CAQ*1 Week 1	CAQ*2 Week 5	CAQ*3 Week 10
Item #16 The use of email helps me learn more	Strongly disagree	23.8%	31.6%	19.0%	15.8%	27.3%	38.1%
	Disagree	28.6%	42.1%	42.9%	42.1%	36.4%	33.3%
	Agree	33.3%	10.5%	19.0%	36.8%	31.8%	19.0%
	Strongly agree	14.3%	15.8%	19.0%	5.3%	4.5%	9.5%
Total			100%			100%	
(Number of Cases)		(21)	(19)	(21)	(19)	(22)	(22)

Note: 4 point scale system from 1 (strongly disagree) to 4 (strongly agree).
*Adapted from Knezek's Computer Attitude Questionnaire. 1999.

TABLE 36.   Combined Gender Attitudes on Email Usage(CAQ Item # 16)

Item # 16 The use of email helps me learn more	CAQ*1 (Week 1)		CAQ*2 (Week 5)		CAQ*3 (Week 10)	
	strongly disagree / disagree	strongly agree / agree	strongly disagree / disagree	strongly agree / agree	strongly disagree / disagree	strongly agree / agree
Boys	52.4%	47.6%	73.7%	26.3%	61.9%	38.0%
Girls	57.9%	42.1%	63.7%	36.3%	71.4%	28.5%

N = 44.
*Adapted from Knezek's Computer Attitude Questionnaire. 1 999.

the boys' positive attitudes about email helping them learn from the time of the first questionnaire (47.6%) to 38% at the time of the third questionnaire.

The girls had a 5.8% point increase of negative attitudes from the time of the first questionnaire to the second questionnaire. There was another 7.7% point increase from the second questionnaire to the third questionnaire. There was a 13.5% point increase of negative attitudes from the time of the first questionnaire to the follow-up questionnaire. The girls showed more negative changes across the three questionnaires than did the boys. It appears that the female students, in general, came away from the case study with more negative attitudes than the boys regarding email usage for learning. A further discussion about the 12 students who used email during the three weeks will be discussed in the section on email use.

Following is a report on the differences in attitudes of the two classes.

Classes I and II differences

Item 3, 6, 17, and 18 were selected to review any differences between the two classes. This study looked at changes across time, therefore cross tabulations were performed on items 3 and 6. Table 37 displays the data from Class I on item 17, "I have a computer at home."

More students from Class II have computers at home than do students from Class I. The data from Class I reveals that 50% of the 20 students whose data were collected have computers at home.

Over three-fourths (87.5%) of the students have computers at home from Class II. There were higher percentages of students (54.2%) from Class II with Internet access at home than those from Class I (45.0%). Table 38 shows that nearly 10% more of these students have access to the Internet even though these students needed more academic support.

It is possible that some of the parents of the students from Class II are concerned about their children's abilities in English and therefore have

TABLE 37. Class I and Class II / Access to Home Computers

| Item #17 | | Classes | |
I have a computer at home	Response	Class I	Class II
	Yes	50.00%	87.50%
	No	50.00%	12.50%
Total		100%	100%
(Number of Cases)		(20)	(24)

TABLE 38.   Access to Internet Connection at Home

Item #18 My computer has Internet access	Response	Classes	
		Class I	Class II
	Yes	45.00%	54.2.%
	No	55.00%	45.80%
Total		100%	100%
(Number of Cases)		(20)	(24)

purchased computers in the hopes that it will help their children succeed. The following are section reports on the data on item 3.

Item 3 asks about the student's opinions whether "I will be able to get a good job if I learn how to use the computer." Cross tabulations were conducted to get a better idea of changes in attitudes of the two classes on item 3. The first and third questionnaires were used to gather the data from Class II (see Table 39).

The data reveals that 100% of those students from Class II who strongly agreed at the first questionnaire changed to agree at the second questionnaire. One hundred percent of those who disagreed at the first questionnaire changed to strongly agree at the second questionnaire. Twenty three percent of those who agreed at the first questionnaire changed to strongly agree at the second questionnaire. The results are statistically significant because the chi-square test statistic and associated p-value are well below the standard cut-off for statistical significance of .05. Table 40 displays the changes in the attitudes of students from Class I.

Nearly 56% of those who agreed at the first questionnaire changed to strongly agree at the second questionnaire. Thirty percent of those who strongly agreed at the first questionnaire changed to merely agree at the second questionnaire. Five percent of those who strongly agreed at the first questionnaire changed to disagree at the second questionnaire. The results are statistically significant because the chi-square test statistic and associated p-value are well below the standard cut-off for statistical significance of .05.

TABLE 39.   Class II and Changes in Attitude on Item 3:
"*I will be able to get a good job*"

(Week 1) Computer Attitude Questionnaire* 1	Responses	(Week 5) Computer Attitude Questionnaire* 2		
		Agree	Strongly agree	Total
	Strongly disagree	100%		100%
	Disagree		100%	100%
	Agree	76.9%	23.1%	100%
	Strongly agree		100%	100%

χ^2 = 8.3 ($p \leq 0.05$), 4 point scale system from 1 (strongly disagree) to 4 (strongly agree).
*Adapted from Knezek's Computer Attitude Questionnaire, 1999.

TABLE 40.   Class I and Changes in Attitude on Item #3:
"*I will be able to get a good job*"

(Week 1) Computer Attitude Questionnaire* 1	Responses	(Week 5) Computer Attitude Questionnaire* 2			
		Disagree	Agree	Strongly agree	Total
	Disagree	100%	100%		100%
	Agree		44.4%	55.6%	100%
	Strongly agree	5.0%	30.0%	70.0%	100%

χ^2 = 20.4 ($p \leq 0.05$), 4 point scale system from 1 (strongly disagree) to 4 (strongly agree).
*Adapted from Knezek's Computer Attitude Questionnaire, 1999.

There were more positive changes in attitudes among students from Class II than from Class I. Students from Class II needed more academic support than students from Class I, but still showed positive changes as compared to students from Class I.

Item 6, which asks if they enjoy lessons on the computer, showed more positive changes over time with students from Class I than with Class II. Table 41 presents the results of Class I.

One hundred percent of those students who disagreed at the second questionnaire changed to agree at the third questionnaire. However, 30% of the students who agreed at the second questionnaire changed to disagree at the third questionnaire. However, 20% of those students who agreed at the

Table 41.   Class I and Changes in Attitude on Item 6:
"I enjoy lessons on the computer"

			(Week 10) Computer Attitude Questionnaire* 3			
(Week 5) Computer Attitude Questionnaire* 2		**Responses**	**Disagree**	**Agree**	**Strongly agree**	**Total**
		Disagree		100%		100%
		Agree	30.0%	50.0%	20.0%	
		Strongly agree			100%	100%

$\chi^2 = 14.8$ ($p \leq 0.05$), 4 point scale system from 1 (strongly disagree) to 4 (strongly agree).
*Adapted from Knezek's Computer Attitude Questionnaire, 1999.

second questionnaire changed to strongly agree at the third questionnaire. The results are statistically significant because the chi-square test statistic and associated p-value are well below the standard cut-off for statistical significance of .05.

Students from Class II showed fewer changes in strong agreement across time than students from Class I. Twenty-five percent of those students from Class II who merely agreed at the second questionnaire changed to strongly agree at the third questionnaire (see Table 42). Fifty-seven percent of those students who strongly agreed at the second questionnaire changed to merely agree at the third questionnaire.

The results are statistically significant because the chi-square test statistic and associated p-value are well below the standard cut-off for statistical significance of .05.

Summary of computer attitude questionnaires

The effect of *Museum Explorer* on student engagement measured using the three computer attitude questionnaires indicated positive attitudes regarding computers and engagement across time. The data gathered on the categories of computer importance and computer enjoyment revealed positive increased changes over time. The categories of computer motivation and persistence showed declining attitudes over time. The girls showed more increased positive changes across time in the categories of computer importance and computer motivation and persistence. The boys showed more increased positive changes across time in the category of email use.

TABLE 42.   Class II and Changes in Attitude on Item 6:
"*I enjoy lessons on the computer*"

| | | (Week 10) Computer Attitude Questionnaire* 3 | | | | |
	Responses	Strongly disagree	Disagree	Agree	Strongly agree	Total
(Week 5) Computer Attitude Questionnaire* 2	Strongly disagree	100%				100%
	Disagree		75.0%	25.0%		100%
	Agree			75.0%	25.0%	100%
	Strongly agree		14.3%	57.1%	28.6%	100%

$\chi^2 = 30.1$ ($p \leq 0.05$), 4 point scale system from 1 (strongly disagree) to 4 (strongly agree).
*Adapted from Knezek's Computer Attitude Questionnaire, 1999.

Class I had more increased positive changes across time than Class II on items 3 and 6.

Teacher Rating Forms

The teacher rating forms were developed from the Bangert-Drowns and Pyke (2002) study on teacher ratings of student engagement with educational software. The study involved the use of a seven-level scale of engagement. Students are often enthusiastic and persistent as they interact with software. Engagement of the student was categorized into various forms or levels, the most basic of which were disengagement, unsystematic engagement, and frustrated engagement. These three levels are easier to rate because their behavioral indicators were most obvious. In the next four levels the student displays increasingly more sophisticated styles of engagement. Teachers in general are able to assess student academic performance adeptly. However, the seven-level scale of engagement was created to help teachers in their assessment of engagement.

The teacher and researcher had discussed the seven-level scale of engagement and the teacher rating forms before the study began. The unexpected problem of the Internet not connecting caused the teacher some anxiety, and on the first week he and the researcher both were kept busy trying to help the frustrated students. He tried to fill out the forms but succeeded in completing only one form.

Although the forms from the regular science teacher may have yielded different and possibly more reliable results, the researcher decided to use the forms filled out by the experienced substitute teacher. The science teacher did not feel comfortable rating all seven modes of engagement without interviewing the students. In addition, the teacher felt that his closer relationship with the students might confound the accuracy of his judgments about his students. The second week the science teacher had gone and the substitute science teacher filled out 15 rating forms (see Appendix E). She filled out forms which represented 34% of the students in both classes. She was urged to base her judgments of engagement on her direct observations of the students' interaction with *Museum Explorer*. She sat behind each student she was observing. She had been asked to limit each observation to only three minutes. She observed 15 students from the two classes. The four-point scale at the lower part of the form asked the teacher to rate her confidence level from very confident to very unsure. She rated herself as confident on all 15 ratings.

Results for modes of engagement

Table 43 displays the modes of engagement, the teacher responses, and the percentages for the combined 15 rating forms.

None of the science teacher's forms were used in this study because he completed only one of them. A possible benefit of the substitute teacher filling out the forms was the advantage of her not extrapolating from her observations based on other knowledge of the students (Bangert-Drowns & Pyke, 2002).

The first three modes are the simplest modes of engagement to observe. Twenty percent of the students on the first mode of learning often showed disengagement. Nearly twenty-seven percent of the students on the second mode of learning often showed unsystematic engagement. However, 80% of the students never or rarely showed disengagement, and over 70% never or rarely displayed unsystematic engagement. Eighty percent of the students never or rarely showed frustrated engagement, and only 20% of the students often displayed frustrated engagement.

The next four modes of engagement are more difficult to detect without interviewing the student. The science teacher had mentioned his frustration with the forms and felt they were too difficult to fill out without interviewing

TABLE 43. Modes of Engagement and Frequencies

Name and Description of Mode	Choices	%
1. Disengagement / Student stops interacting with software	Never	40
	Rarely	40
	Often	20
2. Unsystematic engagement / Student moves from one activity to another without apparent reason	Never	60
	Rarely	13.3
	Often	26.7
3. Frustrated engagement / Student attempts to achieve specific software goals unsuccessfully	Never	33.3
	Rarely	46.7
	Often	20
4. Structure-dependent engagement / Student navigates and operates the software competently to pursue goals communicated by the software or teacher	Rarely	20
	Often	46.7
	Almost always	33.3
5. Self-regulated interest / Student adjusts software features to sustain deeply involved, interesting, or challenging interactions for personally defined purposes	Never	20
	Rarely	13.3
	Often	60
	Almost always	6.7
6. Critical engagement / Student manipulates software to test personal understanding or operational or content-related limitations of software representations	Never	26.7
	Rarely	33.3
	Often	40
7. Literate thinking / Student explores software from multiple, personally meaningful perspectives; uses perspective-sensitive interpretations to reflect on personal values or experience	Never	33.3
	Rarely	26.7
	Often	40

N = 15.
Note: Ratings were made on a 4-point scale (0 = never, 1 = rarely, 2 = often, 3 = almost always).
Adapted from Bangert-Drowns and Pyke, 2002.

the students. The structure-dependent mode of engagement showed that 46.7% of the students often navigated the website competently, and 33.3% of the students almost always navigated the website competently. The fifth mode of self-regulated interest showed that nearly 67% of the students often or almost always displayed this mode of engagement. The sixth mode of critical engagement showed that 40% of the students often displayed this more sophisticated type of engagement with the website, although 26.7% never did and 33.3% rarely did. The seventh mode of engagement dealt with literate thinking, and 40% of the students often engaged in this mode of thinking while working with the website.

The teacher's mean ratings ranged from 0.67 to 2.13 (see Table 44). The highest average frequency rating was for the structure-dependent engagement ($M = 2.13$). The Bangert-Drowns and Pyke (2002) study also showed the highest mean rating to be the structure-dependent engagement mode. The next highest mean rating was for the self-regulated mode of engagement ($M = 1.53$). The two lowest mean ratings were for the unsystematic engagement ($M = 0.67$) and disengagement ($M = 0.80$). Again, the study by Bangert-Drowns and Pyke also showed that their teachers reported the first three "dysfunctional" forms of engagement (disengagement, unsystematic engagement, and frustrated engagement) less frequently than the "functional" forms. Further, the "functional" ratings on their study showed the same responses as this case study, from the highest being self-regulated interest to lowest of literate thinking.

In this study the highest average frequency rating was given to structure-dependent engagement. Relatively low ratings for the "dysfunctional" forms of engagement (disengagement, unsystematic engagement, and frustrated engagement) compared to the "functional" forms of engagement (literate thinking, critical engagement, self-regulated interest, and structure dependence) mean that "dysfunctional" forms of engagement were reported less frequently. The average rating or response from the teacher for literate thinking was *rarely reported*. The average ratings ranged from 0.67 to 2.13.

TABLE 44.   Means and Standard Deviations
for Student Engagement Ratings

Mode of Engagement	M	SD
Literate thinking	1.00	0.88
Critical engagement	1.13	0.83
Self-regulated interest	1.53	0.92
Structure dependence	2.13	0.74
Frustrated engagement	0.87	0.74
Unsystematic engagement	0.67	0.90
Disengagement	0.80	0.77

$N = 15$.

Note: Ratings are on a 4-point scale (0 = never, 1 = rarely, 2 = often,
3 = almost always).

Figure 17 shows the seven engagement ratings given for one student. Two contiguous forms of engagement (structure dependant and self-regulated interest) were given the highest frequency rating for the student.

A sum or average of each student's ratings was not used because each of the seven ratings assessed different behavior. However, these seven ratings formed a continuum from a minimum of disengaged to the maximum of literate thinking.

The ratings peaked as engagement level increased, but dropped off at the highest ratings. This suggests a predominant level of engagement for this student somewhere on the engagement scale between structure dependence and self-regulated interest. Also, the seven ratings form an engagement scale from 1 for disengagement through 7 for literate thinking. Therefore, each student's seven ratings were summarized in a single, frequency-weighted average rating. A new frequency-weighted average score for each student

FIGURE 17.   Ratings of Engagement Frequency for One Student on Each of Seven Types of Engagement

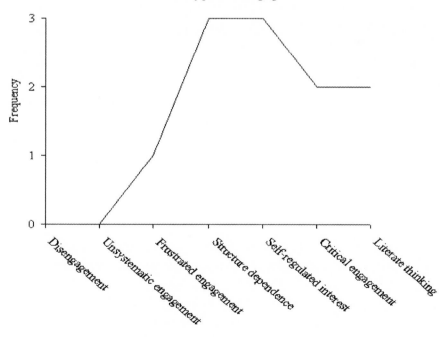

was calculated by multiplying each engagement level (1 to 7) by its teacher rated frequency (0 to 3) and then dividing the sum of these products by the sum of the teacher's frequency ratings.

The seven engagement ratings in Figure 16, which shows the pattern of engagement along the engagement continuum for one student, were thereby transformed to a single score of 5.09. This new frequency-weighted average rating is very positive because it is higher than structure-dependent engagement.

Frequency-weighted average ratings vary. They range from a value of 1 when the student is always disengaged to a value of 7 when the student is always engaged in literate thinking. The students' ratings in this study varied between 2.50 and 5.09. The students were rated positively because only 5 (33%) of the ratings were below structure dependence. However, the mean frequency-weighted average for boys was somewhat higher than for the girls (4.34 for boys and 4.13 for girls).

Summary of teacher rating forms

The teacher rating forms indicate that the students were often or almost always engaged with the website. The data on the four higher modes of engagement indicate that the majority of students often or almost always were actively engaged with the website. Eighty percent of the students displayed the structured dependent mode of engagement. Of these four higher modes of engagement, fewer students (33.3%) displayed literate thinking. These students worked competently as they worked on the website. However, these four modes of engagement also are difficult to rate without either knowing the students well or visiting with them as they work with the software. The students' notebooks also were an indication of the engagement of the students while they used the website.

Student Notebooks

This study defines engagement as students demonstrating positive attitudes and interest in the subject. Engaged students using computers are actively involved in their own learning and actively participate, and show increased interest as they interact with the computer software. The students were encouraged to keep records of their activities on the webpage. They were asked to not only record interesting things they discover on the web site, but monitor their scores on the daily quizzes. The sums of the pages the students used to write or draw pictures is an indicator of their engagement with the website.

All students were given Mead notebooks to use during the three-weeks in the computer lab. They brought the notebooks and a pencil or pen each day to the lab and took them back to their home science classroom after the lab session. Although the students were encouraged to write their own feelings about what they did each day as they explored the website, only two students put down anything other than notes and drawings. Two students wrote things such as, "I wonder why a baby cougar has spots?". All but two students wrote down 100% for each of their quizzes even though it took many of them several tries to arrive at a perfect score. Because of these unexpected events regarding the students' notebooks, it was decided that examining the number of notebook entries could help triangulate the data on student engagement. The students on the first day had the choice of selecting the bears (brown bear and grizzly bear) or the cats (cougar and bobcat). The girls were equally divided in their selection. However, three-fourths of the boys selected the cats.

Analysis of notebook entries

On the last day of the study (in week five) the researcher took all notebooks into the office to be photocopied and then returned them to their teacher to hand back to the students. One boy did not turn his notebook in to be copied. All girls turned their notebooks in to be copied. Forty-three notebooks were photocopied. Table 45 illustrates the numbers of notebook entries for girls and boys.

The average number of pages written by the girls, including both text and drawings, was 13.6 pages. The largest number of pages entered by the girls, including text and drawings, was 25 pages. The largest number of text entries was17. The largest number of drawing entries by the girls was 8. The least number of written pages entered by a girl was 5 pages, and the least number of drawings by a girl was 1 page. The largest number of text entries written by the boys was 11 pages. The largest number of drawings was 11 pages. The largest number of pages written by the boys including both text and drawings was 22 pages. The total number

Table 45.   Notebook Entries: Text, Drawings, and Totals

Girls				Boys		
Text	Drawings	Totals		Text	Drawings	Totals
10	4	14		2		2
5	1	6		9	3	12
16	8	24		3	3	6
8	2	10		1		1
8	2	10		8	1	9
6	3	9		11	4	15
6	3	9		7	7	14
10	2	12		7	1	8
12	3	15		1		1
7	7	14		2	1	3
10	1	11		9	2	11
9	6	15		4		4
7	2	9		9	4	13
14	4	18		4	2	6
9	1	10		7	2	9
9	4	13		5	2	7
11	5	16		11	11	22
17	2	19		8	5	13
12	4	16		8	2	10
12	3	15		5	1	6
11	3	14		5	5	10
12	8	20				
221	78	299	Totals	126	56	182

(N = 22)   (N = 21)

of combined text and drawings of the 22 girls was 299 pages. Two hundred twenty-one pages were text and 78 pages were drawings. The total number of combined pages of text and drawings of the 21 boys was 182 pages. One hundred twenty-six pages were text with 56 pages of drawings. Although there was one more girl who handed in the notebook than boys, there still were 117 more pages of combined text and drawing entries by the girls than by the boys. The girls had 95 more pages of text than the boys and 22 more drawings. The number of notebook entries each day may show that the girls were more actively engaged in their entries than were the boys, particularly writing in text entries. Society encourages girls to write in notebooks and this may be anecdotal evidence why the girls had more entries than the boys. Perhaps the boys were more actively engaged in computer related multimedia tasks and were distracted from the notebooks. Further, some studies suggest that Latino bilingual boys at this age may have fewer writing skills than the girls (Bermúdez & Prater, 1994).

There was a moderate positive correlation between those students who had more total notebook text and drawing entries and their scores on the post-test. Zero indicates no correlation, and 1 indicates a high correlation. The two continuous variables of post-test scores and notebook entries had a Pearson correlation of .342 ($r = .34$) that indicates not a high positive correlation, but nonetheless, some correlation. Figure 18 displays a scatter plot graph of this moderate positive correlation. The data displayed on this graph indicates a moderate positive correlation between the number of notebook entries and the scores on the post-test.

FIGURE 18.   Correlation Between Numbers of Student Notebook Entries and Scores on the Post-Test

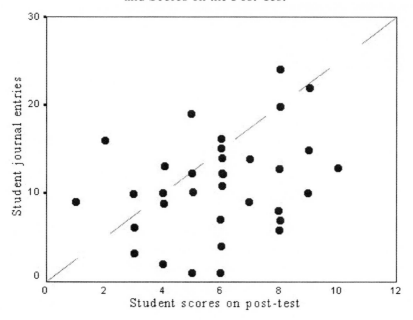

The second day in the computer lab the students were invited at the end of the session to turn in their notebooks if they had entries that they wanted to be put on the *Museum Explorer* website. Their notebooks were returned to them the following day. A total of 12 students (27.2%) turned in their notebooks to have selected pages put in the student class galleries. This number represented nearly one-third of the students. Each day before they began work in the lab the students looked at their class entries online on the large screen at the front of the room. Many of the students also enjoyed looking at the galleries on their own computers in the lab. The website class gallery was designed so that each picture could be enlarged and the entries could be viewed as a photo gallery. They enjoyed discussing what they liked about the various entries. Figure 19 shows one notebook page from Class II that was put in the gallery. This page was created by a girl and was the first student who wanted a notebook entry to be put online. The page is a typical notebook entry done by a girl.

Both girls and boys often mis-spelled words although they were copying from the website. The following entry (see Figure 20) was from one of the twin boys' notebooks. Typically, the boys had more pictures drawn per page than the girls with an average of more than three drawings per page with less text.

Summary of student notebooks

The teacher's plan was actually for the students to express their attitudes in their own notebooks. However, as they did not do this, the use of counted entries per notebook adequately served to measure the effect of the website on engagement. Using counted pages in their notebooks as indicators of student engagement, it was found that the girls were more engaged than the boys. Twelve students put their notebook entries in the student galleries online. Seven of these students also used email to correspond with the assistant curator at the museum.

Description of Open-ended Questionnaires

The open-ended questionnaires were based on a modified version of a study developed by William Beeland (2003). The questions in both the student and teacher open-ended questionnaires helped to measure the effect of the intervention on student content knowledge and engagement. Specific questions

FIGURE 19.   Girl's Notebook Page Posted in Gallery

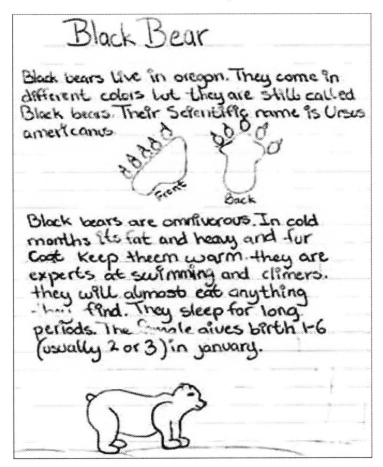

within the questionnaires were designed to answer research questions one, two, and three (see Figure 21).

Student Open-ended Questionnaires

The student open-ended questionnaire was composed of five questions. The students filled out the open-ended questionnaire on the last day of the fifth week. It took the students about 15 minutes to write out their responses.

FIGURE 20.   Boy's Notebook Page Posted in Gallery

Concepts from the responses were coded into manageable content categories. First the researcher decided how many concepts to code for. Next the texts were coded for frequency. The level of generalization was that various words describing an event or thought were put under one concept. For example, if the videos did not work the students used various words to describe this. For instance, one student wrote *the videos froze*. Another student wrote *the movies didn't work*. Both these responses were

FIGURE 21. Questions that Address Research Questions

Questionnaire	Research Question 1	Research Question 2	Research Question 3
Teacher	4 and 5	1, 2, and 3	6
Student		1, 2, and 3	4 and 5

Adapted from Beeland, 2003.

generalized into the category of Internet problems. The students' responses for the five questions were generally only one or two sentences in length. All information was viewed as relevant and important. Table 46 illustrates the five questions in the open-ended questionnaire and the categories derived from the data from each question. Responses to questions 4 and 5 will be discussed in the section on email use.

The following report on questions one, two and three in the student open-ended questionnaire has unedited and unaltered student responses, although italics are added to all inferences of *Museum Explorer.*

Question one: Describe what you liked most when using Museum Explorer Question one asked students to describe what they liked most when using *Museum Explorer.* Twelve students (27.3%) responded that they liked the games and did not mention any other section of the website. The majority of these students were boys, with three girls and nine boys. Six of the students were from Class I and six were from Class II. It may be that the boys play more video games outside the school. The games they referred to were the games on the BBC (British Broadcasting Company) link that was added to the homepage the third week of the study and the second week in the computer lab. Each day the students were given a few minutes to play these games. The teacher liked the games because they were educational, interactive, and challenging. Following are the responses from the twelve students on the games:

- I liked the games because they were cool. The fox game was cool. (boy, Class I)
- Playing the game when you're the wolf. (boy, Class I)

TABLE 46.   Questions and Categories for Student Open-ended Questionnaires

Question	Category	Tally
Question 1:	Games	25
Describe what you liked most when using	Quizzes	13
Museum Explorer.	Information	2
	Videos	8
	Pictures	2
	Notebook writing	1
Question 2:	Internet problems	
Describe what you liked least when using *Museum Explorer.*	Quizzes	5
If you could change one thing about *Museum Explorer,*	No changes	11
what would you change?	Vice reading	9
	More games, animals,	10
	Information	16
Question 3:	Access to information	22
How could using *Museum Explorer* help you learn better	Self-Guided learning	5
than other ways of learning (reading books, watching TV,	Multimedia	12
listening to talks?)	Better	11
	Facts	4
Question 4:	Time limitations	25
Describe your experience on the field trip to the museum.	The curator	2
What was good about it and what was not so good?	Animals	4
	Miscellaneous	11
Question 5:	Answers and information	6
If you emailed the curator at the museum, describe your	Type emails	1
experience.		

- Playing the games was my favorite thing. I liked it because it actually teaches you something. (girl, Class I)
- The games. (girl, Class I)
- What I liked the most of *Museum Explorer* is the computer games. I liked them because they taught me how an animal lives every day. (boy, Class I)
- Playing games. All of the games. (boy, Class I)
- The games. (boy, Class II)
- I like to play the games. (boy, Class II)

- Games were the best thing there. (girl, Class II)
- I liked playing the games because mammal maker was kind of difficult. (boy, Class II)
- The thing I like the most is the game called survival zone because its fun surviving every level. (boy, Class II)
- The games and the games I like to play is mammal maker and the one you are a fox and need to survive. (boy, Class II)

Nine students (20.5%) reported that they liked the quizzes. Seven girls and two boys reported that they liked the quizzes most of all. It is not known why many girls compared to boys liked the quizzes. Note that seven of the responses were students from Class I who were more academically advanced than students from Class II. Only two responses came from Class II. Following are the responses about the quizzes from the nine students:

- The quizzes, because it challenges your mind. And what I liked about the quizzes too was that it had all sorts of tests like crosswords, and missing letters. I think that this was a fun way to test us. (girl, Class I)
- I like most when we did the test because I want to learn more about it. (girl, Class I)
- I liked the quizzes because I never knew a quiz like that. What I'm telling is that I never played a quiz like the ones you made. (boy, Class I)
- I like playing games as in quizzes. (girl, Class I)
- I like the quiz on the bears because I learn more and it helps practice my reading and I know that I have to read so I can answer the questions in the quiz. (girl, Class I)
- The most thing that I liked from the *Museum Explorer* was that it was interesting. Well everything was interesting – the animals, the facts about them, and most of all was the quizzes. It made me feel like I was getting smarter, from each fact. I just love animals. (girl, Class I)
- The quizzes because you learn more. (boy, Class II)
- I really liked doing the quizzes for each animal. (girl, Class I)
- Taking the tests and reading with it so it would help. (girl, Class II)

Two students mentioned the quizzes along with other multimedia aspects such as the movies or games. These two responses were:

- What I liked most was seeing the movies in the *Museum Explorer*. I liked most also the quiz because it showed me that I had learned. (girl, Class II)
- When we need to look in the overview of an animal. The other thing is that the game it had and quizzes too. (boy, Class II)

Sixteen (43.2%) students responded that they liked the various multimedia aspects of the website. There were six girls and ten boys. Nine of these students were from Class I and 7 were from Class II. The responses from these students were:

- What I liked more about *Museum Explorer* was the information they include about every animal and how they show the videos about every animal. (girl, Class I)
- The part I liked most when I was using *Museum Explorer* was the part when the vocabulary they tell you the definition. (boy, Class I)
- What I liked were the games, video clips, audio because the guy read it. (boy, Class I)
- Playing the games, the puzzles, and the word search. My other favorite thing for using the *Museum Explorer* was the pictures of the animals. (boy, Class I)
- What I liked most were the videos. The reason I liked the videos is because I liked how great it shows how bears look. I also liked the games. For example, I liked the game of the fox, which was the best game I have ever used. (girl, Class I)
- I liked the videos. Because I got to see how the animals react when they aren't tamed. (girl, Class I)
- What I liked more when using *Museum Explorer* is how they had the videos to see how or where they keep the mammals. I also liked the games they had. Especially the new ones that you have to memorize the way to go across the maze. (boy, Class I)
- The videos because I did not have to read only the lesson. (girl, Class I)

- What I like doing in *Museum Explorer* were looking at the nice pictures of the animals and the games because they were hard. (girl, Class I)
- The mammal maker and video. They were interesting and the games. (boy, Class II)
- The video of animals. (boy, Class II)
- The games because it is fun to play games. All the information that it has about animals. (boy, Class II)
- Learning about animals. What they eat. (boy, Class II)
- What I liked most when using *Museum Explorer* is how to learn about animals habitat what they like to eat and what they do. (girl, Class II)
- The mammal maker and videos, they were interesting and the games. (boy, Class II)
- We get to find more about animals and games. (boy, Class II)

Eight of these 16 students mentioned that they liked the videos. Eight students mentioned that they liked the games along with other aspects. Other students mentioned that they liked the pictures, the audio text, the vocabulary, information, and learning about animals.

Three students responded with a single answer such as that they like to study different animals, learn new things, or enjoy writing in the notebook. Overall, 43% of the students liked the multi-media aspect of the website. This indicated engagement as they explored the site. Twenty-one percent enjoyed the interactive quizzes and 27% enjoyed the interactive BBC games. All these responses indicate engagement because of the interactive nature of the website.

Question two: Describe what you liked least when using Museum Explorer.

If you could change one thing about Museum Explorer, what would you change?

Question two asked students to describe what they liked least when using *Museum Explorer*. This question produced a larger variety of responses than question one. Ten students (20.4%) responded that they would not change anything. Seven of these responses were from Class I and only three responses were from Class II. Six girls and four boys gave the following responses:

- I don't think there would be something that I could change or add to this program because I think it is already good. (girl, Class I)
- I didn't find anything less interesting. (boy, Class I)
- I liked everything. I also thought nothing was wrong. (girl, Class I)
- Nothing. (boy, Class I)
- What I did not like is nothing. What I mean is that I just loved everything.
- I found everything spectacular. I just have not seen such a great detailed and fun ... (girl, Class I)
- If I could change something from the *Museum Explorer*, what will I change? Nothing. Mindi spent a lot of time on this. Well, that is what I think. She really worked hard, and we owe it all to her. For me, *Museum Explorer* is just very good. I love it. (girl, Class I)
- I wouldn't change anything. Everything was great. (girl, Class I)
- Nothing. (boy, Class II)
- What I like is everything. (boy, Class II)
- Well there's nothing I can change because it is nice. (girl, Class II)

Five boys (11.4%) wanted the quizzes changed. One response was from Class I and four from Class II. It appears that these boys had difficulty for a number of reasons with the quizzes. A website that tracked the number of times students take a quiz could possibly help in understanding why these students had a difficult time with the quizzes. Also, interviewing these students might have contributed to understanding their attitudes. The unaltered responses were:

- The part I didn't really like was the part with the quizzes. (boy, Class I)
- What I did not like that much was the quizzes because they don't help you that much. What I would change would be the quizzes. (boy, Class II)
- Quizzes were the ones, none were difficult. (boy, Class II)
- I will change the quizzes. (boy, Class II)
- Some of the quizzes. (boy, Class II)

Nine students (20.5%) responded that they did not like the voice presentation of the text. Six of these were girls and only three were boys. Seven of the responses were students from Class I, the class with higher academic skills. Why more girls than boys had trouble with the text narration is an issue beyond the scope of this study. The researcher had asked the person who read the text to read slowly, so that the Latino students could understand. It may be that the students in Class I with more proficiency in English simply did not need this extra help with the voice or with the slower reading. These responses indicate the possible need for more buttons on the website that included a slow button for slower reading, a fast button for faster narration, and possibly a "funny voice" narration for more advanced students who like more animated reading. The responses were:

- What I liked least about *Museum Explorer* was the voice they include to read the information. It went too slow. (girl, Class I)
- I really didn't like was the voice. It was too slow when it read the paragraph. (girl, Class I)
- What I like least is hearing the person talking when he reads. I would change the reading so I could read it myself. (girl, Class I)
- I least liked the voice that read the paragraphs because he would go slowly. (girl, Class I)
- What I didn't like when using *Museum Explorer* is the man when he read to us. (girl, Class I)
- Reading the stories of animals. (boy, Class I)
- I would change the voice that narrates the reading part. And he was hard to understand. (boy, Class I)
- The thing that was boring was the guy because he was talking a lot about the animals. (boy, Class I)
- I did not like when the guy kept on talking so fast I would change it by telling him to talk slower next time. (boy, Class II)

Ten students (22.7%) responded to just the last part of the question, "If you could change one thing about *Museum Explorer*, what would you change?". Four of these students were girls and six were boys. Six of the students were from Class II and four from Class I. Since students from Class II have lower

English skills, it may be predicted that more from this class could experience some frustrations while using the website. These responses were:

- I would put more games. I liked the games. I would put interesting games. (girl, Class I)
- There were not enough animals. I would add more animals. (boy, Class I)
- I wouldn't change anything, just maybe make it fun. (girl, Class I)
- I could change it by putting the videos with more action. (boy, Class I)
- The movies. A little bit more excited. (girl, Class II)
- Making it better putting more mammals to compare like a web that animals prey on and so on. (boy, Class II)
- I would just put more animals to select. (boy, Class II)
- What I didn't really like was that sometimes it wouldn't give you so much information in some animals. What I would do to make the *Museum Explorer* better is put more information about animals. (girl, Class II)
- The thing I didn't like was that they didn't let us go to the bobcat. I would change that they should let us get in the bobcat the first time. (boy, Class II)
- Put more games. (boy, Class II)

Five students (11.4%) responded that they did not like it when the videos did not work. Three of these responses were from girls and two from boys. Five responses did not answer the question.

Question three: How could using Museum Explorer help you learn better than other ways of learning (reading books, watching TV, listening to talks)? Question three asked students how using the *Museum Explorer* could help them learn better than other ways of learning (reading books, watching TV, listening to talks). Twenty-two of the student responses to this question dealt with access to information. These responses were:

- Because it provides you with more information about the animal. (boy, Class 1)
- They have real facts. (boy, Class I)

- I think it's better using *Museum Explorer* because it is a program that teaches us to learn specific animal facts. (girl, Class I)
- Using *Museum Explorer* could help me learn better because it gives us more examples about animals, but TV is better because it includes a lot more information. (girl, Class I)
- That it can tell us a lot more. It gave us more facts about the animal. (girl, Class I)
- Using *Museum Explorer* helps you learn because it tells you stuff from right now and not 10 years ago. (girl, Class I)
- It will help me by learning new things. Because by watching TV I won't learn nothing. (girl, Class I)
- It gives me more clearly information about something and I can learn always something new. (girl, Class I)
- Because the program has people that are experienced. In each sentence there was more information. On television etc. they say things like they hunt and don't give enough information. (girl, Class I)
- Because they show a lot about animals and on TV, books, they don't explain that very good. (girl, Class I)
- When I read books, most of them don't have pictures. In *Museum Explorer* they show videos, and explain what they mean. In watching TV, well, I don't really watch TV so it doesn't really help me. And in listening to talks, I can't see what they mean. The way the *Museum Explorer* helps me to learn better, it shows you and explains to you what exactly they mean, so I can learn better than reading books, watching TV, and listening to talks. (girl, Class I)
- They had real facts. (boy, Class I)
- It could help me learn better by knowing different other mammals that I haven't seen. I also enjoyed that they had real facts. (girl, Class I)
- It helps better because it has more details about animals. In the TV there are not games. I like learning better like that. (girl, Class I)
- It could help me more because some times the computer has more information and because it tells you every thing you want to find. (boy, Class II)
- By knowing more about mammals like a cougar and bear. (boy, Class II)

- It would help me more because reading books, watching TV, or listening to talks doesn't explain that much about animals. (girl, Class II)
- Because *Museum Explorer* gives you a lot of information about animals. (boy, Class II)
- I can learn better using *Museum Explorer* because it gives you more information. (boy, Class II)
- You could find go to internet more information. (boy, Class II)Because you can learn what foods the animals eat and how they survive. (boy, Class II)
- It gives more information than just reading and TV you just see it and not et that much information. A computer just gets details. (boy, Class II)
- It explains you better than other stuff. (boy, Class II)
- It helps me better because it gives more information than the books do. (girl, Class II)

Fifteen of these 22 responses used the words *information* or *facts*. The students felt that the website offered more information than the other avenues of learning, which could be expected since they had access online to the many representations of the primary resources at the museum along with detailed information. Five of the responses mentioned that the website had more facts than they could receive from other learning experiences. Eleven responses used the words *better*. Fourteen of the responses were from Class I, with 11 from girls and only three from boys. Eight responses were from Class II with six of those responses from boys and only two responses from girls. One of the girls in particular was very articulate in her response when she said, "When I read books, most of them don't have pictures. In *Museum Explorer* they show videos, and explain what they mean. And in listening to talks, I can't see what they mean. The way the *Museum Explorer* helps me to learn better, it shows you and explains to you what exactly they mean, so I can learn better than reading books, watching TV, and listening to talks." This is a good example of the potential benefits of multimedia web-based materials. These elements of multimedia help engage a learner, keep the learner's interest, and create inquiry.

Five of the responses (13.4%) dealt with self-guided inquiry. Three of the responses were from boys two from girls. The responses were:

- Because you learn whatever you want to learn. (boy, Class I)
- It would help me more because you got to choose the subject you want to read or listen to. (boy, Class I)
- It helps by you have it there till you would need it and learn as far as you can; and read over and over. (girl, Class II)
- Because then they test you on it and see if you learned anything. (boy, Class I)
- Because when you see that it has quizzes you want new stuff so you could get 100%. So then some one asks you a question you answer right. (girl, Class II)

Twelve responses (27.2%) reflected the enjoyment of multimedia over book reading, TV, or lectures. Five of the responses were from boys and seven from girls. Note that several students mentioned the ease of use – just click and see and hear. Several mentioned liking the text read. Five responses were from Class I and seven responses were from Class II. The responses were:

- Because it has quizzes, pictures, and videos about animals; and just click in a dot and it reads the information and it has it all together. (boy, Class I)
- I like to listen to talk because I could understand. (girl, Class I)
- Because in books you could just look up one thing. In TV you have to right fast and you can't rewind. In talk it doesn't say much information. (boy, Class I)
- It is better because it give examples of what it means. It has videos. It has games that they aren't just games but they also teach you something. For example an animals adaptation. (boy, Class I)
- Because people read for you and it's very self explanatory. Everything is described very good. (girl, Class I)
- I don't like reading. I like using the computer. (girl, Class II)

- You don't have to wait. You watch the clips. The information you click and you could hear it instead of reading and making mistakes and take longer. (boy, Class II)
- By the videos and by reading to us. (boy, Class II)
- Because in the TV they say it fast and reading the book about the animal would be a little hard and listening to talks would be hard because you could not understand it by hearing when somebody talks. (girl, Class II)
- Because it has fun games and it tells a lot about how to go use a computer. (girl, Class II)
- By listening or read what it says or what is written in the computer. (boy, Class II)
- Like the bones. They show you bones you could look in maps and their habitat and behavior of the animals. (girl, Class II)

Summary of student open-ended questionnaires

The responses from the first three questions revealed that the students enjoyed the website and were engaged in learning. They particularly were engaged with the various multimedia aspects available on the website such as videos, sound, vocabulary, audio text, and interactive maps, games, and quizzes. The responses of easy access to information using the website, the multimedia nature of the website, and the opportunities for self-guided inquiry reflect strong engagement using the website as compared to other single modes of learning.

Teacher Open-ended Questionnaire

Questions 1 and 3 in the teacher open-ended questionnaire helped to answer the research question regarding the effects of *Museum Explorer* on students' learning engagement (see Appendix C). The teacher was going to fill out his open-ended questionnaire at the time the students were filling out their open-ended questionnaires, but decided to fill it out later and email his responses to me later the next week. Question 1 asked the teacher what he liked most about *Museum Explorer*. Question 2 asked the teacher what he liked least about the website, and because his response is relevant to the future prospects of successful multimedia usage in classroom learning, the researcher has included his response in this section. The discussion on question 4 was in the section for research question one. Questions 5 and 6 will be discussed in the email section.

Question one: What do you like most about the Museum Explorer?
Question one asked the teacher what he liked most about the *Museum Explorer*. The teacher offered interesting insights on the aspects he liked on the website. He wrote:

> My favorite aspect of the site was its holistic approach. There were many different approaches employed towards presenting the targeted concepts. There were reading selections with audio support, and video clips of animals and the researchers who study them; there were representations of skeletons and information about habitat preferences and the adaptations required to live in select habitats. There were links to live cameras at zoos around North America, and interviews with university researchers. By coming at the concepts from so many directions, the program allowed kids many routes towards a more complete understanding. It also allowed individuation for the kids' different learning styles. Graphically inclined kids showed this in their notes by using more sketches and drawings, while more linguistically gifted kids tended to write more. Some kids worked more heavily with the quizzes and games, maybe not taking much in the way of notes, but definitely trying to master the material that would allow them to succeed in those activities.
> The animals were well chosen, starting with raccoon, skunk, beaver, locally accessible animals with which the kids are most likely to have already come into contact. Building from that foundation, the content lead out towards more exotic animals, still featuring the same wide array of resources.

The teacher's attitude towards the website was positive. He described the various aspects that were most appealing to him about the website. The holistic approach appealed to him most of all. The researcher enjoyed his description in particular when he wrote that by coming at concepts from so many directions, the program allowed kids many routes towards a more complete understanding. This is the unique contribution that multimedia offers teachers and students, and the teacher recognized this potential for learning. He believed that the various multimedia avenues for presenting concepts in the website engaged the students. He also liked the different learning styles to meet the needs of the students' learning strategies. For example, he felt that the more graphically inclined students who tended to spend less time with the text material on the website but still worked on the quizzes, were mastering the material.

Question two: What do you like least about the Museum Explorer?

Although this question did not directly address the teacher's views about the engagement of his students, it did provide insight about the negative aspects of the *Museum Explorer* from the perspective of an experienced teacher. It is an important question that needs to be addressed. The successful use of multimedia websites in schools depends on reducing such negative aspects. For example, because the school's Internet bandwidth was limited, intensive use of higher bandwidth multimedia by all students at the same time caused the Internet to stop. The teacher was then frustrated because the videos did not work when the students wanted to see them. He wrote (further interpretation of these comments from the science teacher as well as recommendations will be discussed in Chapter Five):

> The largest problem with the *Museum Explorer* occurred when students had either to wait for problems to be resolved, or to hurry a bit to make up for lost time. Both of those situations are detrimental, of course, to students' attitude and overall learning. The streaming video, being accessed simultaneously by 25 students, at times overloaded the school district's server's capacity to deliver. Given that ours is a relatively new school, that the wiring system is fairly advanced by public school standards, I think this problem might exist in other school buildings. It would be important to plan for the possibility of this kind of situation, given the dependence of *Museum Explorer* on advanced technology, so that if something doesn't work the first time, students are given an alternative activity. Because the software is so rich in options, this isn't too difficult, as some parts of the software are less demanding on the Internet system.

However, I think there would be a way around this problem: rather than keeping the students working together on the same parts of the site, design instruction so that they would be using many different parts of the *Museum Explorer*, reducing the load on system servers. Or perhaps part of the software could be reconfigured to require smaller loads of streaming data.

Question three: Do you believe that your students using Museum Explorer effects the extent to which the students are engaged in the learning process?

The teacher's response to question 3 was shorter than the researcher had anticipated. He wrote:

I find this question difficult to answer. The learning process is a hardwired feature of the human being, something that human beings employ constantly in some manner or another. I am referring to concepts published by Frank Smith, Noam Chomsky, and others about the nature of learning. Using *Museum Explorer* per se doesn't affect their engagement *in the learning process* any more than any other activity I might plan, because the brain is always seeking to learn. But I did see a good degree of engagement with the subject matter of this curriculum. I saw students focused on a number of interesting concepts using software, which allowed them rapid access with the rich array of information.

Summary of teacher open-ended questionnaire

From the analysis of the teacher open-ended questionnaire, the teacher did not feel that using the website affected the students' engagement in the learning process in a particular way. Although he was positive about the learning experience, he felt that as far as a learning process is concerned, the students were no more engaged in the process than in any other activity he might have for them. He did report on a good degree of engagement with the subject matter on the website, and felt that the students were focused on their learning.

Summary of Results for Research Question Two

This study has defined student engagement with computers as students being actively involved in their own learning. They actively participate and show increased interest as they interact with the computer software. In addition, there is improved academic performance that may result from increased student engagement, as demonstrated in the evidence gathered for research question one. The computer attitude questionnaires, the teacher rating forms, the student and teacher open-ended questionnaires, the notebooks, and the emails offered supporting evidence that the *Museum Explorer* website did have a positive effect on student engagement. The increased positive attitudes revealed in the computer attitude questionnaires were interpreted as increased student engagement. The teacher rating forms indicate that the students were often or almost always engaged with the website. The students' notebooks also were an indication of the engagement of the students while they used the website. The use of counted entries per notebook adequately served to measure the effect of the website on engagement. The responses from the student and teacher open-ended questionnaires revealed that the students enjoyed the website and were engaged in learning. Further interpretation of these results will be discussed in Chapter Five.

RESULTS: RESEARCH QUESTION THREE

Research question three: What further engagement is generated by a field trip to the Portland State University Museum biology museum and communication with an assistant curator via email?

This question was answered through examination of the emails the students sent the assistant curator of the museum, the responses of the email users to question 5 in the open-ended questionnaire, question 6 of the teacher open-ended questionnaire, and the examination of the differences between email users and non-email users in the computer attitude questionnaires and pre- and post-tests. Frequencies, percentages, and qualitative analyses were used to examine the data gathered from the measurement instruments.

First, there will be a report on the email correspondence sent by the students to the assistant curator. Next, will be a report on the differences between the email users and non-email users in the computer attitude questionnaires. This is followed by a report on the differences in the pre- and post-tests of the email users and non-email users. Finally, there will be a report on the responses in the student and teacher open-ended questionnaires.

Email Correspondence

Seven boys and five girls took the opportunity to contact the assistant curator at the Portland State University biology museum (see Appendix K). Dr. Luis Ruedas, who served as the PSU liaison to the collaborative, selected the student assistant curator to answer the students' emails. The student assistant curator was a young man of about 30 years of age. He was likable, calm, and loved to teach. He and the researcher spent many days working on the videos that were put in the website. On the videos he talked about the skulls and skins of all the various species that were presented in the website. There was time during each session in the computer lab for the students to email questions that came up as they explored the website. Due to the busy schedule of the science teacher and limited computer access outside of the computer lab time, the students were unable to receive their answers on a regular basis. The science teacher once or twice a week printed out the responses to their questions in their science classroom. The 23 unedited questions (see Appendix J) that the students asked the assistant curator were:

The "how" questions were:

- How can you know the age of the animal just by looking at their teeth?
- How does the skull protect the brain?
- How many cougars can weigh like an elephant?
- How can you tell how old a dog is?
- How many bones does a cougar have?
- How many names does a cougar have?
- How do you know when an animal is pregnant?
- How much weight can they hold in their pouches?
- Can you tell how old an animal is?

The "what" questions were:

- What do you see in the animal's teeth that makes you think the age of it?
- What type of bone is there in the ear?
- What makes cats roar?
- What causes people to have brain tumors?
- What's the oldest animal they have found?
- What is the length and the width of a cougar's skin?
- What are the oldest bones that have been found of a cougar? (As in ancient fossils).
- What's the biggest bone that has been found of any animal?
- What are the ancestors of the cougar?
- What's the smartest animal on earth?

The four more sophisticated questions were:

- Can you tell how long an animal has been pregnant?
- Why don't snow leopards roar?
- When the opossum hangs upside down and the blood rushes down to its brain, does it bother them?
- Do the pouches that the kangaroos have bones?

One boy asked two questions, one girl asked five questions, and one girl asked four questions. Eight questions were *how* type of questions. Ten of the questions were *what* type of questions. One question was a *why* question. One student asked three sophisticated questions such as, "When the opossums hang upside down and the blood rushes down to its brain, does it bother them?"

The students did not have their own email accounts at Edgeview, but the science teacher told the students to use his own email account to send the curator their questions. The main computer was in the middle of the lab and had a large screen on the front wall that was used throughout the study. This computer was used to demonstrate to the students what to do each day on the website and also to email the curator.

The students who used email were not the students who had the most entries in their notebooks. However, seven of these students also put their notebook entries online in the class galleries. Nine students out of the 44 participants entered 15 or more total pages (text and drawings) in their notebooks. However, only 2 of the 12 students who used email entered 15 pages or more of notebook entries. Of the 12 students who used email, the girls had more text and drawings in their notebooks than did the boys. The five girls had more than 10 pages of text in their notebooks, and only one boy had 10 pages of text in his notebook. Both genders drew few pictures compared to non-email users.

Computer attitudes: Email users and non-email users

Tables 47 and 48 present the frequencies and percentages of the email and non-email users on all 16 items in the three computer attitude questionnaires.

In the response for strongly agree the email users had higher percentages in items 1, 2, 5, 6, 9, 10, 11, 12, 13, 14, and 15. On item 6, "I enjoy lessons on the computer," the email users had nearly double the percentages for the strongly agree response than the non-email users. While the non-email users had 32.3% who responded with strongly agree, there were 63.6% of the email users who responded with strongly agree. Item 13, "I enjoy working on a difficult problem," had only 12.9% of non-email users who responded with strongly agree. However, 36.4% of the email users responded with strongly agree on this item. Only in items 3, 4, 7, 8, and 16 did the email users have lower percentages in the strongly agree response. In item 1, "I like using a computer," and item 2, "I am not tired of using a computer," both the email users and the non-email users had no negative responses. The email users had 6 items with no negative responses. These were items 1, 2, 8, 9, 10, and 12. The non-email users had 4 items with no negative responses. These were items 1, 2, 5, and 7. The highest percentage in negative responses of strongly disagree for the email users was item 16, "The use of email helps me learn more." The highest percentage in negative responses for the non-email users was also item 16 with 32.3% of the students who strongly disagreed.

In order to understand better the differences in attitudes between the email users and the non-email users in the computer attitude questionnaires, the increased positive changes were calculated on all items. Table 49 shows

TABLE 47. Frequency Distributions of Email User Responses

Item		CAQ*1 (Week 1)		CAQ*2 (Week 5)		CAQ*3 (Week 10)	
		f	%	f	%	f	%
1. I like using a computer.	Strongly disagree						
	Disagree						
	Agree	2	16.7	4	36.4	1	18.2
	Strongly agree	10	83.3	7	63.6	9	81.8
2. I am not tired of using a computer.	Strongly disagree	1	8.3				
	Disagree						
	Agree	4	33.3	2	18.2	2	18.2
	Strongly agree	7	58.3	9	81.8	9	81.8
3. I will be able to get a good job if I learn how to use a computer.	Strongly disagree						
	Disagree	1	8.3			1	9.1
	Agree	9	75	4	36.4	7	63.6
	Strongly agree	2	16.7	7	63.6	3	27.3
4. I enjoy computer games very much.	Strongly disagree						
	Disagree					1	9.1
	Agree	3	25	4	36.4	2	18.2
	Strongly agree	9	75	7	63.6	8	72.7
5. I learn many new things when I use a computer.	Strongly disagree						
	Disagree	1	8.3			1	9.1
	Agree	4	33.3	6	54.5	4	36.4
	Strongly agree	7	58.3	5	45.5	6	54.5
6. I enjoy lessons on the computer.	Strongly disagree	1	8.3				
	Disagree	1	8.3	1	9.1	1	9.1
	Agree	4	33.3	5	45.5	3	27.3
	Strongly agree	6	50	5	45.5	7	63.6
7. I believe that it is very important for me to learn how to use a computer.	Strongly disagree	1	9.1				
	Disagree					1	9.1
	Agree	3	27.3	6	54.5	5	45.5
	Strongly agree	7	63.6	5	45.5	5	45.5
8. Working with a computer does not make me nervous.	Strongly disagree						
	Disagree	1	8.3				
	Agree	2	16.7	5	45.5	3	27.3
	Strongly agree	9	75	6	54.5	8	72.7
9. Using a computer is not hard for me.	Strongly disagree						
	Disagree	1	8.3	1	10		
	Agree	5	41.7	3	30	3	27.3
	Strongly agree	6	50	6	60	8	72.7

(Continued)

Table 47.   (*Continued*)

Item		CAQ*1 (Week 1)		CAQ*2 (Week 5)		CAQ*3 (Week 10)	
		f	%	f	%	f	%
10. Computers are not difficult to use.	Strongly disagree			1	10		
	Disagree	2	16.7				
	Agree	3	25	3	30	3	27.3
	Strongly agree	7	58.3	6	60	8	72.7
11. I can not learn more from books than from a computer.	Strongly disagree	2	16.7	1	10		
	Disagree	1	8.3	1	10	2	18.2
	Agree	4	33.3	5	50	5	45.5
	Strongly agree	5	41.7	3	30	4	36.4
12. I try to finish whatever I begin.	Strongly disagree						
	Disagree			1	10		
	Agree	7	58.3	3	30	5	45.5
	Strongly agree	5	41.7	6	60	6	54.5
13. I enjoy working on a difficult problem.	Strongly disagree	2	18.2	2	18.2	2	18.2
	Disagree	1	9.1				
	Agree	5	45.5	5	45.5	5	45.5
	Strongly agree	3	27.3	4	36.4	4	36.4
14. I do my homework.	Strongly disagree	2	18.2	1	9.1		9.1
	Disagree	1	9.1	1	9.1	1	9.1
	Agree	2	18.2	2	18.2	3	27.3
	Strongly agree	6	54.5	7	63.6	6	54.5
15. I study hard.	Strongly disagree	2	20	1	9.1	2	18.2
	Disagree	1	10	1	9.1	1	9.1
	Agree	1	10	3	27.3	2	18.2
	Strongly agree	6	60	6	54.5	6	54.5
16. The use of email helps me learn more.	Strongly disagree	4	33.3	3	27.3	4	36.4
	Disagree	3	25	3	27.3	3	27.3
	Agree	3	25	3	27.3	3	27.3
	Strongly agree	2	16.7	2	18.2	1	19.1
		N = 12		N = 11		N = 11	

N = 12.
Note: 4 point scale system from 1 (strongly disagree) to 4 (strongly agree).
*Adapted from Knezek's Computer Attitude Questionnaire, 1999.

Table 48. Frequency Distributions of Non-Email User Responses

Item		CAQ*1 (Week 1)		CAQ*2 (Week 5)		CAQ*3 (Week 10)	
		f	%	f	%	f	%
1. I like using a computer.	Strongly disagree						
	Disagree	1	3.7				
	Agree	8	29.6	11	35.5	8	25.8
	Strongly agree	18	66.7	20	64.5	23	74.2
2. I am not tired of using	Strongly disagree		3.6				
a computer.	Disagree	1	14.3	1	3.2		
	Agree	4	82.1	4	12.9	8	25.8
	Strongly agree	23		26	83.9	23	74.2
3. I will be able to get a good job	Strongly disagree	1	3.6				
if I learn how to use a computer.	Disagree	1	3.6	1	3.2	2	6.5
	Agree	15	53.6	14	45.2	17	54.8
	Strongly agree	11	39.3	16	51.6	12	38.7
4. I enjoy computer games	Strongly disagree	1	3.6	1	3.2		
very much.	Disagree					1	3.2
	Agree	7	25	9	29	6	19.4
	Strongly agree	20	71.4	21	67.7	24	77.4
5. I learn many new things when	Strongly disagree						
I use a computer.	Disagree			2	6.5		
	Agree	13	46.4	15	48.4	16	51.6
	Strongly agree	15	53.6	14	45.2	15	48.4
6. I enjoy lessons on the	Strongly disagree	1	3.6	1	3.2	1	3.2
computer.	Disagree	1	3.6	3	9.7	7	22.6
	Agree	16	57.1	15	48.4	13	41.9
	Strongly agree	10	35.7	12	38.7	10	32.3
7. I believe that it is very	Strongly disagree						
important for me to learn	Disagree	1	3.7	1	3.2		
how to use a computer.	Agree	8	29.6	13	41.9	15	48.4
	Strongly agree	18	66.7	17	54.8	16	51.6
8. Working with a computer does	Strongly disagree						
not make me nervous.	Disagree	3	10.7	1	3.2	2	6.7
	Agree	5	17.9	7	22.6	5	16.7
	Strongly agree	20	71.4	23	74.2	23	76.7
9. Using a computer is not hard	Strongly disagree			1	3.2		
for me.	Disagree	2	7.7	3	9.7	2	6.5
	Agree	8	30.8	9	29	11	35.5
	Strongly agree	16	61.5	18	58.1	18	58.1

(Continued)

TABLE 48. (*Continued*)

Item		CAQ*1 (Week 1)		CAQ*2 (Week 5)		CAQ*3 (Week 10)	
		f	%	f	%	f	%
10. Computers are not difficult to use.	Strongly disagree			4	13.3	1	3.2
	Disagree	6	22.2	2	6.7	3	9.7
	Agree	10	37	10	33.3	10	32.3
	Strongly agree	11	40.7	14	46.7	17	54.8
				N = 32		N = 32	
11. I can not learn more from books than from a computer.	Strongly disagree	3	10.7	4	10	2	6.5
	Disagree	3	10.7	10	26.7	2	6.5
	Agree	11	39.3	9	33.3	18	58.1
	Strongly agree	11	39.3		30	9	29
12. I try to finish whatever I begin.	Strongly disagree						
	Disagree					4	12.9
	Agree	17	60.7	15	50	14	45.2
	Strongly agree	11	39.3	15	50	13	41.9
13. I enjoy working on a difficult problem.	Strongly disagree	3	10.7	1	3.2	5	16.2
	Disagree	8	28.6	11	35.5	9	29
	Agree	11	39.3	14	45.2	13	41.9
	Strongly agree	6	21.4	5	16.1	4	12.9
14. I do my homework.	Strongly disagree	2	7.1			1	3.2
	Disagree	3	10.7	4	12.9	5	16.1
	Agree	13	46.4	15	48.4	13	41.9
	Strongly agree	10	35.7	12	38.7	12	38.7
15. I study hard.	Strongly disagree					1	3.2
	Disagree	3	11.1	6	19.4	5	16.1
	Agree	12	44.4	15	48.4	11	35.5
	Strongly agree	12	44.4	10	32.3	14	45.2
16. The use of email helps me learn more.	Strongly disagree	6	21.4	11	35.5	10	32.3
	Disagree	11	39.3	11	35.5	14	45.2
	Agree	9	32.1	6	19.4	4	12.9
	Strongly agree	2	7.1	3	9.7	3	9.7
		N = 12		N = 11		N = 11	

N = 32.

Note: 4 point scale system from 1 (strongly disagree) to 4 (strongly agree).

*Adapted from Knezek's Computer Attitude Questionnaire, 1999.

the increased changes across time from the first questionnaire to the third questionnaire of email users and non-email users. Notice that the positive increases for both groups are shaded for easier viewing.

The positive changes in computer attitudes of email users suggest that non-email usage may be a computer attitude sentinel. This suggests that

TABLE 49.   Changes in Strongly Agree Responses of Email Users and Non-Email Users

Item	Email Users % Points	Non- Email Users % Points
1. I like using a computer.	−1.5	+7.5
2. I am not tired of using a computer.	+23.5	−7.9
3. I will be able to get a good job if I learn how to use a computer.	+10.6	−.6
4. I enjoy computer games very much.	−2.3	+6.0
5. I learn many new things when I use a computer.	0	−5.2
6. I enjoy lessons on the computer.	+13.6	−3.4
7. I believe that it is very important for me to learn how to use a computer.	−18.1	−15.1
8. Working with a computer does not make me nervous.	−2.3	+5.3
9. Using a computer is not hard for me.	+22.7	−3.4
10. Computers are not difficult to use.	+14.4	+14.1
11. I can not learn more from books than from a computer.	−5.3	−10.3
12. I try to finish whatever I begin.	+12.8	−2.6
13. I enjoy working on a difficult problem.	+9.1	−8.5
14. I do my homework.	0	+3.0
15. I study hard.	−5.5	−.8
16. The use of email helps me learn more.	−7.6	−10.3
Average percentage point gain or loss in attitudes	8.8	−4.3
	$N = 12$	$N = 32$

students who do not use email may be less likely to favor computer usage in every attitude category. The positive change in attitudes observed among email users suggests early familiarity with email technology may result in more positive learning experiences with computers. The greatest increase (23.5% points) of the email users was on item 2, "I am not tired of using a computer." The second greatest increase (22.7% points) was item 9, "Using a computer is not hard for me." The greatest increase (14.1% points) for the non-email users was item 10, "Computers are not difficult to use."

Pre- and Post-Test: Email and Non-email Users

The pre-and post-test scores of the two groups did not reveal outstanding results in differences between email users and non-email users. The questions from both tests were:

1. What animal did this skull come from? (pre-test bear, post-test wolf)
2. Look at the teeth of this animal. What do you think it eats? (deer teeth)
3. Here is a cat skeleton. What one item is not a function of the skeleton?
4. Here is a skin of an animal that lives in Oregon. What do you think it is? (pre-test bobcat, post-test raccoon)
5. Each of these skulls has been given a number. Which number is a rodent? (skulls of beaver, bobcat, wolf, bear)
6. Look at the webbed back feet of this beaver. This helps it swim and is a good example of: (answer: adaptation, skin of beaver)
7. Look at these teeth. You will see a tag on one of the teeth. What is this tooth called? (wolf skull)
8. These bones are called (answer: vertebra, specimen of vertebrae)
9. Deer eat plants. What words best describe its role in the food web? (primary consumer)
10. There are many counties in Oregon. Which county is your school in?
11. When people formulate or make an hypothesis, they are making: (a set of theories intended to explain certain facts)
12. What is not true about mammals? (mammals don't nurse their babies)

Tables 50, 51, and 52 show the results in numbers, percentages, and increased correct answers of the two groups.

On question 7 the email users had the greatest increase (46.9% points) in correct answers, whereas the non-email users had a large drop in correct answers (-23.2% points). However, question 3 showed the non-email users gained at a 14.8% increase while the email users dropped -13.6% points. Question two also shows the email users decreasing in correct answers to -6.8% points while the non-email users increased to 16% points. Question 6 showed the email users increasing in correct answers from the first questionnaire to the third questionnaire 40.1% points, while the non-email users increased only 30.3% points.

Though there were more pronounced differences between these two groups as revealed in the computer attitude questionnaires, the pre- and post-tests did not reveal such positive changes in content knowledge. The

TABLE 50.   Change in Correct Answers for Non-Email Users

Count				Percentage			
Question	Pre	Post	Gain / Loss% Points	Question	Pre %	Post %	Gain / Loss% Points
1	0	3	3	1	0	10.0	+10.0
2	3	8	5	2	10.7	26.7	+16.0
3	8	13	5	3	28.5	43.3	+14.8
4	15	28	27	4	53.6	93.3	+39.7
5	1	15	14	5	3.6	50.0	+46.4
6	13	23	10	6	46.4	76.7	+30.3
7	11	8	–3	7	50.0	26.7	–23.3
8	14	16	2	8	50.0	53.3	+3.3
9	2	13	11	9	7.1	43.3	+36.2
10	17	21	4	10	60.7	70.0	+9.3
11	8	17	9	11	28.6	56.7	+28.1
12	5	15	10	12	17.9	50.0	+32.1

Average gain in correct answers: 8 points (N = 28 pre-test, N = 30 post-test)
Average gain in correct answers: 20 points (N = 28 pre-test, N = 30 post-test)

TABLE 51. Change in Correct Answers for Email Users

Count				Percentage			
Question	Pre	Post	Gain / Loss% Points	Question	Pre %	Post %	Gain / Loss% Points
1	0	0	0	1	0	0	0
2	3	2	−1	2	25.0	18.2	−6.8
3	6	4	−2	3	50.0	36.4	−13.6
4	7	10	3	4	58.3	90.9	+32.6
5	1	5	4	5	8.3	45.5	+37.2
6	5	9	4	6	41.7	81.8	+40.1
7	2	7	5	7	16.7	63.6	+46.9
8	6	6	0	8	54.5	54.5	0
9	4	6	2	9	33.3	54.5	+21.2
10	8	9	1	10	66.7	81.8	+15.1
11	4	5	3	11	33.3	45.5	+12.2
12	2	4	2	12	16.7	40.0	+23.3

Average gain in correct answers: 2 points (N = 12 pre-test, N = 12 post-test)
Average gain in correct answers: 17 points (N = 12 pre-test, N = 12 post-test)

non-email users averaged only 2.3% more in correct answers. Question 5 of the student open-ended questionnaire also provided insight into the attitudes of the email users and their engagement.

Student and Teacher Open-Ended Questionnaires and Email Users

Question five and email users: If you emailed the curator at the museum, describe your experience.

Twelve students elected to use email in the case study, therefore there were potentially only 12 responses to this question. The fifth question on the open-ended questionnaire was, "If you emailed the curator at the museum, describe your experience." Four of the 12 students who used email failed to answer question 5. One student simply wrote that it was ok. Three responses were from students from Class I, and four responses were from students from Class II. The responses were more general than

Table 52.   Differences in Percentage
Point Gains / Losses in Knowledge Tests
Between Email and Non-Email Users

Questions	Email Users	Non-Email Users
1.	0	+10.0
2.	−6.8	+16.0
3.	−13.6	+14.8
4.	+32.6	+39.7
5.	+37.2	+46.4
6.	+40.1	+30.3
7.	+46.9	−23.3
8.	0	-3.3
9.	+21.2	+36.2
10.	+15.1	+9.3
11.	+12.2	+28.1
12.	+23.3	+32.1
Averages	17.4	19.7
	N = 12	N = 30

were expected. The seven responses were:

- I liked sending him an email because I got to type, which I like. I felt like if every time I was confused I would get to type. (girl, Class I)
- Yes, I did email _____, and the experience emailing him was really cool because I was actually talking to a curator person. Wow! (girl, Class I)
- It was great getting an answer from a professor. I wish I could ask him more questions to get more answers. (boy, Class I)
- They were really good and know how to answer. (boy, Class II)
- He tells about the animals and he has learned with more experience about the animals. (girl, Class II)
- He answers the question and he is good and he is smart. (boy, Class II)
- It was good because we could get more information about what we want to learn. (girl, Class II)

These students enjoyed this alternative mode of getting answers to their questions. Most of the responses dealt with getting answers to their questions from the assistant curator or getting information about something they wanted to learn. Interviewing the 12 students who used email could have helped in understanding the benefits derived from email usage. Question 6 in the teacher open-ended questionnaire offered more in-depth evaluation about what the students experienced using email. Following is the teacher's response.

Question six and teacher evaluation of email users: In what ways, if any, did the field trip to the Portland State University biology museum and contact with the graduate student via email enhance and / or contribute to the students' engagement?

This question helped to better understand the students' experience with email usage. The science teacher responded:

> The contact with the assistant curator via email was a big plus for those kids eager to learn more from an acknowledged authority. They especially seemed to enjoy having an information source who would answer almost any question about mammals, not only about the concepts presented in the software. One girl just seemed to enjoy the act of typing the letters and reading the responses as much as the information contained, while other students seemed really interested in the content information. This was a big plus, and in a more leisurely setting this arrangement could be a real plus for any classroom.

The teacher enjoyed this opportunity for his students to contact an authority figure at the university. If the application phase of the learning cycle had been adhered to more closely, particularly discussions between teacher and students and expanding their interests, the students may have been more excited about the emails. Also, several days the teacher forgot to print out the answers from the curator for his students. There may have been some lost potential for learning and engagement through the use of email.

Question four: Describe your experience on the field trip to the museum.
What was good about it and what was not so good?
Question 4 asked students to describe their experience on the field trip to
the museum and what they thought was good and what was not so good.
Although the plan had been to spend an hour at the biology museum at
Portland State University, the Oregon Zoo trip interfered with this plan.
When the students arrived at the museum there were only a 15 minutes
until they had to leave. This disappointment caused many of the students
to mention the time limitation of their visit in response to the part of the
question about what was not so good. Five students mentioned this disappointment along with what they thought they had missed. Three of these
students were boys and two were girls. All five were from Class I. Their
comments were:

- We didn't have much time. That was kind of sad because we couldn't
  give more questions. (boy, Class I)
- We did not have enough time. We did not get to touch anything. (boy,
  Class I)
- It was not so good because it was only five minutes and there was
  only a few things in one room. (boy, Class I)
- Something was that we didn't have enough time to ask questions and
  look at the different animals that they had out. (girl, Class I)
- Well, we didn't have a lot of time to understand things clearly. (girl,
  Class I)

There were 25 students who responded to both parts of the question and
expressed what they liked and did not like about the field trip to the museum.
They usually expressed liking the skulls, furs, skeletons, and listening
to the assistant curator. All 25 of these students expressed that they wanted
more time in the museum. Following are a few of the responses that were
interesting. The first response is from the young boy whom the teacher
described as the one who needed the most help academically because of
his low English language skills. He is also the one whom the teacher had
visited during lunch and had asked him what the scientific name for the
cougar was, and the boy had responded correctly. It was particularly

interesting that he was able to see both good and bad in the limited time factor. The second response is from one of the 13 year-old girls who was very expressive and articulate and was described by the teacher as being extremely social, but less interested in academics. The main pattern found in the 25 responses was that the students were engaged in the museum experience but disappointed with the limited time factor. The responses were:

- It was good because we at least got to see it and spent 15 minutes. It was not good because we only stayed there for 15 minutes.
- My description of my experience on the field trip to the museum was really cool, what I mean by that is that I love animals and skeletons. What was good about it is that Aaron answered my question in real life — that's cool. What was not good is that we didn't have enough time to see and ask more questions and Aaron to show us more stuff. But at least he answered my questions in real life.
- We did not have much time. I found the bones interesting and fun. (girl, Class I)
- I liked how the bones looked. I wondered how they put it so the bones won't fall apart. I did not like that we only had a little bit to listen to the guy. (girl, Class II)
- It was good because in spite that we were there for a little time there was good questions and great answers that helped me learn more. The bad thing was that there was not much time and that I wanted to stay longer. (girl, Class I)

The responses from question four revealed that the students enjoyed this contact with the primary resources that they had been studying about. It also indicated that the students developed positive feelings about the curator, and perhaps even felt a connection with him which cannot be measured. The experience at the museum did increase their engagement, although they were disappointed with the short duration of the visit. The response from the teacher in question six in the open-ended questionnaire gives more insight into the experience at the museum.

Question six: In what ways, if any, did the field trip to the Portland State University biology museum and contact with an assistant curator via email enhance and / or contribute to the students' engagement?

The teacher's response was interesting in that he looked beyond the moment to the future of these students. Before the field trip and while still in the computer lab stage of the study, on several occasions the researcher heard the students talking about going to the university and that they had never seen a university before. So this experience put them in touch with another new dimension in their learning.

The science teacher wrote:

> The lab / classroom visit at PSU was very interesting, as much for the ambience of the room and university as for the actual presentation. I say that because our Mexico-born students, though they may have heard quite often that college is an important option for their future, have largely never seen a university campus, and have no mental image of what that experience might be like.

Summary of Results for Research Question Three

Research question three sought to examine the further engagement that resulted from the students' contact via email with the assistant curator of the biology museum and the field trip. The data could only be analyzed qualitatively through careful examination of the responses in the open-ended questionnaires and the emails sent to the curator. Overall, the results indicated further increased engagement amongst the 12 students who used email to contact the curator. These 12 students had remarkable positive increases in computer attitudes across time. The field trip added another dimension in their engagement. Although the students' time in the museum was cut short, they saw the primary resources they had been studying about, they met the assistant curator whom they had emailed and had seen and listened to on the videos, and many of them visited a university for the first time. All these things contributed to increased learning engagement.

Conclusion

At the beginning of this chapter, three research questions were set forth. The purpose of this case study was to answer these three research questions:

1. What is the effect of *Museum Explorer* (a virtual biology museum used in conjunction with a museum / school partnership) on middle school students' content knowledge?
2. What is the effect of *Museum Explorer* on middle school students' learning engagement?
3. What further engagement is generated by field trips to the Portland State University biology museum and communication with an assistant curator via email?

Data gathered during the course of the study were carefully examined for evidence that answers these questions. These research questions were investigated using frequencies and descriptive statistics. The instruments chosen to detect and measure these changes were the content knowledge pre-test and post-tests, two questions in the teacher open-ended questionnaire, and the notebook assignment. The methodology for research question two was to use not only quantitative methods but also use qualitative analysis. Descriptive statistics, frequency distributions, means and standard deviations, cross tabulations, correlations, and qualitative analysis were used to analyze the results from these measurement instruments and identify causal relationships between *Museum Explorer* and students' engagement. Finally, the methodology for research question three was to use frequencies, percentages, and qualitative analyses to examine the data gathered. This question was answered through examination of the emails the students sent the assistant curator of the museum, the responses of the email users to question five in the open-ended questionnaire, question 6 of the teacher open-ended questionnaire, and the examination of the differences between email users and non-email users in the computer attitude questionnaires and pre- and post-tests. In review, Table 53 summarizes the test instruments and the data collection methods used to investigate each research question.

TABLE 53.   Data Collection Methods and Research Questions

Research Questions	Pre- / Post-Tests	Student Questionnaires	Teacher Questionnaire	Teacher Rating Forms	Notebooks & Emails
1.	√		√		√
2.		√	√	√	√
3.		√	√		√

As the above table shows, the first research question, "What is the learning effect of *Museum Explorer* on middle school students' content knowledge?" was answered using pre-tests and post-tests, the science teacher's responses on the open-ended questionnaires, and the notebook assignment. The data was analyzed quantitatively using statistical analysis. The combined classes averaged 20% more in increased correct answers on the post-test. The effect of *Museum Explorer* on student content knowledge was greater for the girls than the boys, and greater for Class II than Class I. The teacher open-ended questionnaire and the notebook assignment gave evidence of the positive effect the website had on student content knowledge.

The second research question, "What is the effect of *Museum Explorer* on student learning engagement?" was answered through student computer attitude questionnaires, the teacher ratings of student engagement, open-ended questionnaires, and notebooks. The effect of *Museum Explorer* on student engagement using the three computer attitude questionnaires indicated positive attitudes and engagement across time. The teacher rating forms indicated that the students were often or almost always engaged with the website. The responses to the open-ended questionnaire revealed that the students enjoyed the website and were actively engaged in learning. The teacher's responses to the open-ended questionnaire indicated the belief that his students were engaged with the subject matter on the website, and felt that the students were focused on their learning. The count of text notebook entries indicated that the girls were more actively engaged with the website. The girls had 299 total pages and the boys had 182 total pages.

The third research question, "What further engagement is generated by field trips to the Portland State University biology museum and communication with university graduate students via email?" was answered through examination of the open-ended questionnaires as well as the data gathered on the email users and non-email users. The engagement that was generated by the use of email by the 12 students was positive, particularly examining the attitudes of the students as revealed in the computer attitude questionnaires as compared to the non-email users.

The following chapter discusses in more detail the results and implications of the study along with recommendations for further research.

Chapter Five

Summary and Discussion

This chapter gives an overview of the case study and summarizes the results. First, the research problem will be restated as well as the methodology used in this study. Second, an overall summary of the case study findings and conclusion will be presented. Finally, there will be a discussion of the interpretation of the findings, the relationship of this study to previous research, recommendations for practice, and suggestions for further research.

Purpose of the Study

Life science teachers need better computer technology resources to support their science instruction. A middle school science teacher's job is to interest and instruct students in science with the goal of meeting state science standards. However, recent studies report that science is a subject in which teachers feel unprepared. Further, teachers feel they lack sufficient resources. Given this lack of sufficient science resources and teachers feeling unprepared to teach science, computer technology may provide a promising teaching support framework. Computer technology, in particular

Internet-based science instruction, can empower teachers in areas they feel less qualified to teach, introduce interactive multimedia that is interesting to students, and save money by building museum / school partnerships that deliver a powerful and flexible means of learning over the Internet.

This case study began during the spring of 2004 and continued for 10 weeks, which included the follow-up computer attitude questionnaire after the first five weeks. The purpose of the follow-up questionnaire was to see if there had been changes in attitude as the students took the second questionnaire five weeks earlier. The students took part in the study as an extension of their regular science curriculum. A total of 10 weeks were spent at the Edgeview Middle School and Meridian Elementary School.

The purpose of this case study was to determine if there was any noticeable positive relationship between biology learning and engagement and the use of interactive computer-based materials. In particular, the project aimed to identify a relationship between student learning and engagement and the use of dynamic and interactive computer-based media. The goal in the creation of the website was to create a dynamic and interactive computer-based learning environment that increased students' understanding of basic biology facts in a dynamic and open-ended way as well as to increase students' engagement. As the participants of the study were middle-school students, attention was focused on designing an environment that engaged students of this age in an interactive way, motivate learning, and increase interest in biology.

RESEARCH DESIGN, METHODOLOGY, AND INTERVENTION

This research issue was reduced to three research questions which were:

- Research Question One: What is the effect of *Museum Explorer* (a virtual biology museum used in conjunction with a museum / school partnership) on middle school students' content knowledge?
- Research Question Two: What is the effect of *Museum Explorer* on student learning engagement?
- Research Question Three: What further engagement is generated by a field trip to the Portland State University biology museum and communication with an assistant curator via email?

Answers to these questions were sought by funneling the analysis for each question through a set of measurement instruments. Each instrument set was the result of careful research design aimed at using quantitative and qualitative research tools to produce an answer to that research question. For example, research question one was answered by evaluating the measurement outputs of three testing instruments: (1) pre-test of biology content knowledge, (2) post-test of biology content knowledge, (3) a teacher open-ended questionnaire, and (4) notebook assignment. Figure 2 (reproduced from Chapter Three), depicts a model that could describe this process.

FIGURE 2.   Research Model

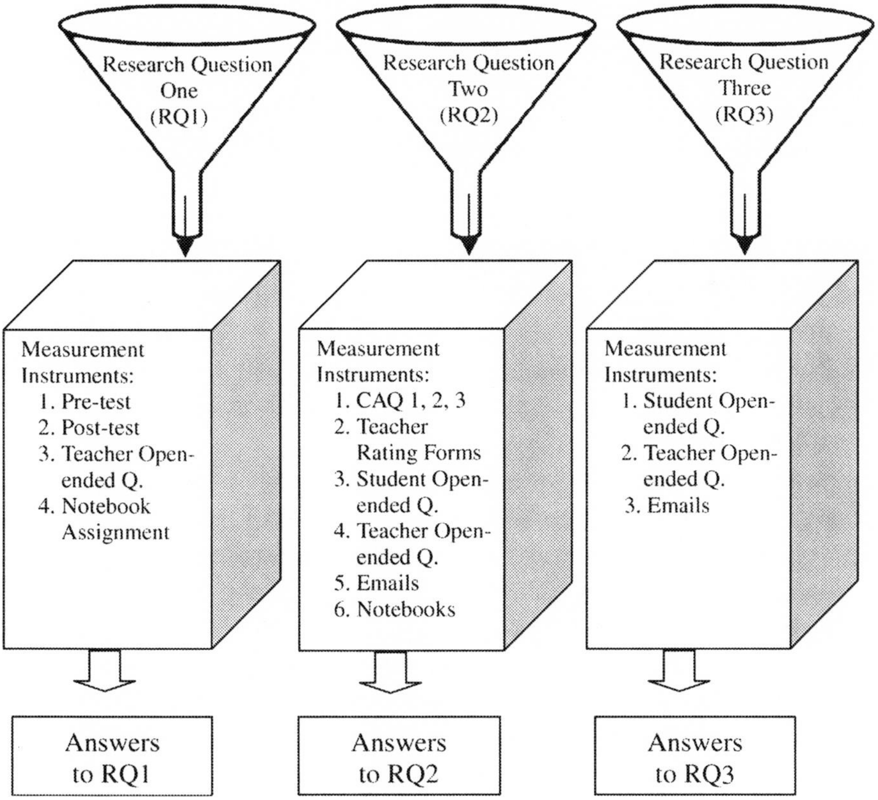

Research Design

Because this study dealt with both the contemporary issue of computer technology use in the science classroom and the unique intervention of an online biology museum integrated into the middle school science curricula, it was well suited for an empirical case study within such a context. Further, this case study relied on multiple sources of evidence from several instruments, thus establishing a clear chain of evidence (Yin, 1993). Therefore, this study was well suited for using quantitative as well as qualitative methodologies. The unique intervention of an online biology museum integrated into the middle school science curricula was well suited for a case study using both quantitative and qualitative methodologies.

Many other studies have explored questions about computer technology on student engagement. However, the online museum developed by the researcher in this case was a unique and innovative supplement for science curricula designed specifically for the case study. Further, the digital instructional application was designed to meet both the instructional requirements of the state and also meet the particular needs of students in the two Latino classrooms.

Because this supplement was a little-known innovative system, more than just quantitative data was needed. The great value in the qualitative method is the openness to rethink and find new themes that explain the participant's experiences. In fact, qualitative research methods do collect information from exactly the type of attitude questionnaires, notebook entries, and other observations available in this study. Such information can also be used to formulate a particular paradigm or perspective.

Furthermore, qualitative research methods are particularly important for studies where the participant's experiences are outside of a societal norm, such as the Latino students in this study's grade-school biology classes whose primary language is not English. Qualitative research allows the researcher to understand the meanings of the lives of the students unfiltered by external standards of what is "normal" (Janesick, 1994). Qualitative research enriches quantitative research. Therefore, a mixed method research design was selected. The measuring instruments included knowledge pre- and post-tests, questionnaires, teacher rating forms, student notebooks, and emails.

Methodology

The resulting data was used to explore both whether the introduction of the *Museum Explorer* influenced learning engagement and content knowledge as well as those factors associated with that influence. It also addressed further engagement that may have been generated by the field trip and communication with graduate students at Portland State University biology museum. Table 7 (reproduced from Chapter Four) summarizes the areas of inquiry and the data collection methods used to investigate each area. Note the sources of evidence for the areas of inquiry that were selected to facilitate triangulation of data.

Intervention: Museum Explorer

Museum Explorer is an interactive online computer-based biology learning application developed for this research project. The application was created by the author, currently under the direction and control of the author, was hosted by Portland State University's Office of Information Technology, and was accessible online at www.museumexplorer.org. The *Museum Explorer* was designed for middle school grades and was hosted temporarily for the duration of the research project. It was developed and hosted using freely available Open Source software that included Apache web server, PHP web scripting language, and various free java scripts. Graphics and other multimedia content were obtained, with permissions, from various sources. Content included images and videos of specimens taken within the Portland State University biology museum, archived media from faculty, and public domain media available for not-for-profit use by other teaching institutions and websites.

TABLE 7.   Data Collection Methods and Research Questions

Research Questions	Pre- / Post- Tests	Student Questionnaires	Teacher Questionnaire	Teacher Rating Forms	Notebooks & Email
# 1	√		√		√
# 2		√	√	√	√
# 3		√	√		√

The conclusion indicated increased content learning and student engagement as a result of the intervention of this interactive multimedia website. The analysis also indicated some differences in the genders and between the two classes. An unexpected and surprising result indicated significant differences in computer attitudes between the 12 email users and non-email users.

RESULTS

Research Question One

Research Question One: What is the effect of Museum Explorer (a virtual biology museum used in conjunction with a museum / school partnership) on middle school students' content knowledge?

The scope of this research question was to examine the effect of the online interactive website on middle school students' content knowledge. The effect of *Museum Explorer* was defined as changes in students' content knowledge, or the level of basic biology understanding. Four measurement tools were used to detect and measure these changes. These instruments were the pre-test, the post-test, the teacher open-ended questionnaire, and one homework assignment given by the teacher to the students during the last week in the computer lab.

The pre-test measured content knowledge before the intervention of the *Museum Explorer*, and the post-test measured any changes in content knowledge after the intervention. The post-test showed significant increases in content knowledge. The daily interactive quizzes the students engaged in gave them opportunity to learn biology facts in various interactive ways. The interactive nature of the website permitted the students to study the various biology facts through multiple avenues of exploration such as quizzes, videos, listening to the text read, and print-outs. The researcher was not aware of further discussions the teacher had with his students in the science classroom, nor was the researcher aware of the topics the students had studied prior to the case study. These extraneous variables could have an effect on content learning.

The combined classes averaged 20% points more in increased correct answers on the post-test. The effect of *Museum Explorer* on student content knowledge was greater for the girls than the boys, and greater on Class II than Class I.

FIGURE 22.   Percentage of Combined Scores of Pre-Test and Post-Test

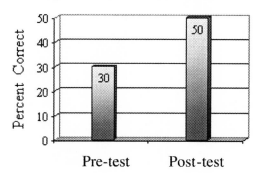

The teacher open-ended questionnaire and the notebook assignment gave evidence of the positive effect, the website had on student content knowledge. Figure 22 above illustrates the overall gains in correct answers of the combined classes.

Though the above figure depicts a good gain in increased correct answers, the girls had slightly more correct answers than the boys. The girls had an overall average of 27% point gains of correct answers whereas the boys had only 18.2% point average total gains in correct answers. Without the scores from the students' standard achievement and reading tests to compare, it was difficult to detect variables or attributes to explain these gender differences. Figures 23 and 24 display graphs illustrating the boys' and the girls' pre- and post-test percentages of correct answers.

The students in the two classes scored differently on the individual pre- and post-test questions as well. However, the overall scores were very similar. Students from Class II scored slightly higher (18.8% points) in overall increased correct answers than students from Class I (17.6% points). However, the students from Class II (those who need more academic support) had higher percentages of correct answers on both the pre-test and the post-test as shown in Figures 25 and 26.

Data from two other measurements helped to answer research question one. Two questions from the teacher open-ended questionnaire and the notebook assignment added insight into student engagement in this case study.

FIGURE 23.   Girls Percentage of Correct Answers

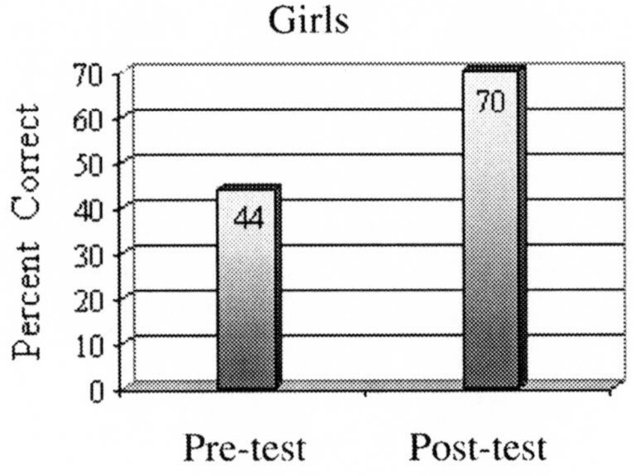

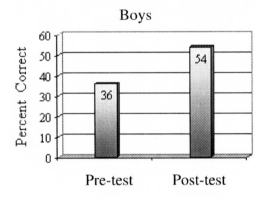

FIGURE 24.   Boys Percentage of Correct Answers

Although there was no way for the science teacher to precisely assess the effect of *Museum Explorer* on student content knowledge, his responses in the open-ended questionnaire were positive about the website contributing to student learning. The teacher mentioned several important learning modes such as self-guided learning, mastery, and increased engagement leading to inquiry. It should be noted that the teacher indicated the need for these learning modes to be coupled with other learning experiences. He wrote that the power of the medium was the employment of visual, auditory, and tactile modes of learning as the students interact with the program.

FIGURE 25. Class I: Percentage for Pre- / Post-Test

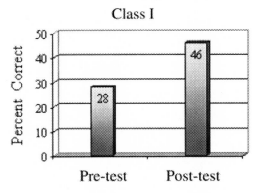

FIGURE 26. Class II: Percentage for Pre- / Post-Test

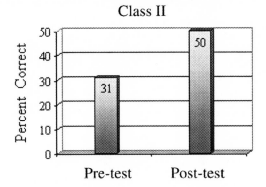

The notebook assignment, although not part of the original research design, was added by the teacher in the science classroom to the activities during the last week and was to be completed in the computer lab. Because the students entered the assignment into their notebooks, it was decided to use this as part of the research measurements. The essays and pictures by the students showed a surprising ability to use the information from the website as well as information gathered from class discussions with their teacher in the science classroom.

Summary of results

Overall, research question one results provide strong evidence that the intervention of the *Museum Explorer* increased student content knowledge. Although the pre-test had measured content knowledge before the intervention of *Museum Explorer*, the post-test measured increased positive changes in content knowledge after the intervention. The combined classes averaged 20% more in increased correct answers on the post-test. There was slightly greater increased content knowledge for the girls than the boys, as well as slightly greater increases for Class II than for Class I. The pre-test, post-test, teacher open-ended questionnaire, and the notebook assignment all gave clear evidence that the website did have a positive effect on student content knowledge. Although extraneous variables could skew the results one way or another, the changes that occurred from the time of the pre-test to the post-test were positive.

In this setting, the absence of control and treatment groups made precise evaluation of the results impossible. Further, the participants were all of Latino descent, and the researcher was not well acquainted with possible ethnic considerations regarding biology understanding and / or use of computer technology. The science teacher had an unusual interest in hands-on biology learning in his classroom, which was made evident by all the physical science models displayed throughout the classroom. This could have an effect of the students as they related to the intervention.

Research Question Two

Research question two: What is the effect of Museum Explorer on student learning engagement?

The scope of this research question was to examine the effect of the online interactive website on middle school students' learning engagement. The instruments chosen to detect and measure student engagement were three computer attitude questionnaires, open-ended response questionnaires for students and teacher, the teacher rating forms, student notebooks, and email use. Descriptive statistics, frequencies, cross tabulations, and qualitative analysis were used to measure the effect of *Museum Explorer* on students' engagement.

The results from the computer attitude questionnaires show increased engagement across time in the form of increased positive attitudes regarding computer importance and enjoyment. The teacher rating forms indicated that the students were often or almost always engaged with the website. The count of text notebook entries indicated that the girls were more actively engaged with the website. The girls had 299 total pages and the boys had 182 total pages. The responses from the student open-ended questionnaires revealed that the students enjoyed the website and were actively engaged in learning. Responses from the teacher open-ended questionnaires indicated a belief that the students experienced a high degree of engagement with the subject matter on the website, and demonstrated that they were focused on their learning.

Summary of results

Overall, research question two results indicate that students actively participate and show increased engagement, that is, active involvement in their own learning, as they interact with multimedia teaching tools like the *Museum Explorer*. In addition, there is improved academic performance that may result from increased student engagement, as demonstrated in the evidence gathered for research question one. The computer attitude questionnaires, the teacher rating forms, the student and teacher open-ended questionnaires, the student notebooks, and the emails offered supporting evidence that the *Museum Explorer* website did have a positive effect on student engagement.

The effect of *Museum Explorer* on student engagement using the three computer attitude questionnaires indicated positive attitudes and engagement across time. The increased positive attitudes revealed in the computer attitude questionnaires were interpreted as increased student engagement. The teacher rating forms indicate that the students were often or almost always engaged with the website. The students' notebooks also were an indication of the engagement of the students while they used the website. The use of counted entries per notebook adequately served to measure the effect of the website on engagement. The responses from the student and teacher open-ended questionnaires revealed that the students enjoyed the website and were engaged in learning. The responses from the student and teacher open-ended questionnaires revealed that the students enjoyed the website and were engaged in learning.

Research Question Three

Research question three: What further engagement is generated by a field trip to the Portland State University biology museum and communication with an assistant curator via email?

The scope of research question three was to examine the effect of the field trip to the museum and correspondence with the assistant curator on the students' engagement. This question was answered through examination of the emails the students sent to the assistant curator of the Portland State University biology museum, the responses of the email users to question 5 in the open-ended questionnaire, question 6 of the teacher open-ended questionnaire, and the examination of the differences between email and non-email users in the computer attitude questionnaires and pre- and post-tests. Frequencies, percentages, and qualitative analyses were used to examine the data gathered from these measurement instruments. Twelve students corresponded through email to the assistant student curator of the university biology museum. Therefore, any positive effect of email use on student engagement was confined to those students. These students showed engagement through the interesting questions they asked him. The changes in the computer attitude questionnaires of the email users revealed dramatic positive changes across time compared to the non-email users.

Overall, while the pre-test and post-test did not reveal positive changes in content knowledge in the email users, the computer attitude questionnaire revealed pronounced differences between the two groups (email users and non-email users). The open-ended questionnaires revealed an attitude about the use of computer technology to indirectly and virtually touch resources that was similarly positive to their attitude about direct contact with primary resources.

Summary of results

First, the open-ended questionnaire revealed that these students enjoyed email correspondence to get answers to their questions. Most of the responses talked about the enjoyment of getting answers to their questions from the assistant curator, or getting information about something they wanted to learn. Second, the teacher's response in the open-ended questionnaire about the use of email revealed a highly positive attitude. Contact with the assistant curator via email was a big plus for his students who were eager to learn more from an acknowledged authority. The teacher also felt that in a more leisurely setting the arrangement could be a real plus for any classroom. Finally, the field trip to the museum was a positive experience for the students. The responses in the open-ended questionnaire revealed that the students enjoyed this contact with the primary resources that they had been studying about. It also indicated that the students developed positive feelings about the curator, and perhaps even felt a connection with him, which cannot be measured. The experience at the museum did increase their engagement, although they were disappointed that the visit was shorter than anticipated. The overall result is one showing increased engagement from contact with primary resources, as well as indirectly through the virtual contact made possible through the interactive multimedia of computer technology. The effect of the field trip to the museum on the students' engagement was strongly positive.

Overall summary of results for research questions one, two and three

The combined classes averaged a 20% point gain in increased correct answers on the post-test. The effect of *Museum Explorer* on student content knowledge was greater for the girls than the boys, and greater in Class II than Class I. The teacher open-ended questionnaire and the notebook assignment gave evidence of the positive effect the website had on student content knowledge. The effect of *Museum Explorer* on student engagement using the three computer attitude questionnaires indicated positive attitudes regarding computers and engagement across time. The teacher rating forms indicated that the students were often or almost always engaged with the website. The count of text notebook entries indicated that the girls were more actively engaged with the website. The girls had 299 total pages and the boys had 182 total pages. The responses from the student open-ended questionnaires revealed that the students enjoyed the website and were actively engaged in learning. The responses from the teacher open-ended questionnaires indicated a belief that his students were more engaged with the subject matter on the web site, and felt that the students were focused on their learning. The engagement that was generated by the use of email by the 12 students was positive, particularly examining the computer attitude questionnaires as compared to the non-email users.

Discussion

The following quotation summarizes the overall response the science teacher had to the introduction and use of *Museum Explorer* in his classroom:

> Yes, I'm sure that *Museum Explorer* contributes to student learning. I overheard conversations that indicated learning, and watching kids take the quizzes showed me that they were mastering some of the material at the time. Coupled with other learning experiences, I believe *Museum Explorer* can help develop learning that is retained over time, encourages kids to seek and comprehend more learning about our North American native mammals, and to be better informed about the concept of adaptation and the role of the physical environment in shaping animal adaptations. (Participating Science Teacher, May 13, 2004)

Interpretation of Findings

Given the response above, the researcher will now discuss the overall interpretation of the study. The results from the gathered data were interesting and at times surprising. As an example, while the students appeared eager to get busy with the website throughout the three weeks in the computer lab, the second and third computer attitude questionnaires showed declining enjoyment of computer lessons across time. The extraneous variable of the Internet not working the last day in the lab could have affected their responses the following day for the administration of the second computer attitude questionnaire. This unfortunate occurrence could have affected the students' responses on many of the items in both the computer attitude questionnaires and the open-ended response questionnaires. Another unexpected variable which may have affected the student responses was the substitute teacher filling in for a full week in the middle of the study. Further, surprised at suddenly being faced with a substitute teacher may have unconsciously altered my attitude during those days in the computer lab, which in turn affected the students. Teacher training was in session during that third week of the case study, but somehow the science teacher had forgotten to let me know earlier that he would be unavailable during that week. The substitute teacher had not been aware of the case study until the morning of her arrival, and therefore there was little time to discuss in detail the teacher rating forms. However, she felt confident that she could fill them out and was successful in filling out 15 of the forms. Only her 15 rating forms were examined in the final analysis.

Being a participant observer allowed me to work along with the students on a daily basis. During the five weeks at the school, the researcher learned many things about them. For example, it was surprising that the student whom the teacher had described as requiring the most academic support because of the low English proficiency appeared to be the most intense and engaged in the activities, seldom taking his eyes off the screen.

Another surprise was the dramatic positive changes in computer attitudes of email users. The results suggested that non-email usage may be a computer attitude sentinel. That is, students who do not use email may be less likely to favor computer usage in every attitude category. The positive change in attitudes observed among email users suggests early familiarity with email technology may result in more positive learning experiences with computers.

Present Study and Previous Research

This study began at a time when interactive virtual biology museums were not as common on the Internet as they are now. The creation and hosting of virtual museums found online today far outnumber what was available just five years ago. This exponential growth indicates both a desire to use this type of computer technology and a readiness to give students opportunity to be more participatory in their learning and not merely recipients (Papert, 1993). Teachers can facilitate learning using computer technology designed to enhance the collaborative and interactive experience of the students.

Previous studies have suggested that students are motivated to seek solutions to problems if computer activities provide intellectual challenge, stimulate curiosity, and give a sense of independent control and mastery (Bowen, 2003; Hinrichsen & Jarrett, 1999; Kulik, 1994; Lepper, 1985). Though there are many studies that have explored computer technology use in the middle school classroom, this study was unique in that the online museum was developed by the researcher as an innovative supplement for the participants in this case study.

Limitations of the Study

However reliable the results are in this study, general conclusions are severely limited. Bias may have inadvertently been inserted into the study. The new experience mid-year for the students could explain some variations. Also, variables such as prior knowledge gained during the first part of the school year as well as differences in classroom instruction of the two classes may have influenced learning. Implementation of the study was more variable and less faithful to the research design than anticipated. Nevertheless, the study may provide a valuable textured insight into the realities of implementing interactive Internet-based multimedia teaching tools into a predominantly Latino grade-school science classroom. Furthermore, although a quarter century ago there was wide belief that single studies could resolve major issues of causation in the social sciences, current scholarship suggests research synthesis of conclusions from many smaller studies may be more valid with respect to inferences about the generalizability of effects (Light & Pillemer, 1984; Cooper & Hedges, 1994). Hence, the value of this study may primarily lie in the synthesis of its conclusions with other similar studies.

Recommendations for Practice

Museum Explorer is a high technology learning tool. As such, it depends on a high technology infrastructure; something quite expensive to maintain properly for most schools. Even when the proper infrastructure is provided, the complicated systems may not always work properly at critical times. For example, in anticipation of another Internet shutdown, the researcher placed a copy of the *Museum Explorer* on a CD in each computer on the second day in the computer lab. Although problems with the Internet bandwidth were resolved and the local copies were not used, the experience made it obvious that Internet teaching tools become useless when the Internet connection slows or quits. In addition, variations in software installed on classroom computers created confusion when some computers failed to support the multimedia. It would seem helpful for any teaching tool that depends on multimedia content and the Internet to require as a prerequisite uniform software package, or for the teaching tool to be java or flash-based. Further, to ensure the Internet connection does not become a bottleneck for serving multimedia content, redundancies must be built into the system. Naturally, the first choice is to ensure the Internet connection does not fail and does not cause a bottleneck. The second choice, should Internet bandwidth remain inadequate, would be for local school servers to be configured to serve the multimedia demands directly through the school's own local area network. Alternatively, the multimedia content could be provided on CDs to each computer in the classroom. In short, effective use of Internet-based multimedia content for teaching requires special care to be taken to ensure the infrastructure works properly.

Teachers should take advantage of these powerful new teaching tools. These tools show potential to solve the stated problem that this case study hoped to address. Life science middle school teachers need better computer technology resources to support their science instruction. As quoted at the beginning of this discussion, the science teacher felt that coupled with other learning experiences, *Museum Explorer* could help develop learning that is retained over time and encourage kids to seek and comprehend more.

Recommendations for Future Research

By the nature of this powerful teaching tool, there is a connection to a university biology department where funds to service this infrastructure might be more readily available. The most positive future scenario for the implications of this study would be the following:

- Develop a more complete and expanded version of *Museum Explorer*
- Put the website in service in connection with a university teaching museum
- Make it available to all public schools in the state
- Conduct further studies such as this present study and monitor the results

One of the most important extensions of the project would be to engage experienced and new teachers in the further design and development of websites such as the one created for this study. Good projects normally require insights from a variety of experienced people. Following the completion of the study in the middle school, the researcher met some of the faculty of the Science Resource Team, a division of the Child Services Center in Portland, Oregon. They viewed the website and suggested that they supply a team of science teachers to be organized for further development and implementation. However, they felt that without a joint grant with a local university, the possibilities would be limited.

Another step would be to incorporate teacher lesson plans and student activities into the webpage design for teachers in various grade levels. Because Oregon public schools begin the study of animals and their habitats in the second grade, creating the webpage at different levels would be an important addition. Also, there should be a teachers' page that would be password-protected for teachers such as links, supplementary material, and teacher forums.

Conclusion

This case study revealed that computer technology along with interactive and teacher-supported multimedia can increase the engagement and learning of middle school students. The study also demonstrated the ways in which a virtual biology museum combined with a museum / school partnership could enhance classroom science learning experience. It supports the premise that computer technology may help activate the student's curiosity, wonder, and the desire to search for solutions.

Although research on the effect of computer technology use in the science classroom is inconsistent, many studies stress the need for computers to play a major role in the teaching and learning of science. A major component in understanding how to increase computer use in the science classroom is to study the effect of computer technology on student engagement and learning. The need for more research studies on the effect of computer technology use on student engagement and learning in middle school science classrooms implemented through partnerships warrants investigation.

The interactive nature of the computer program used in this study created interest and engagement. Not only did the students interact with *Museum Explorer*, but time was given before the lab began to share what they were learning. In addition, they had opportunity to contact a biology student who served as temporary assistant curator at the university biology museum, and whom they later met on the field trip to the physical museum. Visiting the museum after working with the virtual museum added an engaging element. The students not only saw first-hand the primary resourcesthey studied on the website, but had opportunity to visit with the assistant curator with whom they had been corresponding.

This case study revealed the ways in which a virtual biology museum combined with a museum / school partnership could enhance classroom science learning experience. The *Museum Explorer* allowed students, some of whom may have difficulty following structured lectures or scheduled reading assignments, to more freely pursue topics of interest to them, yet remain within the framework of the larger unit. Results from this study do offer insights into the improvement of how teachers teach. Such improvement can be gained through increased awareness of computer resources and the role that museums can play in science programs.

In the end, the ultimate value of this study may lie more generally in the demonstration that computer and Internet Technologies can be far more powerful teaching tools in the hands of educators than has been widely seen in today's classroom. However complex or difficult using these technologies may seem both to teachers and administrators, as teaching best practices merge with information management practices, education policy has little choice but to also harness these powerful forces of mass delivery of interactive multimedia. This study suggests that interactive multimedia delivered through the Internet can not only provide an engaging teaching medium but can supplement, maybe even replace in certain instances, teacher lecture time. Traditional knowledge transfers, which rely on the transport of mass (books) and expenditure of costly human resources (teacher lecture time), can be transformed into mass-less transactions of a new Teaching Information Management System (TIMS). The potential for heightened student engagement, increased student content knowledge, and cost-savings are enormous. Results from this study offer insights into the improvement of how teachers teach. That improvement can be gained through increased awareness of computer resources and the role that museums can play in science programs.

APPENDIX A

COMPUTER ATTITUDE QUESTIONNAIRE

This survey contains 20 brief questions. Read each statement and then circle the number which best shows how you feel.

Example: I like chocolate ice cream

1	2	3	④

1. = ☹ Strongly Disagree (SD) 2. = ☹ Disagree (D)
3. = ☺ Agree (A)   4. = ☺ Strongly Agree (SA)

		☹ SD	☹ D	☺ A	☺ SA
(1)	I like using a computer.	1	2	3	4
(2)	I am tired of using a computer.	1	2	3	4
(3)	I will be able to get a good job if I learn how to use a computer.	1	2	3	4
(4)	I enjoy computer games very much.	1	2	3	4
(5)	I learn many new things when I use a computer.	1	2	3	4
(6)	I enjoy lessons on the computer	1	2	3	4
(7)	I believe that it is very important for me to learn how to use a computer.	1	2	3	4
(8)	Working with a computer makes me nervous.	1	2	3	4
(9)	Using a computer is hard for me.	1	2	3	4
(10)	Computers are difficult to use.	1	2	3	4

(Continued)

TABLE. (*Continued*)

	SD ☹	D ☹	A ☺	SA ☺
(11) I can learn more from books than from a computer.	1	2	3	4
(12) I believe that it is very important for me to learn	1	2	3	4
(13) I enjoy working on a difficult problem.	1	2	3	4
(14) I do my homework.	1	2	3	4
(15) I study hard.	1	2	3	4
(16) The use of email helps me learn more.	1	2	3	4

Please put a check next to the best answer

(17) I have a computer at home   yes _____   no _____

(18) My computer has Internet access   yes _____   no _____

(19) If you have a computer at home, how many hours a week do you use it?

    0 – 2 hours _____
    2 – 4 hours _____
    4 – 6 hours _____
    More than 6 hours _____

(20) Please check below

    I am a girl _____   I am a boy _____
    I am _____ years old
    I am Hispanic _____
    I am Russian _____
    I am both Hispanic and Russian _____

APPENDIX B

STUDENT OPEN-ENDED QUESTIONNAIRE

Name _____   Code # _____

Please answer the following questions in writing:

Q 1)   Describe what you liked most when using *Museum Explorer.*

Q 2)   Describe what you liked least when using *Museum Explorer.* If you could change one thing about *Museum Explorer,* what would you change?

Q 3)   How could using *Museum Explorer* help you learn better than other ways of learning (reading books, watching TV, listening to talks?)

Q 4)   Describe your experience on the field trip to the museum. What was good about it and what was not so good?

Q 5)   If you emailed _____ at the museum, describe your experience.

Modified and Adapted from: Beeland, Jr. (2003) Student engagement, visual learning and technology: Can interactive white-boards help? Action Research Exchange. Retrieved 10 / 12 / 03 from http://chiron.valdosta.edu/are/

APPENDIX C

TEACHER OPEN-ENDED QUESTIONNAIRE

Please answer the following questions:

Question 1.   What do you like most about the *Museum Explorer*?

Question 2.   What do you like least about the *Museum Explorer*?

Question 3.   Do you believe that your students using *Museum Explorer* effects the extent to which the students are engaged in the learning process?

Question 4.   Do you believe the use of *Museum Explorer* contributes to student learning? Why or why not?

Question 5.   In what ways, if any, did the interaction with *Museum Explorer* address the three modalities of learning: visual, auditory, and tactile?

Question 6.   In what ways, if any, did the field trip to the Portland State University Museum of Vertebrate Biology and contact with the graduate student via email enhance and / or contribute to the students' engagement?

Modified and Adapted from: Beeland, Jr. (2003) Student engagement, visual learning and technology: Can interactive whiteboards help? Action Research Exchange. Retrieved 10 / 12 / 03 from http://chiron.valdosta.edu/are

APPENDIX D

CONTENT KNOWLEDGE TEST (PRE / POST-TEST)

Name _____ Code # _____

Please circle the number you think is the best answer. You may touch the items, but please do not pick them up.

Q 1) What animal did this skull come from?

1. Bear
2. Cougar
3. Raccoon
4. Wolf

Q 2) Look at the teeth of this animal. What do you think it eats?

1. Plants
2. Insects
3. Meat
4. Fish

Q 3) Here is a cat skeleton. What one item is **not** a function of the skeleton?

1. Support
2. Heat regulation
3. Protection
4. Movement

Q 4) This is a skin of an animal that lives in Oregon. What do you think it is?

1. Wolf
2. Beaver
3. Bobcat
4. Cougar

Q 5)   Each of these skulls has been given a number. Which number is a rodent?

1.

2.

3.

4.

Q 6)   Look at the webbed back feet of this beaver. This helps it swim and is a good example of:

1.   Adaptation
2.   An hypothesis
3.   Environmental control
4.   Evolution

Q 7)   There is a tag on one of the teeth. What is this tooth called?

1.   Canine
2.   Incisor
3.   Molar
4.   Premolar

Q 8)   These bones are called:

1.   Arm bones
2.   Leg bones
3.   Ribs
4.   Vertebrae

Q 9)   Deer eat plants. What words best describe its role in the food web?

1.   Primary producer
2.   Secondary consumer
3.   Primary consumer
4.   Tertiary consumer

Q 10)　There are many counties in Oregon. Which county is your school in?

    1.　Clackamas County
    2.　Marion County
    3.　Washington County
    4.　Multnomah County

Q 11)　When people formulate or make a hypothesis, they are making:

    1.　A wild guess
    2.　A set a theories intended to explain certain facts
    3.　A statement of something already proven
    4.　A decision

Q 12)　What is **not** true about mammals?

    1.　Mammals give birth to live young
    2.　Mammals don't nurse their babies
    3.　All mammals have backbones
    4.　All mammals are vertebrates

ALTERNATE POST-TEST

Name _____　Code # _____

Please circle the number you think is the best answer. You may touch the items, but please do not pick them up.

Q 1)　What animal did this skull come from?

    1.　Bear
    2.　Cougar
    3.　Raccoon
    4.　Wolf

Q 2)   Look at the teeth of this animal. What do you think it eats?

1. Plants
2. Insects
3. Meat
4. Fish

Q 3)   Here is a cat skeleton. What one item is **not** a function of the skeleton?

1. Support
2. Heat regulation
3. Protection
4. Movement

Q 4)   This is a skin of an animal that lives in Oregon. What do you think it is?

1. Wolf
2. Beaver
3. Raccoon
4. Cougar

Q 5)   Each of these skulls has been given a number. Which number is a rodent?

1. support
2. heating
3. protection
4. movement

Q 6)   Look at the webbed back feet of this beaver. This helps it swim and is a good example of:

1. Adaptation
2. An hypothesis
3. Environmental control
4. Evolution

Q 7)   There is a tag on one of the teeth. What is this tooth called?

1.   Canine
2.   Incisor
3.   Molar
4.   Premolar

Q 8)   These bones are called:

1.   Arm bones
2.   Leg bones
3.   Ribs
4.   Vertebrae

Q 9)   Deer eat plants. What words best describe its role in the food web?

1.   Primary producer
2.   Secondary consumer
3.   Primary consumer
4.   Tertiary consumer

Q 10)   There are many counties in Oregon. Which county is your school in?

1.   Clackamas County
2.   Marion County
3.   Washington County
4.   Multnomah County

Q 11)   When people make an hypothesis, they are making:

1.   A wild guess
2.   A set of theories intended to explain certain facts
3.   A statement of something already proven
4.   A decision

Q 12)   What is **not** true about mammals?

    1.   Mammals give birth to live young
    2.   Mammals don't nurse their babies
    3.   All mammals have backbones
    4.   All mammals are vertebrates

APPENDIX E

TEACHER RATING FORM

Student ID _____

For each of the seven statements below, indicate how often you have seen the student engaged in the identified behavior (Adapted from Bangert-Drowns & Pyke, 2002)

1. Student stops interacting with the software. Student may sit and tinker with the software in a seemingly purposeless or disinterested way with little or no response to feedback from the computer. Or, student may in fact turn away from the software or resist using it at all.

    Almost always   Often   Rarely   Never

2. Student moves from one incomplete activity to another without apparent reason.
    Student successfully completes simple tasks within the software but does not link tasks for higher-order goals.

    Almost always   Often   Rarely   Never

3. Student tried to effectively interact with the software, but unsuccessfully. Student might manifest frustration in negative comments, confusion, aggressive behavior, erratic behavior, or signs of agitation, distress, or anxiety.

    Almost always   Often   Rarely   Never

4. Student pursues goals communicated by the software. Student may not yet display full mastery of software features, but response to operational, navigational, or content organization.

    Almost always   Often   Rarely   Never

5. Student stimulates and maintains deeply involved interactions with the software. Student adjusts software features to sustain interesting or challenging interactions and creatively uses software for personally defined purposes.

Almost always   Often   Rarely   Never

6. Student manipulates software features, keenly observes the effects of the manipulations, and integrates the results in future interactions. These manipulations seem designed to test personal understanding of the software content or the limitations of the software presentations.

Almost always   Often   Rarely   Never

7. Student explores and develops multiple interpretations of a software experience. Student manipulates software features to explore different perspectives. In verbal statements, student describes different perspectives and use of software interactions as an opportunity to reflect on personal values or experience.

Almost always   Often   Rarely   Never

How Confident are you of your ratings above?

Very confident   Confident   Unsure   Very unsure

APPENDIX F

Informed Consent Forms: Student

A Case Study of the Effects of a Virtual Biology Museum on Middle School Students' Learning Engagement and Content Knowledge

Student's first name and last initial _____

Your parents have said that it is okay for you to take part in a project being conducted by Mindi Donaldson. The project is a part of Mr. _____'s science class. You will use an online biology museum in the computer lab for several science classes, and then go on a field trip to Portland State University biology museum. Mindi is trying to find out how using an online biology museum will affect your learning. Choosing to participate in this project will not affect your science grade, nor will choosing not to participate.

If you choose to do it, you will be asked to take a simple pre-test about what you know about animals and their lives. You will also take a questionnaire at the beginning and end of the study. For three weeks you will go to the computer lab and work on the online biology museum Mindi calls *Museum Explorer*. In the last week of the study you will take a post-test to find out if using the online museum helped you learn. There are online quizzes for you to take and keep scores in your journal. The journal will have the scores from your quizzes each week. You will take the field trip during the fifth week. There will also be a place in the questionnaire at the end of the study where you can write and describe in your own words your experience participating in the project.

If you get tired during any of the time while you take the tests, questionnaires, work in the computer lab, or when you are on the field trip, just tell me or your teacher — you won't get into any trouble! If you are having trouble during class time, your teacher can give you something else to do. If you have any questions about what you will be doing during the project, ask me to explain. I am the only one who will be seeing your questionnaires and tests, and the final results will not be connected to you. Further, the name of your school will not be used in the report.

Please sign your name below if you want to try it. If you don't want to sign your name, then you will need to follow the rest of the class in the activities, but the information from your tests and questionnaires will be left out of the study. If you get too tired working on the computers, your teacher can assign you another activity. Please remember that if you get tired, you can stop and rest at any time, and if you decide not to take part anymore, let me know.

Signed _____

Date _____

APPENDIX G

INFORMED CONSENT FORMS: PARENTAL: (ENGLISH AND SPANISH VERSIONS)

January 5, 2004

Dear Parents,

My name is Mindi Donaldson and I would like to include your child in a research project on the effects of an online biology museum on student learning and engagement. I am a doctoral student at Portland State University, Department of Curriculum and Instruction.

Mr. _____'s students in two science classes will be participating in this study project for parts of five weeks. The project will be integrated into Mr. _____'s regular science curriculum. If you choose to let your child participate, it will not affect the grades at all. If you choose to now allow your child to participate, all responses from the tests, questionnaires, and online quizzes your child takes will not be entered into the final data analysis, and it will not affect your child's grades. During the fifth week of the project the class will be taking a school field trip with Mr. _____ and me to the Portland State University Museum of Vertebrate Biology in Portland, Oregon. Here they will see the things they have been looking at in the online museum. The distance is 30 miles from _____. The students will be well supervised and will be visiting the museum on campus for around two hours.

I will be the only person viewing the responses from the questionnaires, pre- and post-tests, and online quizzes. Neither you nor your child's name will appear in any reports of this research. You have a right to review a copy of any survey, questionnaire, or quiz being administered to your child.

Participation in this project is voluntary and involves no unusual risks to you or your child. You may change your choice to allow your child to participate at any time during the project with no negative consequences. Your child can withdraw at any time from this project with no negative consequences. Again, this would mean that no responses from your child will be entered into the data analysis. If your child becomes tired during the computer time in the lab, he / she can tell Mr. _____ and he will offer an alternative activity.

Your child's participation in this project will further teachers' knowledge to enhance their teaching methods. Please indicate your decision on the following page by signing your name and give back to your child to be delivered to Mr. _____ by March 15, 2004. A more detailed description of the project is attached as well as a brochure in case you need more information to help you decide.

Sincerely,

Mindi Donaldson

Please indicate below your decisions regarding your child's participation

Yes ____ I give permission for my child to participate in this project.

No ____ I do not give permission for my child to participate in this project.

_____

(Parent / Guardian printed name)

_____

(Parent / Guardian signature)

Date _____

Please have your child return this signed paper to Mr. _____ by March 15, 2004.

PURPOSE, DESCRIPTION, AND TIMELINE OF STUDY

The purpose of this mixed-method case study is to examine the impact of an online museum / school science curriculum called *Museum Explorer!* developed by the researcher on middle school students' content knowledge and learning engagement. Specific goals of the study are to: (a) identify the learning content impact on middle school students of a virtual biology museum implemented through a museum / school partnership, (b) examine the learning engagement of students using *Museum Explorer!*, an online digital biology museum, and (c) determine what further engagement is generated by field trips to the museum and communication with biology graduate students through email correspondence at school.

Museum Explorer! is an online biology museum and is designed as a supplement to the life science curriculum. The components of the content in the online museum fall within the common science curriculum goals for the state of Oregon. This study will give students an enriched learning experience using varied multimedia such as video, sound, 3D images, and the accumulated store of facts on northwest vertebrates. They will have opportunity to view videos of the living animals, hear the sounds they make, see habitat and biotic province maps, view rotation of skulls, hear short lectures, take quizzes to test their own understanding, and much more.

The virtual biology museum unit at _____ Middle School will begin during the winter of 2004 and will continue for five weeks as shown below in Figure 3. Parts of two class periods during the first week will include the pre-test, which will take around 20 minutes, and the questionnaire, which will take around 20 minutes. Weeks two, three, and four will each have three days to use the online biology museum. Week five will involve one day for the school field trip to the Portland State University Museum of Vertebrate Biology, one class period for the post-test which will take 20 minutes, and one day for the questionnaire, which will take 35–40 minutes.

De enero el 24 de 2004

Padres Queridos,

Mi nombre es Mindi Donaldson y quisiera incluir a su niño en un proyecto de investigación sobre los efectos de un museo en línea de la biología en el estudiante que aprende y contrato. Soy un estudiante doctoral en la universidad de estado de Portland, departamento del plan de estudios e instrucción.

Los estudiantes de Mr. _____ en dos clases de la ciencia participarán en este proyecto del estudio para las partes de cinco semanas. El proyecto será integrado en plan de estudios regular de la ciencia de Sr. _____. Si usted elige deja a su niño participar, no afectará los grados en todos. Si usted elige ahora permitir que participe su niño, todas las respuestas de las pruebas, de los cuestionarios, y de los concursos en línea sus tomas del niño no serán incorporadas en el análisis de datos final, y no afectará sus grados de los child?s. Durante la quinto semana del proyecto la clase llevará un disparo al campo de la escuela con Sr. _____ y yo el museo de la universidad de estado de Portland de la biología vertebrada en Portland, Oregon. Aquí verán las cosas que han estado mirando en el museo en línea. La distancia está a 30 millas de _____. Supervisarán y visitarán a los estudiantes bien el museo en el campus por alrededor dos horas.

Seré la única persona que ve las respuestas de los cuestionarios, diarios, las pruebas pre y del poste, y los concursos en línea. Ni usted ni su nombre de los child?s aparecerá en cualquier informe de esta investigación. Usted tiene una derecha de repasar una copia de cualquier examen, cuestionario, o concurso que es administrado a su niño.

La participación en este proyecto es voluntaria y no implica ningún riesgo inusual a usted o a su niño. Usted puede cambiar su decisión para permitir que su niño participe en cualquier momento durante el proyecto sin consecuencias negativas. Su niño puede retirarse en cualquier momento de este proyecto sin consecuencias negativas. Una vez más esto significaría que no se incorporará ningunas respuestas de su niño en el análisis de datos. Si su niño hace cansado durante el tiempo de computadora en el laboratorio, he / she puede decir a Sr. _____ y él ofrecerá una actividad alternativa.

¿Su participación de los child?s en este proyecto fomentará a profesores? conocimiento para realzar sus métodos de la enseñanza. Indique por favor su decisión en la página siguiente firmando su nombre y dé de nuevo a su niño que se entregará a Sr. _____ antes del de enero 30 de 2004. Una descripción más detallada del proyecto se une así como un folleto en caso de que usted necesite más información ayudarle a decidir.

Si usted tiene concierne o los problemas acerca de su niño'la participación de s en el estudia o su niño'los derechos de s cuando un sujeto de investigación, complace contacta la Investigación Humana de Sujetos Revisa el Comité, la Oficina de Investigación y Patrocinó Proyectos, 111 Vestíbulo de Cramer, la Universidad del Estado de Portland, (503) 725-4288. Si usted tiene las preguntas acerca del se estudia, complace contacta el investigador, la Mindi Donaldson, en 5015 NE decimoquinto, Portland, Oregon, 97211, (503) 249-1756.

Sinceramente,

Mindi Donaldson

Indique por favor debajo de sus decisiones con respecto a su participación de los child?s

_____ doy sí el permiso para que mi niño participe en este proyecto.

Ningún _____ no doy el permiso para que mi niño participe en este proyecto.

(nombre impreso Parent / Guardian)

(firma de Parent / Guardian)

Haga por favor que su niño vuelva este papel firmado a Sr. papa antes del de enero 30 de 2004.

PROPÓSITO, DESCRIPCIÓN, Y TIMELINE DEL STUDIO

¡El propósito de este estudio de caso del mezclar-me'todo es examinar el impacto de una ciencia en línea Museum llamado plan de estudios Explorer de museum / school! ¿convertido por el investigador en estudiantes de la escuela media? contrato contento del conocimiento y el aprender. Las metas específicas del estudio son: (a) identifica el contenido el aprender afecta en estudiantes de la escuela media de un museo virtual de la biología puesto en ejecucio'n con una sociedad de museum / school; (b) examina el contrato el aprender de estudiantes usando a explorador del museo!, un museo digital en línea de la biología; y (c) se determina lo que es generado más lejos el contrato por disparos al campo al museo y a la comunicación con los estudiantes graduados de la biología a través de la correspondencia del email en la escuela.

¡Explorador Del Museo! es un museo en línea de la biología y se diseña como suplemento al plan de estudios de la ciencia de vida. Los componentes del contenido en el museo en línea caen dentro de las metas comunes del plan de estudios de la ciencia para el estado de Oregon. Este estudio dará a estudiantes una experiencia de aprendizaje enriquecida usando multimedia variados tales como vídeo, sonido, las imágenes 3D, y el almacén acumulado de hechos en animales del noroeste. Tendrán oportunidad de visión videos de los animales vivos, oyen los sonidos que hacen, ven el habitat y los mapas biotic de la provincia, opinión la rotación de cráneos, oyen conferencias cortas, concursos de la toma para probar su propia comprensión, y mucho más.

La unidad virtual del museo de la biología en la escuela media de Valor comenzará durante el invierno de 2004 y continuará por cinco semanas según lo demostrado abajo en el cuadro 3. Las partes de dos períodos de la clase durante la primera semana incluirán la preprueba que tomará alrededor 20 minutos, y el cuestionario, que tomará alrededor 20 minutos. Las semanas dos, tres, y cuatro quieren cada uno tienen tres días para utilizar el museo en línea de la biología en el laboratorio de la computadora. La semana cinco implicará una mañana o tarde para el disparo al campo de la escuela al museo de la biología de la universidad de estado de Portland, a un período de la clase para la prueba del poste que tomará 20 minutos, y a un día para el cuestionario, que tomará 35–40 minutos.

¡Explorador Del Museo! Proyecto Timeline

Tarea	Semana #1	Semana #2	Semana #3	Semana #4	Semana #5
Entrenamiento de profesor	viernes				
¡Puesta en práctica del explorador del museo! Y Grado Del Profesor		3 días 35 minutos (cada día)	3 días 35 minutos (cada día)	3 días 35 minutos (cada día)	
Cuestionario Del Profesor					viernes
Cuestionarios Del Estudiante	viernes				viernes
Pre y post-Tests	viernes				viernes
Disparos al campo					jueves

Cuadro 3. Hora proyectada para el estudio

APPENDIX H

INFORMED CONSENT FORMS: PRINCIPAL

_____, Principal
_____ Middle School
_____ Road
_____, Oregon 97071

January 5, 2004

Dear Mr. _____,

You are invited to participate in a research study conducted by Mindi Donaldson from Portland State University, Department of Curriculum and Instruction. Under the supervision of Dr. Dannelle Stevens and in partial fulfillment of requirements for a doctoral degree in Educational Leadership, the researcher seeks to examine the impact of an online virtual biology museum on middle school students' content knowledge and learning engagement. Your school was selected to participate in this project because of the expressed interest of your science teacher, Mr. _____. Mr. _____ came in contact with Mindi at the Oregon Science Teachers' Conference two years ago. He has expressed interest in computer use in the classroom and uses innovative strategies for teaching science.

The *Museum Explorer!* is an online virtual museum designed by the researcher to be a partial supplement for science curricula for sixth grade students. It is an accessible and cost-effective means of conveying information from Portland State University Museum of Vertebrate Biology's primary resources to students and teachers. The components of the content in the online museum fall within the common science curriculum goals for the state of Oregon.

The case study will involve two science classes for a period of five weeks, three days each week. Mr. _____has agreed for two science classes to participate in the study, which will begin in February. Student subjects will be told that although they will be required to participate in the study as part of their daily science class schedule, the data from their participation will be withheld from the study if they don't agree to fully participate. Whether they agree to full participation or not, their grades will not be affected. If they experience difficulty in the computer lab, assistance will be given to them, or the teacher may allow them to engage in other relevant science activities.

WEEK ONE

Week one will consist of teacher training time when the teacher will have a chance outside of class time to try *Museum Explorer* online and go over the schedule for the five weeks. During this week the teacher and students will take separate questionnaires regarding their attitudes toward computers and should take 30 minutes. On a different day this first week the students will take a simple content knowledge pre-test on simple biology facts. The test should take 30 minutes.

WEEKS TWO THROUGH FOUR

Weeks two through four consist of student computer time in the lab, three class periods each week. The teacher, Mr. _____ will randomly select 15 students from each class to rate engagement with the software. He will observe each target student for 5 minutes before moving on to the next student. During this time Mindi will be in the lab with the students, but the teacher is welcome to participate as they navigate through the *Museum Explorer*. Each day the students will take one of the online quizzes and they will put down their scores in a small quiz journal they will be given to keep for the three weeks.

WEEK FIVE

Week five includes the school field trip to Portland State University Museum of Vertebrate Biology. If the field trip is not possible during this week, the final questionnaire must be postponed until after the trip is taken. However, the multiple choice post-test can be taken the fifth week as it covers the biology content of *Museum Explorer,* which they have already worked with.

Five weeks after the initial five-week study there will be a follow-up questionnaire, which is the same questionnaire the students took during the study. This is to help determine if there has been any change in attitude toward computers during this time.

Any information that is obtained in connection with this study and that can be linked to you, your two classes, your school, or the school district will be kept confidential by using a coding format.

The second questionnaire will have open-ended questions about the student's learning and engagement during the study. You will find these questions attached. He will come on the field trip and will remain with the students each class time. The students' participation in the five-week project will not affect their grades. If a student feels they are getting tired in the computer lab, Mr. _____ will provide alternative activities equivalent in time and effort of the research project.

The following chart on the following page shows the proposed time line for the research.

FIGURE 11. *Museum Explorer* Project Timeline

Task	Week #1	Week #2	Week #3	Week #4	Week #5
Teacher Training	Friday				
Implementation of *Museum Explorer*		3 Days (180 min. total)	3 Days (180 min. total)	3 Days (180 min. total)	
Teacher Questionnaire					Friday
Student Questionnaires	Friday				Friday
Pre- and Post-Tests	Friday				Friday
Field Trip					Thursday

The proposed study is not potentially high-risk to the subjects, nor is it of a controversial nature. None of those participating in the research project will be identified in the final report. This includes the school district, _____ Middle School, and the individual students and teacher participating. A copy of the completed study will be submitted to the District Superintendent as well as yourself.

If you grant permission for this study, a letter requesting parental permission will be sent home with each student. Attached is a copy of the child's assent letter, a copy of the informed consent letter that would be mailed to the district superintendent, and the letter to Mr. _____. Also attached are the surveys and questionnaires.

There are several potential benefits to the subjects. The students may have an enriched learning experience using the online biology museum and contact with the graduate students at the Portland State Museum. The field trip will provide a real-life experience for the students where they can see first hand the things they have been looking at online. The questionnaires will give both teacher and students time for introspection as they answer the questions regarding their own attitudes toward computers. Finally, the experience will provide insight to enhance classroom science learning, and will provide a useful lens for science educators as they learn to integrate technology into the curricula.

The final dissertation will contain a special note of thanks to the subjects' participation in this study. The individual names, however, will not be given, but rather recognition for the two classes and teacher as a whole.

If you have concerns or problems about your participation in this study, please contact the Human Subjects Research Review Committee, Office of Research and Sponsored Projects, 111 Cramer Hall, Portland State University, (502) 725-4288. If you have questions about the study itself, contact Mindi Donaldson at 5015 NE 15th, Portland, Oregon 97211 or by telephone at (503) 240-1756.

Thank you very much for your consideration in this matter.

Sincerely,

Mindi Donaldson

APPENDIX I

INFORMED CONSENT FORMS: TEACHER

A CASE STUDY OF THE EFFECTS OF A VIRTUAL BIOLOGY MUSEUM ON MIDDLE SCHOOL STUDENTS' LEARNING ENGAGEMENT AND CONTENT KNOWLEDGE

January 7, 2003

Dear participant,

You are invited to participate in a research case study conducted by Mindi Donaldson from Portland State University, Department of Curriculum and Instruction. Under the supervision of Dr. Dannelle Stevens and in partial fulfillment of requirements for a doctoral degree in Educational Leadership, the researcher seeks to examine the impact of an online virtual biology museum on middle school students' content knowledge and learning engagement. You were selected to participate in this project because of your expressed interest in computer use in the classroom and your use of innovative strategies for science learning.

The *Museum Explorer* is an online virtual museum designed to be a partial supplement for life science curricula for sixth grade students. It is an accessible and cost-effective means of conveying information from Portland State University Museum of Vertebrate Biology's primary resources to students and teachers. The case study will involve five weeks of science class time, three days each week, and you will be committing to the five-week period. Five weeks after the initial study there will be a follow-up questionnaire identical to the questionnaire given during the study. This is to help determine if the students' attitudes toward computers has changed during the five weeks. Your students' participation in this research project will be a part of their regular science studies for the five weeks and will not affect their final grades in any way. If a student tires in the computer lab you will need to provide alternative activities suited both in time and effort to that of working on the project.

The risks in this study would be that introducing such a unique innovation into your class schedule could cause unforeseen responses in your students such as anxiety or frustration. While you may not receive any direct benefit from taking part in this study, participation in the study may help to increase knowledge in ways that enhance and inform teaching practices.

If you decide to participate, week one will consist of teacher training time when you will have a chance outside of class time to try *Museum Explorer* online and go over the schedule for the five weeks. During this week your students will take questionnaires regarding attitudes toward computers and should take 30 minutes. On a different day this first week your students will take a simple content knowledge pre-test on simple biology facts. The test should take 30 minutes.

Weeks two through four consist of student computer time in the lab. During this time Mindi will be in the lab with the students, but you are welcome to participate as they navigate through the *Museum Explorer*. Each day the students will take one of the online quizzes and they will put down their scores in a small quiz journal they will be given to keep for the three weeks. During this time you will select at random 15 students from each class whom you will rate their engagement. Five minutes will be given for each target student rating. You will learn how to do this during the first week.

Week five includes the field trip to Portland State University Museum of Vertebrate Biology. If the field trip is not possible during this week, the final questionnaire must be postponed until after the trip is taken. However, the post-test can be taken the fifth week and is multiple choice that will cover the biology content of *Museum Explorer.*

Any information that is obtained in connection with this study that can be linked to you, your two classes, your school, or the school district will be kept confidential by using a coding format.

Your participation is voluntary. If you have concerns or problems about your participation in this study or your rights as a research subject, please contact the Human Subjects Research Review Committee, Office of Research and Sponsored Projects, 111 Cramer Hall, Portland State University, (503) 725-8182. If you have questions about the study itself, please contact Mindi Donaldson at 5015 NE 15th, Portland, Oregon 97211 or by telephone at (503) 249-1756.

Your signature indicates that you understand the above information and agree to take part in this study. Please understand that you may withdraw your consent at any time without penalty, and that, by signing, you are not waiving any legal claims, rights, or remedies. The researcher will provide you with a copy of this form for your own records.

Thank you,

Mindi Donaldson

Signature _____

Date _____

APPENDIX J

Human Subjects Review

(Memorandum and Outline for Application Proposal)

Portland State University HSRRC Memorandum

To: Mindi Donaldson

From: Cathleen Davidson, HSRRC 2004

Date: February 9, 2004

Re: HSRRC waived review of your application titled, "A Case Study of Effects of a Virtual Biology Museum on Middle School Students' Learning Engagement and Content Knowledge"

Your proposal is exempt from further Human Subjects Research Review Committee review, and you may proceed with the study.

Even with the exemption above, it was necessary by University policy for you to notify this Committee of the proposed research, and we appreciate your timely attention to this matter. If you make changes in the research protocol, the Committee must be notified in writing, and changes must be approved before being implemented.

If you have questions or concerns, please contact the HSRRC in the Office of Research and Sponsored Projects (ORSP), (503) 725-4288, 111 Cramer Hall.

cc: Dannelle Stevens

Waiver memo

I. Project Title and Prospectus

Title: A Case Study of the Effects of a Virtual Biology Museum on Middle School Students' Learning Engagement and Content Knowledge

Part of the elementary school teacher's job is to interest and instruct students in a variety of subjects. Studies report that science is a subject in which teachers feel less prepared, less effective, and have limited classroom resources. This research project evaluates the effectiveness of an online digital biology museum to transfer knowledge and increase engagement in middle school students.

The purpose of this mixed-method case study is to examine the impact of an online museum / school science curriculum called *Museum Explorer* developed by the researcher on middle school students' content knowledge and learning engagement. Specific goals of the study are to: (a) identify the learning content impact on middle school students of a virtual biology museum implemented through a museum / school partnership; (b) examine the learning engagement of students using *Museum Explorer*, an online digital biology museum; and (c) determine what further engagement is generated by field trips to the museum and communication with biology graduate students through email correspondence.

The case study will last five weeks and will involve two sixth-grade classes and their science teacher at Edgeview Middle School in _____, Oregon. The experiences for the students include a pre-test and post-test, two questionnaires on computer attitude (one of which includes open-ended questions), a trip to the physical museum at Portland State University Museum of Vertebrate Biology, and contact with graduate students in the museum using email. The teacher will take a computer attitude questionnaire at the beginning of the study and a repeat questionnaire end of the study. There will be six open-ended questions at the end of the last questionnaire.

II. Exemption Claim for Waiver of Review

I am requesting a waived review under the following exemption on page nine of the Application Guidelines for Research Involving Human Subjects.

> *Research conducted in established or commonly accepted educational settings, involving normal educational practices, such as (i) research on regular and special education instructional strategies, or (ii) research on the effectiveness of or the comparison among instructional techniques, curricula, or classroom management methods.*

Rationale

The waived review appears most applicable for this case study because the study will be conducted in a typical classroom during normal school hours.

Further, the students use computers each week in the computer lab, so the intervention of the online museum will not be outside their experience. The students will be taking part in this project as an extension of their regular science curriculum. The components of the content in the online museum fall within the common science curriculum goals for the state of Oregon. Confidentiality will be assured by strict adherence to coded format of pre-tests, post-tests, and questionnaires.

III. SUBJECT RECRUITMENT

Subjects are two classes of sixth grade students with one science teacher for both classes. The school is Edgeview Middle School in _____, Oregon. The science teacher, _____, has taught science at Edgeview for many years. The Principal Investigator has visited with the principal of Edgeview in person, and he has expressed interest in his teachers and students taking part in the project. Student subjects will be told that although they will be required to participate in the study as part of their daily science class schedule, the data from their participation will be withheld from the study if they so choose. If they experience difficulty in the computer lab, assistance will be given to them, or the teacher may allow them to engage in other relevant science activities. Mr. _____ has agreed for two science classes to take part in the study. He will be part of the study by way of questionnaires, both Likert-type and open ended, will come on the field trip, and will remain in the class each day. The students' participation in the five-week project will not affect their grades. Should a student decide that they are getting tired in the computer lab, Mr. _____ will provide alternative activities equivalent in time and effort of the research project.

IV. INFORMED CONSENT

Student subjects will sign the attached letter, which explains that their participation is voluntary. The letter of consent explains to the students that the results of the questionnaires and tests will not affect their grades. The letter explains that their teacher has chosen that this five-week project will be part of their regular science class schedule, and if they get tired for some reason, they can inform their teacher. The subjects are informed that the results will be held in confidentiality.

V. First Person Scenario

Student

Recently my science teacher told me about Mindi Donaldson, a doctoral student at Portland State University who is asking me and the other students in science class to participate in her upcoming study concerning an online virtual museum she has made. Mindi came to my class and told us she wants to see how using the online museum and taking a field trip to the university's biology museum influences my learning. Also, I will have a chance to email graduate students at the Portland State Museum biology museum and ask them questions. Mindi said we will take a test the first week to find out what we know right now about animals, and then we will take another test after we use the online museum to see what we have learned. We also will take a questionnaire about how we feel about computers, and at the end of the project we will have a chance to describe our feelings about the project in writing.

Teacher

I met Mindi Donaldson at the Oregon Science Teachers' Conference two years ago where she had a booth. We spent some time visiting about her upcoming research introducing a virtual online biology museum in a middle school classroom. I became interested in the proposed study and suggested we consider using my science class at Edgeview Middle School in _____, Oregon. Since that time we have corresponded via email on several occasions and she came down to my school to observe the classes about four months ago. She is interested in examining the effects of her online museum on the students' learning engagement and content learning. She also wants the classes to take a school field trip up to the Portland University Museum of Vertebrate Biology in Portland, Oregon. This will give the students, she says, an opportunity to see first-hand what they have been studying online for three weeks. Part of the study includes opportunity for the students to contact graduate students using email when they have questions they are interested in learning about.

The first week the students will take a pre-test on their knowledge about animals and then on another day a questionnaire about computer attitudes. Both pre-test and questionnaires will take around 25 minutes. I will also be taking a questionnaire about computer attitudes during the time the students are taking their questionnaires. The next three weeks I will take the classes into the computer labs where they can explore the online museum. They will be given notebooks where they will put down their scores each day after taking the quizzes. Mindi will be in the computer lab each day to help the students if they have any difficulty. The fifth week the students will take a 25-minute post-test based on information from the online museum. Before taking the final questionnaire on computer attitudes the students will take a field trip to the physical museum in Portland. The final day of the research the students will take the same questionnaire they took the first week, but there will be an additional section with 5 open-ended questions for the students to describe their experiences. I will also take the same questionnaire I had taken the first week called Teacher Attitudes Toward Computers, but there will be an additional six open-ended questions for me to describe my feelings about the five weeks of the study.

VI. POTENTIAL RISKS AND SAFEGUARDS

This proposed case study is not potentially high-risk to the subjects, nor is it of a controversial nature. The main concerns with risk would involve the protection of confidentiality. The possibility of fatigue going on the field trip to Portland State University biology museum or fatigue from computer use during the class periods could be possible risk factors. Both the teacher and the researcher will be on hand at all times during the science class times and field trip to monitor the students and offer help if needed.

To protect student identity, names will be coded when the data is entered into the software program. The only person entering data will be the researcher. The original files containing the questionnaires, pre and post-tests, and quiz journals will be stored in files for three years and will be inaccessible to anyone but the researcher.

VII. Potential Benefits

There are several potential benefits to the subjects. The students may have an enriched learning experience using the online biology museum and contact with the graduate students at the Portland State Museum using email. The field trip will provide a real-life experience for the students where they can see first hand the things they have been looking at online. The questionnaires will give both teacher and students time for introspection as they answer the questions regarding their own attitudes toward computers. Finally, the experience will provide insight to enhance classroom science learning, and will provide a useful lens for science educators as they learn to integrate technology into the curricula.

The final dissertation will contain a special note of thanks to the subjects' for participation in this study. The individual names, however, will not be given, but rather recognition for the two classes, the teacher, and the school as a whole.

VIII. Records and Distribution

The records from this case study will be kept in the Principal Investigator's home office. The final dissertation will not use specific names.

APPENDIX K

EMAILS: STUDENTS AND CURATOR

EMAIL QUESTIONS AND ANSWERS

What's the oldest animal they have found?

I'm not quite clear on whether you're asking about the age of an individual animal or the earliest known example of any animal, so I'll try to answer both questions.

Individual animals can be very hard to age. The dating methods that work for fossils only tell us how long something has been around after it died, not how long it lived before that, and some animals simply don't show any signs of aging once they reach maturity. For example, sea anemones (which you can see at the coast, at the Oregon Zoo in the marine mammal exhibit, and in most aquaria) are potentially immortal! The oldest individual on record was well over a hundred years old when its aquarium was bombed during World War II. Turtles are famously long-lived, and there are claims of some having lived for several hundred years, but these claims are very hard to authenticate. The only way to tell for certain is to have an animal of known age animal marked or in captivity, and observed over a long period of time; this has not been done for more than a hundred years or so for any one animal. I don't know which animals have been monitored like that, so I can't honestly say which has been documented to live the longest.

The oldest animals in the fossil record include strange, poorly-preserved things that look more or less like sheets of tissue, dating from about 700–750 million years ago. Because they were soft-bodied, it's very hard to tell much about them. There are also very old sponge fossils, from about the same time, and it is generally thought that sponges are the oldest lineage of animals still around today.

What is the length and the width of a cougar's skin?

That depends on the cougar! There is a lot of variation in most animals, and cougars are such a wide-ranging species that they are more variable than most. I'd give you some examples, but unfortunately, I'm writing this from at home, so I can't go over to the cougar cabinet and take a skin out and measure it. I can make a note to do that later and get back to you; or perhaps I can bring some out when you come and visit, and you can help me measure them yourself!

How many bones does a cougar have?

If you don't count the individual parts of fused bones (the pelvis consists of six bones fused together, for instance, which I'll count as one because you can't take them apart), there are about 200. The exact number varies from one animal to another, because the length of the tail (and so the number of bones in the tail) is somewhat variable.

How many names does a cougar have?

Cougars have gone by many names – even only considering those in English! The most common are "cougar", "puma", and "mountain lion". Cougars are also called "panthers", "painters", and "catamounts". (The name "panther" here means something different from what most people think of, which is an all-black leopard or jaguar. I don't know why a tan cougar would get named after a black leopard!) I've read that there are other, less common names as well, but I don't know what they are or how many of them there are. Probably if you went around in the mountains with a picture of a cougar and asked every old person living in a shack what it was, you'd get a lot of different answers, but I don't know what they are!

Cougars are cursed with multiple names even in science, where these things are supposed to be standardized. Originally, the cougar's scientific name was Felis concolor, but Puma concolor was also proposed, and scientists still haven't agreed which one is the better name!

What's the oldest bones that have been found of a cougar? (As in ancient fossils)

The oldest bones that we know definitely came from a cougar are probably about half a million years old. They've been excavated from about 30 different sites.

What's the biggest bone that has been found of any animal?

The biggest single bone would probably be the humerus (upper arm bone) of a dinosaur called _Brachiosaurus_, which could measure well over eight feet in length. However, if you consider a skull to be a single bone (it's actually a composite of over two dozen), the largest bone found would probably be the skull of a sperm whale, which can reach close to twenty feet long!

What are the ancestors of the cougar?

I'll have to answer this question indirectly, so bear with me. The cougar is fairly closely related to a group of cats including the ocelot and the margay, which are small-to-medium-sized cats with spots somewhat like those on a jaguar. This group shared a recent common ancestor with the cougar and another cat (the jaguaroundi), but which split off from the family tree first, and what the common ancestor looked like, I don't know that anyone knows. It is probably placed in the genus _Felis_, like the cougar itself often still is, although feline nomenclature is (and has for some while been) the subject of heated debate!

How can you know the age of the animal just by looking at their teeth, what do you see in the animal's teeth that makes you think the age of it?

Well, for one thing, most mammals have two sets of teeth, just like we do: deciduous (baby or milk) teeth and permanent (or adult) teeth. These look different from one another, and usually the deciduous teeth don't fall out until the permanent teeth start to develop anyway, so it's easy to tell when an animal still has its first set of teeth. Since scientists have kept track of when the average member of a species loses its first set of teeth, we can use this as an estimate of the animal's age.

For another thing, if the animal is missing teeth, we can generally assume that it's pretty old, especially if the bone has healed over the empty socket. Whether through disease or injury, teeth generally aren't lost when an animal is young.

The best thing to look for, though, is tooth wear. The surfaces of the teeth that match other teeth grind against one another, and eventually this wears them down. The amount of wear is a pretty good indicator of an animal's age: most mammals eat every day (unless they're hibernating, ill, or otherwise indisposed) and so the rate of tooth wear can be considered fairly constant.

I'll show you some examples of this when you come and visit!

How does the skull protect the brain?

You can think of the cranium (or braincase, the part of the skull that surrounds the brain) as a sort of helmet for the brain. It's made of thin but hard bone, and its round shape makes it resistant to cracking easily. Inside the skull are several layers of membranes, each filled with fluid (sort of like a water balloon with another water balloon inside it), so the brain has a fair amount of cushioning between it and the cranium. This means that there is a sort of shock absorber between the delicate brain and the sturdy bone.

By the way, the idea of thinking of the cranium as a helmet is so useful that people have used animal crania as bases for designing helmets!

What type of bone is there in the ear?

There are two types of bones in the ear. One is the hard bony structure that protects the delicate sensory parts, and is called the auditory bulla. It is made of the densest bone found in the body, and is the hardest structure in the vertebrate body after the teeth! This density is important because it isolates the various sensory parts of the ear from extraneous vibrations, so that the ear hears as little as possible that doesn't come through the ear canal.

The other type of bone is much more typical in structure, but not so typical in size. These are the ossicles, or middle ear bones: the malleus, incus, and stapes. There is one of each of these in each ear, and they act as levers to amplify the sound waves that hit the eardrum. It's hard to describe exactly how each one moves, and in fact modelling of the system has shown it to be more complex than anyone expected!

It's interesting to note, by the way, that only mammals have three pairs of ear ossicles. Birds, reptiles, and amphibians have only one pair. The one bone that they have on each side is called the columella, and is the same thing as the stapes in mammals. What would be the other two ossicles are actually part of the jaw in these animals!

What makes cats roar?

Roaring, like purring, is incompletely understood. It is thought that both result from the vibration of a series of bones in the throat collectively known as the hyoid apparatus. This is cartilaginous in cats that purr and bony in cats that roar. From this you might expect that cats that roar can't purr, and cats that purr can't roar, and this is indeed the case, although there are some that do neither. Roaring cats also have an elastic ligament that connects to the hyoid bones and probably is involved as well in roaring. In any event, though, it's quite possible (although again, not known for sure) that the vocal cords are not used at all when a cat roars!

Why don't snow leopards roar?

Snow leopards don't have the bony hyoid apparatus that I just mentioned, although they do have that elastic ligament. (I don't know whether they can purr!) They are in fact a good example of why the hyoid apparatus needs to be bony in order to roar!

What causes people to have brain tumors?

A tumor is a mass of cells that reproduce uncontrollably. Tumors can be caused by any number of things, including exposure to certain chemicals, radiation, and malfunction in a single cell. Determining exactly which of these is responsible for starting a tumor can be difficult. It is known that individuals from some families are more likely to get tumors than those from others; in other words, there is a genetic component. So certain genes are involved as well, and there has been a lot of research to investigate how they work. Exactly what causes a particular tumor, though, may or may not be possible to determine. There's a bright future ahead for anyone that wants to do cancer research!

How can you tell how old a dog is?

Can you tell how old an animal is?

I'll answer both of these questions at the same time. One of the first things that most mammalogists look at when studying a particular animal is the teeth. When an animal is young, the adult teeth aren't all grown in yet, and then an animal is old, teeth may be missing or worn down. Sometimes teeth become discolored with age as well. There are other things to look at as well. Many animals become more susceptible to certain diseases or injuries as they age, although this can vary from one species to the next, so you need to know what to look for. Many animals go through visible changes as they reach maturity, so (for instance) you can get a good idea of how old a male deer is by looking at his antlers. Of course, females don't have antlers, and males shed them every year, so this may not be very helpful! But it is an example.

For dogs, aside from the teeth, you would look at the eyes, joints, and coat. Older dogs often lose their eyesight, and arthritis is a common problem. Meanwhile, as any animal's health deteriorates, it will be less able to maintain itself, and this is apparent in many mammals as a dull coat. There may be other things as well, but a veterinarian would know more than I about them!

In most cases, it isn't possible to tell an exact age, but rather just a life-stage. In other words, I couldn't look at an animal and tell you that it's four years old, but I might be able to tell you whether it's an infant, a juvenile, or an adult, and if an adult, whether it's young, medium, or old. How many years each of these categories translates to depends not just on the species but also on how hard a life the animal has led and on its own particular family history.

When the opossum hangs up side down and the blood rushes down to it's brain does it bother them?

Not really. Opossums are much smaller than we are, and so the difference in blood pressure between the top and bottom of their bodies isn't anywhere near as great as in ours. Because of this, their blood doesn't do much rushing when they're upside down, and I doubt that they even notice it.

How many cougars can weigh like an elephant?

Well, that depends on the cougar and the elephant. Female cougars can weigh from 36 to 60 kg and males can weigh from 67 to 103 kg. Elephants are more complicated, because there are two species. For the Asiatic (or Indian) elephant, females weigh 2720 (on average) and males about 5400 kg.

For the African elephant, females weigh from 2400 to 6000 kg and males from 4000 to 7500 kg.

What all this means is that if you have a bunch of small female cougars, it would take over 208 of them to equal the weight of a large male African elephant, but if you had a bunch of large male cougars, it would take only 26 or 27 of them to equal the weight of an average female Asiatic elephant. (I'll leave the other calculations for you, if you're really eager to do them!)

On average, though, you're probably looking at 60 to 80 cougars to the elephant. Just keep in mind that these figures can vary tremendously!

Interesting questions — keep them coming!

How can you tell that someone has a brain tumor?

It's tricky: the symptoms can differ according to which part of the brain the tumor is in, and so brain tumors are often misdiagnosed. There are two main methods used to confirm the existence, location, and severity of a brain tumor. One is to take a biopsy of the tissue, which means cutting out a bit of it, and then examining it under the microscope. Since healthy tissue looks different from cancerous tissue, this is a pretty good method, but it's a bad idea if the tumor lies beneath the outer surface of the brain. The other method is to use imaging technology, which means taking either an MRI scan (which uses magnets and radio waves) or a CAT scan (which is a really fancy sort of X-ray). Biopsies are invasive (it's brain surgery, after all!), and imaging is very expensive, so neither procedure is used unless symptoms are already present. This isn't as bad a problem as it might sound, because early detection doesn't seem to make a very big difference in treatment of brain tumors (a very different situation from most other cancers, by the way!).

Another, newer, method is genetic screening. Certain genes are known to be associated with brain tumors, and can be detected with a simple blood test. This method doesn't say that someone *has* a brain tumor, though, only how likely one's chances are of *getting* one; and of course it can tell nothing at all about where it is in the brain, or how big, or what type. It is used only in conjunction with a diagnosis of symptoms to tell us that there is or is not likely a brain tumor, and if there is, the other methods are used to determine other important information.

How do you know when an animal is pregnant?

When an animal becomes pregnant, her hormone levels change, and they don't return to "normal" until after she weans her young. These hormonal changes are present in both blood and urine, so a sample of either can be collected and tested to determine whether the animal is pregnant.

Of course, a late-term pregnancy may be obvious from a visible bulge, and of course if the animal is in for surgery or is dead and being dissected, the uterus will be bigger and lumpier than normal. A fetus may also show up in an X-ray, and it can be seen with ultrasound (sort of like the sonar used by submarines); ultrasound is often used with pregnant women so that they can "see" their unborn children! These techniques are expensive, though, so they aren't used much except with zoo animals and pets, and then only when there might be some complication with pregnancy.

Can you tell how long an animal has been pregnant?

Not always, and almost never exactly. The only sure way to know how long an animal has been pregnant is to know when she became pregnant, but of course that information isn't usually available, so we use other methods.

The hormonal levels that I mentioned change over the course of a pregnancy, and if you know what their levels are over time for the animal that you're looking at, you might be able to determine how long the animal has been pregnant. You can also use ultrasound or take an X-ray to see how big the fetus(es) is/are.

The catch here is that you need to know what the hormonal levels are throughout pregnancy, or how quickly the fetus grows and how large the newborn is likely to be, in order to use this information. Many, many mammals are very poorly studied, and there simply isn't any way to interpret data without some reference! In these cases, you can use closely related animals as substitutes for the species you're looking at, but there's always the chance that you've got something that differs more than you expect from your model.

You also need to know how long a pregnancy usually lasts, in order to place your data into context. Pregnancies vary from three weeks in mice to a year and a half in some marine mammals! In the case of the mice, of course, it's pretty easy to tell; the changes are rapid and obvious. In the case of a marine mammal, it's often the best we can do to get it down to which month she became pregnant!

What's the smartest animal on earth?

That's an easy question: humans! We are easily, by any measurement, the most intelligent animals on the planet.

You might have been thinking of non-human animals, though, and there the question isn't quite so easy. There are a few contenders. One is our closest living relatives, the great apes: the chimpanzee, the bonobo, the gorilla, and the orangutan. These animals have complex social interactions and make simple tools, and they can be taught to "speak" in sign language and to solve complex problems. Which is smartest amongst them is debated, and I don't think that it'll be settled any time soon.

The best evidence is that they're all about as smart as each other, but that their brains work in different ways: chimpanzees are very creative, for instance, but get distracted or bored very easily, while gorillas will stick to a problem for much longer, although they might not be as insightful.

Another group of very smart animals are the cetaceans – the whales, dolphins, and porpoises. They are harder to test for intelligence, but all indications are that they are very, very smart. As to whether they are smarter than apes, nobody has yet proven one way or the other.

Other smart animals include some of the carnivores (cats and dogs being notables there) and hoofed animals (the champions in those groups are pigs and horses). All of these are mammals, of course, and it's likely that they are smarter than any non-mammals as well. Not so much has been done outside of mammals, though, so we can't be sure.

Do the pouches that the Kangaroos have bones and how much weight can they hold in their pouches?

There are no bones in the pouches of kangaroos (or other marsupials), but there are bones near them. It has been hypothesized that these bones help support the pouch, but there is a fair amount of evidence that says otherwise as well; my feeling is that they have a different function. They are still called "marsupial bones", though.

I'm not aware of any research investigating the weight capacity of a kangaroo's pouch! My guess is that it would be similar to a leather bag, which can hold quite a lot of weight. How much exactly, though, I don't think anyone knows!

These are interesting questions! I look forward to answering more.

APPENDIX L

DESCRIPTION OF *MUSEUM EXPLORER* DEVELOPMENT

Five requirements guided development of the *Museum Explorer* (www.museumexplorer.org): economy, scalability, easy administration, modular design, and support for multimedia. Meeting the economy requirement would allow the project to get done and the application to be maintained on a limited budget. The scalability requirement would allow the application to be later expanded to meet the growing needs of a biology museum without fundamental changes to application architecture. The easy administration requirement would allow for any museum staffer to update the application with information from the latest specimen without any specialized knowledge in programming or design software. The modular design requirement would allow the application to be easily expanded and altered through modules to meet changing needs of teachers and curators. Finally, the multimedia requirement would ensure the continued support for the addition of the multimedia content identified in the study as enhancing the student content knowledge and contributing to student engagement.

Developing the *Museum Explorer* application with free tools met the economy requirement. The limited budget of the research project rendered development using commercial content management systems prohibitively expensive. Instead, the architecture of the site was designed around readily available open-source software. The term open-source software describes a relatively new phenomenon in software development: transparent development methodologies. Traditional copyright protected software developed for distribution through commercial markets is characterized by proprietary source code and licensing terms designed to maximize profits. In contrast, open-source software is characterized by free distribution, full access to source code, unrestricted derived works, and nondiscrimination to maximize contributions (Bruce Perens, "Open Source Definition," Open Source Initiative, 2005 (www.opensource.org). Sometimes called copyleft protected software, open-source software is characterized by freely available source code and licensing terms that do not require royalties or other fees for use. However, this does not mean open-source software is on the fringes of the information technology landscape. Today, the revenue generated by open-source software is now in the billions of dollars and growing (Introduction, "Open Source Software," IBM Systems Journal, Volume 44, No.2, 2005). Even NASA's Acquisition Internet Service department chose open-source to save money, saving nearly $180,000 by using MySQL database server software (Maria Winslow , "The Practical Manager's Guide to Open Source," Lulu Press, 2004). One key to this projects successful implementation is that these open-source developments reach a critical point in maturity at the same time this research project was implemented. Between 2000 and 2004, open-source application development tools and open-source server software was finally available, viable, and widely supported by an ever expanding open-source development and support community. Projects that depend on Information Technology finally had access to tools similar to those that were previously proprietary, very expensive and largely limited to commercial enterprise class projects with big budgets.

Developing the *Museum Explorer* as a website using standard Internet technologies instead of a proprietary workstation based application using tools like Visual Basic were the first step to satisfy this scalability requirement. The *Museum Explorer* could potentially contain records for tens of thousands of specimen records in the Portland State University biology museum. It was essential that the technologies chosen in the initial demonstration phase not prohibit the expansion from a handful of specimen records to later thousands. The second step to scalability was to design the *Museum Explorer* website as a database driven website rather than merely a web of flat hyperlinked HTML pages. This would allow one-time creation of a website front-end, back-end database to hold specimen details, and scripts to respond to viewer requests through a web browser and automatically fetch requested content from the database. The added bonus of this approach is easy administration of the *Museum Explorer* website that does not require continual creation of new specimen content pages with specialized skills in traditional webpage editors like Macromedia Dreamweaver, Microsoft Frontpage or Adobe GoLive. Instead, new content can be entered into predefined fields through simple website administration forms in any web browser.

Three specific open source software tools were identified as the most viable options to realizing these requirements of economy, scalability, and easy administration in the development of the *Museum Explorer* website. They would also address the two other requirements of modular design and multimedia support. The tools used to create and operate the *Museum Explorer* website were (1) Apache web server (httpd.apache. org), (2) MySQL database server (www.mysql.com), and (3) PHP hypertext pre-processing language (www.php.net). First, Apache web server was used because it is the server platform Portland State University's Office of Information Technology provided access to for this project. Apache is the most common software used worldwide to server Internet web sites ("Web Server Survey," Netcraft (news.netcraft.com/archives/web_server_survey. html), April 2005). Second, MySQL database server was chosen because it is supported on the Apache web servers provided for the study by Portland State University and because it is widely considered the world's most popular open source database. Over six million servers worldwide use MySQL database server to power high-volume Web sites and other critical business systems, including Google, Sony, The Associated Press, Yahoo, and NASA ("MySQL Customers by Industry," MySQL AB (www.mysql.com), 2005).

Finally, PHP scripts were used both because Portland State University's servers support PHP scripts and because PHP scripts can provide a Web interface to the potentially large database of biology specimen records to be used in this research project. PHP has broad support of databases, including Oracle, IBM DB2, and MySQL (Ibid.). In February 2005, 54% of Apache web servers included the PHP scripting language ("Apache Module Report_PHP," Security Space, March 2005, www.securityspace. com/s_survey/data/man.200503/apachemods.html?mod=UEhQ), accounting for nearly 20 millions distinct Internet website domains worldwide (http:// www.php.net/usage.php). PHP has now surpassed Microsoft's ASP to become the most popular server-side scripting language (Web scripting technology on the Internet. PHP is a widely-used server-side scripting language for accepting Internet browser requests, dynamically generating web pages and other content, and presenting the results to the Internet viewer's browser

("PHP Manual: Introduction," The PHP Group (www.php.net), April 2005). Numerous open-source PHP scripts are now freely available as integrated content management systems, as well as modules that perform most of the functions required for the *Museum Explorer*. The scripts adapted for the purposes of the *Museum Explorer* include PHPBB Forum, MD-Pro CMS, Gallery, and many other smaller scripts cited within the website's code.

REFERENCES

Aksoy, N. (1998). *An overview of elementary education in the United States: Past, present, and future with its organization, nature of program and teaching strategies.* (ERIC Digest No. ED424956)

Baker, E., Gearhart, M., & Herman, J. (1993). Evaluating the apple classrooms of tomorrow. In Baker, E. & O'Neil, H. (Eds.), *Technology assessment in education and training* (pp. 173–197). Hillsdale, NJ: Lawrence Erlbaum.

Bangert-Drowns, R., & Pyke, C. (2002). Teacher ratings of student engagement with educational software: An exploratory study. *Educational Technology Research and Development, 50*(2), 23–38.

Barnum, C.R., & Kotar, M. (1989). The learning cycle. *Science and Children, 26*(7), 29–32.

Becker, H. (2000a). Pedagogical motivations for student computer use that lead to student engagement. *Educational Technology, 40*(5), 5–17.

Becker, H. (2000b). *Findings from the teaching, learning, and computing survey: Is Larry Cuban right? 8*(51). Retrieved September 9, 2003 from Education Policy Analysis Archives Web site: http://epaa.asu.edu/epaa/

Beeland, W. (2003). *Student engagement, visual learning, and technology: Can interactive whiteboards help?* Retrieved September 20, 2003, from the Valdosta State University Web site: http://chiron.valdosta.edu/are/Artmanscrpt/vol1no1/beeland_am.pdf

Beisenherz, P., & Dantonio, M. (1996). *Using the learning cycle to teach physical science: A hands-on approach for the middle grades.* Portsmouth, NH: Heinemann.

Bermúdez, A., & Prater, D. (1994, Summer/Fall). Examining the effects of gender and second language proficiency on Hispanic writers' persuasive discourse. *Bilingual Research Journal, 3*(18), 47–61.

Borg, W., & Gall, M. (1989). *Educational research: An introduction.* New York: Longman.

Bowen, E. (2003). *Student engagement and its relation to quality work design: A review of the literature.* Retrieved November 11, 2003, from the Valdosta State University Web site: http://chiron.valdosta.edu/are/vol2no1/pdf%20articles/StewartR_AM.pdf

Bradsher, M., & Hagan, L. (1995). The kids network: Student-scientists pool resources. *Educational Leadership, 53*(2), 38–43.

Bransford, Brown, & Cocking, 2000. How People Learn: Brain, Mind, Experience, and School. Retrieved April 19, 2003, from National Academies Press Web site: http://www.nap.edu/openbook/0309065577/html/index.html

Byers, A., & Fitzgerald, M. (2002). Networking for leadership, inquiry, and systemic thinking: A new approach to inquiry-based learning. *Journal of Science Education and Technology, 2*(1), 81–91.

Campbell, D., & Stanley, J. (1963). *Experimental and quasi-experimental designs for research*. Chicago, IL: Rand-McNally.

Christie, A. (2004). *How adolescent boys and girls view today's computer culture*. Paper presented at National Educational Computing Conference. Retrieved April 30, 2004, from the Arizona State University Web site: http://www.west. asu.edu

Clark, K. (2000). Urban middle school teachers' use of instructional technology. *Journal of Research on Computing in Education, 33*(2), 178–195.

Cooper, H., & Hedges, L. (Eds.). (1994). *The handbook of research synthesis*. New York: Russell Sage Foundation.

Cordell, L. (2000). Finding the natural interface: Graduate and public education at one university natural history museum. *Curator, 43*(2), 111–121.

Creswell, J. (1998). *Research design: Qualitative & quantitative approaches*. Thousand Oaks, CA: Sage Publications.

Cuban, L. (1986). *Teachers and machines: The classroom use of technology since 1920*. New York: Teachers College Press.

Cuban, L. (1996). Myths about changing schools and the case of special education. *Remedial and Special Education, (17)*, 75–82.

Cuban, L., & Kirkpatrick, H. (1998, Summer). Computers make kids smarter—right? *TECHNOS Quarterly for Education and Technology, 7*(2), 26–31. Retrieved August 18, 2003, from TECHNOS Web site: http://www.technos.net

David, C., & Matthews, B. (1995). The teacher internship program for science (TIPS): A successful museum-school partnership. *Journal of Elementary Science Education, 7*(1), 16–28.

Dede, C. (1998). The scaling-up process for technology-based educational innovations. In Dede, C. (Ed.), *Learning with Technology* (pp.199–215). Alexandria, VA: Association for Supervision and Curriculum Development.

Dewey, J. (1915). *John Dewey: The school and society and the child and curriculum*. Chicago: University of Chicago Press.

Diamond, J. (2000). Moving toward innovation: Informal science education in university natural history museums. *Curator, 25*(2), 93–102.

Forsyth, D., & Archer, R. (1997). Technology assisted instruction and student mastery, motivation, and matriculation. *Teaching of Psychology, 24*(3), 207–212.

Frankel, D. (1995). True needs, true partners. In E.C. Hirzy (Ed.), *True needs, true partners: Museums and schools transforming education* (pp. 9–14). Washington, DC: Institute of Museum Services.

Freire, P. (1972). *Cultural action for freedom.* London: Penguin Books Ltd.

Guzzetti, B. (1993, December). *Critical review of qualitative research on conceptual change from science education.* Paper presented at the forty-third Annual Meeting of the National Reading Conference, Charleston, SC.

Hannon, K., & Randolph, A. (2001). *Collaborations between museum educators and classroom teachers: Partnerships, curricula, and student understandings.* (ERIC Digest No. ED448133)

Hede, A. (2002). An integral model of multimedia effects on learning. *Journal of Educational Multimedia and Hypermedia, 11*(2), 177–191.

Hein, G. (2001). *Informal science supporting education reform: Theory and practice/ beliefs and actions.* Keynote lecture delivered at the Fifth Annual Northeast Informal Science Education Network Conference. Worcester, MA.

Hinrichsen, J., & Jarrett, D. (1999). *Science Inquiry for the classroom: A literature review.* Retrieved May 13, 2003, from the Northwest Regional Educational Laboratory Web site: http://www.nwrel.org

Hirzy, E. (1996). (Ed.).*True needs, true partners: Museums and schools transforming education.* Washington, DC: Institute of Museum Services.

Iding, M., Crosby, M., & Speitel, T. (2002). Teachers and technology: Beliefs and practices. *International Journal of Instructional Medial, 29*(2), 153–170.

Janesick, V. (1994). The dance of qualitative research design: Metaphor, methodology, and meaning. In N. Denzin & Y. Lincoln (Eds.), *Handbook of qualitative research* (pp. 209–219). Thousand Oaks, CA: Sage Publications.

Knezek, G., Christensen, R., & Miyashita, K. (1999). *Computer attitude questionnaire, version 5.25.* Denton, TX: The University of North Texas.

Knezek, G., Christensen, R., & Miyashita, K. (2000). *Instruments for assessing attitudes toward information technology.* Denton, TX: Texas Center for Educational Technology.

Krajcik, J., Soloway, E., Blumenfeld, P., Marx, R., & Fishman, B. (2000). *Inquiry based science supported by technology: Achievement among urban middle school students.* Ann Arbor, MI: University of Michigan, School of Education. (ERIC Document No. ED443676)

Kulik, J. (1994). Meta-analytic studies of findings on computer-based instruction. In E.L. Baker, and H.F. O'Neil, Jr. (Eds.), *Technology assessment in education and training* (pp. 9–33). Hillsdale, NJ: Lawrence Erlbaum.

Kyle, W., & Bonnstetter, R. (1992). *Science curriculum improvement study: Profile of excellence*. Hudson, NH: Delta Education.

Lawson, A.E. (2001). Using the learning cycle to teach biology concepts and reasoning patterns. *Journal of Biological Education, 34*(4),165–169.

Lento, E., O'Neill, D., & Gomez, L. (1998). Integrating internet services into school communities. In C. Dede (Ed.), *Learning with technology* (pp.171– 198). Alexandria, VA: Association for Supervision and Curriculum Development Yearbook.

Lepper, M. (1985). Microcomputers in education, motivational, and social issues, *American Psychologist, 40*(1), 1–18.

Light, R. J., & Pillemer, D. B. (1984). *Summing up: The science of reviewing research*. Cambridge, MA: Harvard University Press.

Lincoln, Y., & Guba, E. (1985). *Naturalistic inquiry*. Newbury Park, CA: Sage Publications.

Lourenco, M. (2001, July). *Are university collections and museums still meaningful?* Paper presented at the International Council of Museums General Conference in Barcelona, Spain.

Mann, D., & Schafer, E. (1997). *An investment in technology pays off in student performance*. Retrieved November 18, 2003, from the American School Board Journal Web site: http://www.asbj.com/199707/asbj0797.html

Marek, E., & Cavallo, A. (1997). *The learning cycle: Elementary school science and beyond*. Portsmouth, NH: Heinemann.

Marshall, C., & Rossman, G. (1999). *Designing qualitative research* (3rd Ed.). Thousand Oaks,CA: Sage Publications.

Mayer, R., & Moreno, R. (1998). *A cognitive theory of multimedia learning: Implications for design principles*. Retrieved November 15, 2003, from the University of New Mexico Web site: http://www.unm.edu/~moreno/PDFS/chi.pdf

McKenzie, J. (1997). Building a virtual museum community. In D. Bearman & J. Trant (Eds.), *Museums and the Web97* (pp. 77-86). Pittsburgh,PA: Archives & Museum Informatics.

Melber, L., & Cox-Peterson, A. (2001, April). *Teacher professional development and informal learning environments: Investigating partnerships and possibilities*. Paper presented at the annual meeting of the American Educational Research Association. Seattle, WA.

Melber, L., & Abraham, L. (2002). Science education in U.S. natural history museums: A historical perspective. *Science and Education, 11*, 45–54.

Merriam, S. (1990). *Case study research in education: A qualitative approach*. San Fransisco, CA: Jossey-Bass Publishers.

Molnar, A. S. (1997). *Computers in education: a brief history.* Retrieved February 23, 2003, from *T. H. E. Journal (Technological Horizons in Education)* Web site: http://www.thejournal.com/magazine/vault/A1681.cfm

Mousavi, S., Low, R., & Sweller, J. (1995). Reducing cognitive load by mixing auditory and visual presentation modes. *Journal of Educational Psychology, 87*(2), 319–34.

Museums and the web. (2003). Retrieved February 18, 2003, from Archives and Museum Informatics Web site: http://www.archimuse.com/mw2003/

National Center for Education Statistics. (2003). *Internet access in U.S. public schools and classrooms: 1994 – 2000.* Retrieved April 17, 2003 from National Center for Education Statistics Web site: http://nces.ed.gov

National educational technology standards for teachers: Preparing teachers to use technology (2003). Retrieved June 23, 2003, from International Society for Technology in Education Web site: http://cnets.iste.org

National Middle School Association. (2003). *The position paper of national middle school association middle level curriculum: A work in progress.* Retrieved April 16, 2003, from National Middle School Association Web site: http://www.nmsa.org/

National Research Council. (1996). *National Science Education Standards.* Retrieved April 19, 2003, from National Academies Press Web site: http://www.nap.edu/books/0309053269/html/

National Science Teachers Association. (2002). *The Use of Computers in Science Education.* NSTA Position Statement. Retrieved October 21, 2002, from NSTA Web site: http://www.nsta.org/positionstatement&psid=4

Newmann, F. (1986). Priorities for the future: Toward a common agenda. *Social Education, 50*(4), 240–250.

Newmann, F. (Ed.). (1992). *Student engagement and achievement in American secondary schools,* New York: Teachers College Press.

Olson, S., & Loucks-Horsley, S. (Eds.). (2000). *Inquiry and the national science education standards: A guide for teaching and learning.* (addendum for the 1996 NSES) Retrieved May 3, 2003, from National Academies Press: http://books.nap.edu/html/inquiry_addendum/

Oregon Department of Education. (2003). *Science Teaching and Learning to Standards.* Retrieved June 6, 2003, from Oregon Department of Education Web site: http://www.ode.state.or.us/teachlearn/specialty/pre-post/sci-tlss200405.pdf

Papert, S. (1993). *The children's machine: Rethinking school in the age of the computer.* New York: Basic Books.

Paris, S., Yambor, K., & Packard, B. (1998). Hands-on biology: A museum-school-university partnership for enhancing students' interest and learning in science. *The Elementary School Journal, 98*(3), 267–88.

Patton, M. (2002). *Qualitative research and evaluation methods.* Thousand Oaks, CA: Sage Publications.

Piaget, J. (1970). *Science of education and the psychology of the child.* Translated from the French by Derek Coltman. New York: Orion Press.

Ross, C. (1993). *Girls as constructors in the early years: Promoting equal opportunities in math, science, and technology.* Stoke-on-Trent, UK: Trentham.

Sandholtz, J., Ringstaff, C., & Dwyer, D. (1994). *Student engagement: Views from technology-rich classrooms.* Retrieved August 8, 2003, from ACOT Web site: http://a1712.g.akamai.net/7/1712/51/1403b36e54106d/www.apple.com/education/k12/leadership/acot/pdf/rpt21.pdf

Schacter, J. (2001). *The impact of education technology on student achievement: What the most current research has to say.* Santa Monica, CA: Milken Exchange on Education Technology.

Skramstad, H. (1999). An agenda for American museums in the twenty-first century. *Daedalus, Journal of the American Academy of Arts, 128*(3), 109–128.

Slavin, R. (1986). *Educational psychology: Theory and practice.* Needham Heights: MA: Allyn & Bacon.

Smith, W., Butler-Kisber, L., LaRocque, L., Portelli, J., Shields, C., Sparkes, C., & Vibert, A. (1998). *Student engagement in learning and school life: National project report.* Montreal: McGill University Office of Research on Educational Policy.

Stanovich, K. (2000). *Progress in understanding reading: Scientific foundations and new frontiers.* New York: Guilford Press.

Templeton, M. (1999). *What America thinks about science education reform: An analysis of the Bayer Facts of Science Education I-V.* Retrieved August 18, 2003, from Bayer Web site: http://www.bayerus.com/msms/news/pages/factsofscience/analysis.html

Tirrell, P. (2001). A synopsis and perspective of concerns and challenges for the international community of university museums. *Curator, (43)*2, 157–180.

Tomic, W., & Kingma, J. (Eds). (1998). *Conceptual issues in research on intelligence.* Greenwich, CT: JAI Press.

Yellis, K. (1990). Museum education. In M. Shapiro (Ed.), *The museum: A reference guide* (pp. 167–197). New York: Greenwood Press.

Yin, R. (1993). Application of case study research. *Applied Social Research Methods Series* (vol. 34). Newbury Park, CA: Sage Publications.

Young Children's Computer Inventory. (1994). Handbook for young children's computer inventory. Retrieved June 25, 2003, from Texas Center for Educational Technology Web site: http://www.tcet.unt.edu

Wade, C. (2003). *The Oregon Educational Technology Plan (OETP)*. Retrieved November 20, 2003, from Oregon Department of Education Web site: http://www.ode.state.or.us/teachlearn/subjects/technology/oetpsurvey.pdf

Wasserstein, P. (1995). What middle schoolers say about their school work. *Educational Leadership, 53*(1), 41–43.

West, R. (2000). Princeton University closes natural history museum. *The Informal Learning Review. 45*(2), 1.

INDEX

DOWNLOAD MUSEUM EXPLORER

Museum Explorer can be downloaded at
www.cambriapress.com/museumexplorer
The access code is APDME888.

Printed in the United States
70597LV00002B/175-210